D0566841

A ...

... Business Administration
1441 L Street, N.W.
Washington, D.C. 20416

C Export-Import Bank
of the United States
811 Vermont Avenue, N.W.
Washington, D.C. 20571

D Office of the U.S. Trade
Representative
Winder Building
600 17th Street, N.W.
Washington, D.C. 20506

E U.S. Trade and Development
Program
Rosslyn Plaza East
1621 North Kent Street
Rosslyn, Virginia
(Mailing Address:
Washington, D.C. 20523)

F Agency for International
Development
Department of State Building
320 21st Street, N.W.
Washington, D.C. 20523

G Department of Commerce
14th Street between Constitution
Avenue and E Street, N.W.
Washington, D.C. 20230

H Department of Agriculture
14th Street and Independence
Avenue, S.W.
Washington, D.C. 20250

Map artwork provided courtesy of D.C. Department of Transportation.

WASHINGTON'S BEST KEPT SECRETS

WASHINGTON'S BEST KEPT SECRETS

A U.S. GOVERNMENT GUIDE TO INTERNATIONAL BUSINESS

Edited by

William A. Delphos

Vice President, Operations
Overseas Private Investment Corporation
Washington, D.C.

JOHN WILEY & SONS
New York · Chichester · Brisbane · Toronto · Singapore

Library of Congress Cataloging in Publication Data:

Delphos, William A. (William Arthur), 1951–
　　Washington's best kept secrets.

　　　1. Corporations, American—Government policy—
Information services—United States. 2. International
business enterprises—Information services—United
States. 3. Industrial promotion—Information services—
United States. 4. United States—Commerce—
Information services. I. Title

　　HD2785.D385 1984　　　353.0082′7　　　83–16671
　　ISBN 0–471–87944–4

Printed in the United States of America

10 9 8 7 6 5 4 3 2 1

This book is an integral part of "Operation Opportunity"—a special effort undertaken by the federal government in 1983 to make available to the American business community information about various U.S. government programs and services that can assist Americans doing business abroad.

The following federal agencies, co-sponsors of Operation Opportunity, participated in the compilation of this information:

Department of Agriculture
Department of Commerce
Office of the U.S. Trade Representative
Agency for International Development
Export-Import Bank of the United States
Overseas Private Investment Corporation
Small Business Administration
U.S. Trade and Development Program

FOREWORD

If a single word can be used to describe today's world, it is *interdependence*. That interdependence represents a great challenge and an opportunity for the U.S. business community, particularly for smaller- and medium-sized companies ready to expand into new markets.

When Control Data was founded in 1957, we faced the whole array of problems that confront any small business, and they are formidable. At the same time, however, we believed that the problems could be solved if we accelerated the growth of our business by entering overseas markets as quickly as possible.

We have been very pleased with the success of this strategy, especially in developing countries. Obviously, there were unusual risks involved in establishing operations in those countries, risks that would not enter into any decision about domestic expansion or establishing operations in a foreign industrialized nation. Given the potential of third world markets and the manageability of these risks, this was a sound business decision.

We believe that adoption of this strategy by other companies in the U.S. private sector can lead to the kind of public–private partnerships that are needed in developing countries. Jamaica is a case in point. Working with the U.S. Business Committee on Jamaica, appointed by President Reagan to assist Prime Minister Seaga's economic recovery program, we have been very active in bringing private-sector investment to this island country. What is needed in Jamaica, as well as in other developing countries with market economies, are public–private partnerships that can bring about structural change in their economies.

Especially needed are private-sector efforts that can support education and training, agriculture, and small business development.

The less developed nations contain nearly three-fourths of the world's population and much of its natural wealth. They have a vast reservoir of human resources. The hopes and aspirations of the people of these countries depend on the opportunity to learn, earn, and create a better quality of life for their families.

Today, those needs and opportunities have multiplied far beyond any expectations. In 1969, for example, the developing nations accounted for about $11 billion in U.S. exports. By 1982, that volume had reached some $100 billion—and that is just a fraction of the potential.

One-tenth of our national income stems from exports, and one-fifth of U.S. jobs depend on trade. Two-fifths of our agricultural production is sold abroad, and one-third of our corporate profits are generated by international operations.

At a time when domestic unemployment is of concern, some people question the propriety of encouraging U.S. investment abroad. But without restoring the momentum of economic development throughout the world, we cannot sustain the growth needed to solve our own problems. Like it or not, interdependence is a fact of life that is here to stay.

The most practical and immediate answer to this dilemma is the acceleration of private participation, and more developing countries are seeking to attract U.S. companies to enter into business ventures by offering a wide variety of incentives. Many of them are well aware that their economies are not large or diversified enough to attract multinational corporations, and are gearing their promotion efforts toward smaller companies whose capacities are compatible with their needs and potential. This trend represents a great opportunity, but that opportunity is no secret. The businessmen of the other industrialized nations are aware of the potential and are wasting no time in cultivating this potential.

For the U.S. business community, the time has come to restore our competitive edge, which has eroded alarmingly in recent years.

Admittedly, it is no simple task for the smaller-business executive to readjust from thinking in purely domestic terms to the broader dimensions of the overseas marketplace. Because we live and work in the world's greatest marketplace, many smaller companies tend to view overseas markets as the exclusive province of the multinational, but the world has changed. Where yesterday's growth came from domestic expansion, tomorrow's will come from the markets of Asia, Africa, the Caribbean, South America, and the Middle East.

U.S. expertise in management and technological know-how is generally regarded as the finest in the world and can make significant contributions to the development process. Further, the physical presence of U.S. companies directly benefits host countries by improving production capabilities, creating jobs, generating foreign exchange, teaching new skills, and offering people the opportunity to help themselves.

Strangely enough, many people overlook, or simply do not understand, the critical role investment plays in stimulating U.S. exports. In reality, the two go hand-in-hand. Overseas affiliates and subsidiaries of U.S. companies account for some 40 percent of our total annual exports, and estimates are that every billion dollars in exports creates 40,000 new domestic jobs. Clearly, it is in the national interest to pool our resources more effectively to meet the challenge. There is no time to be lost.

For any business executive considering overseas investment, the first step is to learn about the many and varied services available through the U.S. government. It is unfortunate, but true, that the business community tends to be critical of U.S. government incentives as compared to those provided by Japan and the European nations. In reality, all too few corporations actually know what is available.

Taken on an overall basis, the United States offers many business encouragement programs, but information about these services has not been easy to come by.

Because the key services are administered by various divisions and branches of the Departments of Agriculture and Commerce, the Export-Import Bank, Small Business Administration, Agency for International Development, Office of the U.S. Trade Representative, U.S. Trade and Development Program, and the Overseas Private Investment Corporation, information has been unobtainable from a single source.

At long last, this guide compiles information on all of the services offered to exporters and investors, organized by type of assistance, rather than under agency headings. It provides such nuts and bolts as names and telephone numbers for direct contact, which alone can save the businessperson time and a good deal of frustration. In short, it is organized along lines familiar to the business community rather than to the government bureaucracy.

Organized and coordinated by the Overseas Private Investment Corporation, *Washington's Best Kept Secrets* is required reading for any executive whose company is either involved in, or contemplating, operations in the international marketplace.

WILLIAM NORRIS
Chairman and Chief Executive Officer
Control Data Corporation

PREFACE

Imagine, if you will, walking into the neighborhood grocery store to buy a jar of chunky peanut butter. As you enter the store, you're stunned to discover that the aisles have been rearranged. Instead of familiar product groups, the displays are organized by manufacturer—Procter & Gamble, General Foods, Del Monte, Beatrice Foods, and so forth.

What should have been a simple shopping excursion has now become a bizarre hunting expedition, where success rests on a combination of dogged determination and almanaclike knowledge. Who manufactures peanut butter? Which one makes chunky peanut butter? And who makes chunky peanut butter in a reusable plastic tub?

While the grocery store scenario may seem to be a bit far-fetched, it is an all too realistic description of the dilemma facing American businesses today when they attempt to shop at Uncle Sam's agencies for assistance in operating overseas.

This book is designed to unscramble the scores of U.S. government programs available for American firms seeking to do business abroad— taking them off the shelves now marked Department of Commerce, Export-Import Bank, Small Business Administration, Overseas Private Investment Corporation, and so forth, and putting them onto more logical shelves such as financing, insurance, and market information.

Eight federal agencies currently offer most of the key programs in this particular area of business assistance. Another half-dozen agencies provide a limited number of services for U.S. businesses seeking to enter the international marketplace. All have contributed to this guide in the desire to make information about government assistance more accessible to the American business community.

While it would be an exaggeration to suggest this publication is all-inclusive, every effort has been made to include detailed descriptions of the major government programs available for U.S. businesses considering overseas operations. It is our hope that it will make a significant contribution to strengthening the working partnership between the private sector and the government—a critical need if we are to compete successfully in the international marketplace.

WILLIAM A. DELPHOS

Washington, D.C.
September 1983

ACKNOWLEDGMENTS

Many people made this book possible, and I would like to express my gratitude for their contributions.

This book would never have become a reality had it not been for the support of Malcolm Baldrige, Secretary of Commerce; John R. Block, Secretary of Agriculture; William E. Brock, United States Trade Representative; William H. Draper III, President and Chairman, Export-Import Bank of the United States; Elise R.W. du Pont, Assistant Administrator, Bureau for Private Enterprise, Agency for International Development; Christian R. Holmes, Director, U.S. Trade and Development Program; M. Peter McPherson, Administrator, Agency for International Development; James C. Sanders, Administrator, Small Business Administration; and Craig A. Nalen, President, Overseas Private Investment Corporation.

Our diligent and dedicated research team spent many hours checking, organizing, and compiling an enormous amount of material. Donna L. Brodsky, who headed the team, deserves special credit for her leadership and unswerving focus on detail. Also my thanks to those who assisted her, including Elizabeth J. Dribben, Gordon E. Hunt, Karen F. Kornbluh, Lynn A. Ksanznak, Graham Williams, and Brenda S. Wilson.

For their help in producing an easy-to-understand book, appreciation is extended to writers Juan M. Cameron and Kevin P. Power. My gratitude also goes to Robert Jordan for his contributions to the introduction, and to Deloitte Haskins & Sells for its section on taxes and host-country incentives.

In putting together such a work, it is imperative that information be carefully reviewed and early drafts clarified. Thanks go to the unfailing eyes of our reviewers, including Leo Phillips, Josephine Martin, and Barbara Miller, who also contributed in many other areas.

Special thanks go to those who offered their considerable knowledge and effort: Michael A. Potterf and Richard H. Davis of the Commerce Department; Phyllis O. Bonanno and Edward J. Stucky of the Office of the United States Trade Representative; Alan T. Tracy, Robert P. Scherle, Jimmy D. Minyard, Thomas H. Lederer, and Richard F. Rortvedt of the Department of Agriculture. My appreciation is also extended to Arthur J. Obester of the Export-Import Bank; Richard A. Tropp, Hawthorn I. Munson, and Bruce E. Bouchard of the Agency for International Development; Michael E. Deegan of the Small Business Administration; and John V.E. Hardy, Jr. of the U.S. Trade and Development Program.

I am also indebted to other government agency people who supported us in this effort, including John A. Barcas, Department of State; Brian Gorman, National Oceanic and Atmospheric Administration; Bill Gschwend, Peace Corps; Phillip Keif, Department of Energy; Chris Keilach, Peace Corps; Edmund T. McMurray, Internal Revenue Service; Diana M. Montgomery, Department of State; John Roth, Customs Service; William A. Russell, Jr., Federal Communications Commission; Lee Skillington, Patent and Trademark Office; Harold Sundstrom, U.S. International Trade Commission; James Taylor, Department of Labor; Jan Verschuur, Department of State; and Harvey J. Winter, Department of State.

Finally, appreciation must be extended to Roberta Wojton and Elaine Lewis for their patience and dedication in typing the many pages of manuscript.

W.A.D.

CONTENTS

WASHINGTON'S BEST KEPT SECRETS

CHAPTER ONE

WINNING OVERSEAS

Now that time and distance have been so compressed that an American can fly to Paris for lunch and return the same day, "business as usual" has a decidedly new dimension. New technologies in communication, not to mention instant access to an almost limitless supply of information, have triggered a revolution posing tremendous challenges and opportunities for the modern business executive.

Only a few years ago, a company could seek new markets by exploring opportunities in other cities and other states. Although some of the nation's larger companies looked for growth in other nations, the majority of American businesses thought the magic of the U.S. marketplace was enough. Today, the character of the U.S. marketplace is vastly different. Investors from foreign countries are flocking to the United States in increasing numbers, while our whole structure is shifting from a "smokestack" economy to a more sophisticated, technologically oriented society. The U.S. business executive now must look for new avenues of growth, and many are facing the reality that the best opportunities may lie beyond the water's edge.

The Potential

Multinational corporations have long recognized the potential of overseas expansion, and their investments have made enormous contributions to accelerating trade and economic growth in many areas of the world. But if the United States is to maintain a competitive position in world commerce, we must broaden our investment base by encouraging more small and medium-sized firms to enter international markets, especially those of the developing world, which are today's fastest growing markets for U.S. goods and services.

Overseas investment is a two-way street that strengthens developing economies by creating employment, teaching new skills, and infusing much-needed capital into countries whose economies are just beginning to grow. At the same time, overseas enterprises accelerate growth in the United States by opening new markets, creating jobs, and making a positive return to our balance of payments.

While massive government-to-government assistance programs have done much to alleviate some basic problems in the developing world, they are a beginning, not an end. Used primarily for establishing basic infrastructure such as dams, roads, power complexes, and other

3

public-sector projects, these programs are the base for a private-sector superstructure that can create permanent jobs, ongoing productivity, and new opportunity. Unfortunately, at a time when needs are accelerating, concessional aid is declining, and many nations have been forced to curtail critical development programs.

Like many problems, this one holds the seeds of its own solution. Developing nations, many of which have been hostile to or at least highly suspicious of foreign private investment, increasingly see it as the most immediate and practical answer to maintaining growth. The result has been a recasting of investment laws and a broadening of the incentives offered to attract foreign capital.

Winning at Home

The stage is now set for a new era of growth and opportunity, and the U.S. business community has an uncommon chance to restore its competitive leadership. It would be difficult to overestimate the importance of this effort. To a great extent, our success will depend on teamwork between the government and the business community. Effective use of federal services can make the difference between success and failure.

This book is designed as a ready reference manual, compiling information on the scores of government-supported business assistance programs classified by some as "Washington's best kept secrets." This wall of secrecy has not been built by government alone, although government has made a significant contribution by isolating both programs and information into various departments and agencies. At least some of it can be attributed to the business community's previous lack of interest in international operations. This guide seeks to tear down that wall, putting all the pieces in one place so that the array of government programs becomes a solution rather than a puzzle.

About the Book

Virtually all of the trade and investment incentive programs designed to help American business compete overseas are administered by eight agencies—the Departments of Agriculture and Commerce, Office of the U.S. Trade Representative, Agency for International Development, Export-Import Bank, Overseas Private Investment Corporation, Small Business Administration, and the U.S. Trade and Development Program. Brief descriptions of their functions as they relate to promoting international business development can be found at the end of this chapter.

Until now, businesses seeking the appropriate federal assistance program or individual to help them overseas were forced to wander through the bureaucratic labyrinth of these Washington agencies in hopes of finding an answer. With this reference guide, however, the maze of agency authority lines has been erased. In its place is a "repackaged" presentation of government programs for business, arranged according to type of assistance available rather than by agency. To further illustrate how these programs can best be used by American businesses, case studies are highlighted in each chapter.

Readers unfamiliar with the overseas marketplace should notice that the chapters logically flow from "getting started" information to the nuts-and-bolts of putting a business deal together.

Chapter 2, for example, outlines the wide array of business information available to U.S. firms considering operations overseas, including market background reports, statistical profiles, country economic analyses, and international demographic data.

In Chapter 3, discussions of specific programs—data banks, search services, and contract bid notifications—are designed to help businesses identify trade and investment opportunities that currently exist overseas.

Chapter 4 is devoted to outlining government programs that help plan for or support reconnaissance trips overseas.

Chapter 5 provides detailed descriptions of the various programs available for obtaining feasibility study funding and assistance.

In Chapter 6, the regulations and requirements of doing business overseas are explored, and programs available for obtaining foreign government approvals are discussed. At the end of this chapter is a useful consideration of taxation issues.

Chapter 7, "Financing the Deal," sets forth the dozens of loan, loan guarantee, and letter of credit programs available to U.S. businesses with sights on overseas markets, including information on eligibility, interest rates, and terms.

Chapter 8 details how the business executive can obtain insurance or other forms of guarantee to protect an overseas venture.

Chapter 9 discusses programs for initiating actual operations overseas and for expanding such operations at a later stage.

In addition to the contact individuals noted throughout the book, a listing of key regional federal offices and U.S. embassy contacts overseas is provided in the appendix.

Obviously, no single volume could begin to describe the scope and diversity of the thousands of overseas enterprises involving U.S. firms or the hundreds of government programs that have been used to help those undertaking such enterprises. Nevertheless, every effort has been made to present as much information as possible in an easy-to-understand form that can help make business investment decisions more effective and productive.

The following federal agencies administer the bulk of programs designed to assist American businesses wishing to compete in the international marketplace.

Department of Agriculture.   Through its Commodity Credit Corporation, the Department of Agriculture administers export sales and donations for foreign use through other agencies as well as providing export guarantees to foreign buyers. Its Foreign Agricultural Service gathers worldwide information through representatives stationed in 70 U.S. embassies, develops export data to support trade, and works to reduce trade barriers. Its Office of International Cooperation and Development is responsible for international and technical cooperation for development assistance programs.

Department of Commerce.   The Department's International Trade Administration coordinates issues relating to trade administration, international export policies, and trade programs. It also organizes trade missions and trade fairs and generally works to strengthen the U.S. trade position. Background information on all countries is provided through the Department's U.S. Commercial Service, with 48 district offices throughout the country. The Foreign Commercial

Service gathers detailed information on local conditions through 127 posts in 67 countries.

Office of the U.S. Trade Representative. This Cabinet-level agency is responsible for the direction of trade negotiations, formulation of overall trade policy, and bilateral and multilateral negotiations pertaining to trade. It represents the United States at meetings of the General Agreement on Tariffs and Trade (GATT) and the Organization for Economic Cooperation and Development (OECD) and in negotiations with the United Nations Conference on Trade and Development (UNCTAD).

Agency for International Development. AID offers loans and grants on concessional terms to less developed countries to further development plans, and it provides assistance for programs relating to population growth, housing, and market-oriented development. Assistance sectors include agriculture, health, population control, education, human resources, housing, and private volunteer organizations. Its Bureau for Private Enterprise supports projects involving local private-sector resources. AID maintains posts at 64 U.S. embassies abroad.

Export-Import Bank of the United States. This agency provides support for facilitating exports, offers export credits and guarantees, and offers direct credit to borrowers outside the United States. Through the Foreign Credit Insurance Association, Eximbank provides credit protection for U.S. exporters; these policies insure repayment in the event of default by a foreign buyer and may be used as collateral for bank loans. The agency also guarantees repayment to commercial banks that provide financing to exporters covering service contracts, leases, and other special situations.

Overseas Private Investment Corporation. OPIC encourages U.S. private investment in developing countries by providing political risk insurance and finance services. Its insurance provides protection against the risks of inconvertibility of local currency, expropriation or nationalization, and losses resulting from war, revolution, insurrection, or civil strife. Finance services include direct loans of up to

$4 million to smaller businesses (companies not ranked in the "Fortune 1000"), loan guarantees of up to $50 million, and financing of up to $100,000 for feasibility studies. Programs are available for new projects or expansion of existing facilities. OPIC operates its programs in more than 90 developing countries.

Small Business Administration. SBA offers financial assistance, counseling, export workshops and training to help U.S. companies enter international markets. It provides loans and loan guarantees to U.S. companies for equipment, facilities, materials, and working capital for selected export market development activities. Export counseling services and marketing information are available at no cost from the agency's Service Corps of Retired Executives and Active Corps of Executives, and by university students who participate in the Small Business Institute Program. In addition, Small Business Development Centers based at universities offer business counseling and assistance. SBA has 79 district offices throughout the United States.

U.S. Trade and Development Program. This agency is responsible for the administration of planning services leading to reimbursable programs with U.S. agencies, or direct host-government contracts with U.S. private firms, for project implementation. The program includes support for project identification, design, feasibility studies, and design engineering.

CHAPTER TWO

THE MARKETS

Before considering an overseas venture, most businesses want to ascertain the market potential for their products or services. In many cases, the U.S. government can provide U.S. firms with important market data at little or no charge. Various federal resources for obtaining such market information are reviewed in this chapter, categorized into three major subject areas:

Global Information. International economic and demographic statistics as well as worldwide agricultural data.

Industry/Commodity Information. In-depth reports and services for analyzing the factors affecting commodity shipments, and markets for products of specific industry sectors.

Country Information. Economic and demographic reports for specific countries, country seminars, market research reports, and country risk assessment.

GLOBAL INFORMATION

International Economic Indicators

International Economic Indicators is a quarterly report providing basic data on the economies of the United States, France, West Germany, Italy, the Netherlands, England, Japan, and Canada. It includes current statistics for 68 economic indicators, including gross national product, industrial production, trade, prices, finance, and employment. Annual trends since 1970 and recent quarterly changes are presented for various time intervals. The publication assesses the United States' relative international economic position, providing an overall view of international trends. It can be used as a basis for more detailed analyses of the economic situation in major industrial countries.

Cost
Annual subscription $15 in U.S.; $18.75 foreign. Single copies $4.75 in U.S.; $5.95 foreign. Order no.: S/N 003-025-80001-9.

Contact
Superintendent of Documents
U.S. Government Printing Office
Washington, DC 20402
(202) 783-3238

International Demographic Data

The U.S. Bureau of the Census collects and analyzes worldwide demographic, social, and economic data that can assist companies in identifying potential markets for their products. Demographic measures for each country are published in summary form in the biennial *World Population* series. (1979 is the latest edition.)

Cost
$11.00 in U.S.; $13.75 foreign. Order no.: S/N 003-024-02805-1.

Contact
Superintendent of Documents
U.S. Government Printing Office
Washington, DC 20402
(202) 783-3238

Additional data on a wide variety of topics, including population size and growth rate, fertility, mortality, migration, urban/rural residence, population age structure, marital status, education, literacy, economic activity, health indicators, and household measures, are stored in a computerized data base. This information is compiled for 70 variables for each country in the data base, which will eventually include all countries.

Cost
$5.50 per copy.

Contact
> Sylvia Quick, Chief
> Data Evaluation Branch
> Scuderi Building, Room 407
> U.S. Bureau of the Census
> Washington, DC 20233
> (202) 763-4086

International Agricultural Data

Several divisions of the Department of Agriculture provide international agricultural data.

The Economic Research Service

The Economic Research Service's International Economics Division collects and analyzes extensive information on foreign country and commodity markets for U.S. agricultural products, forecasts changes in these markets, and conducts research on longer term agricultural supply, demand, and trade issues. Regional branches study individual country markets as well as such regional groupings as the European Community (EC) and the Association of South East Asian Nations (ASEAN). Analysts also collect and interpret current information on developments in commodity markets and foreign government policies that can influence internationally traded commodities.

The Trade Policy Branch furnishes current information on trade strategies of major agricultural trading countries and on activities of international organizations such as the Food and Agriculture Organization (FAO), Organization for Economic Cooperation and Development (OECD), General Agreement on Tariffs and Trade (GATT), and United

Nations Conference on Trade and Development (UNCTAD). The Branch also analyzes alternative trade policies and their implications for U.S. agricultural trade.

The World Analysis Branch regularly generates and distributes a wide variety of world price and quantity data for commodities of major interest to U.S. exporters, such as grains and livestock products. This Branch maintains a large data base of agricultural export and import statistics for many countries and regions.

The Agricultural Development Branch makes available analyses and data on the economic development and future market needs of the developing countries.

Contact

The appropriate branch chief:

Branch	Branch Chief	Telephone
Africa/Middle East	Cheryl Christensen	(202) 475-3443
Asia	Carmen Nohre	(202) 447-8860
Latin America	Oswald Blaich	(202) 447-9110
Western Europe	Reed Friend	(202) 447-6809
Eastern Europe/U.S.S.R.	Anton Malish	(202) 447-8380
North America/Oceania	Donald Seaborg	(202) 447-8376
Trade Policy	Vernon Roningen	(202) 447-8470
World Analysis	John Dunmore	(202) 382-9818
Agricultural Development	Lon Cesal	(202) 447-8926

The Economic Research Service also issues the following publications on a regular basis:

The Foreign Agricultural Trade of the United States (bimonthly)

World Agricultural Outlook and Situation (quarterly)

Outlook for U.S. Agricultural Exports (quarterly)

Food Aid Needs and Availabilities (annually)

Regional Situation and Outlook Reports (annually) for the following areas:

North America/Oceania
Latin America

Middle East and North Africa
Sub-Saharan Africa
East Asia
South Asia
Southeast Asia
China
Eastern Europe
The Soviet Union
Western Europe

Contact

Information Division
U.S. Department of Agriculture
Room 1664-S
Washington, DC 20250
(202) 447-4230; 447-8590

Foreign Agricultural Service

The Foreign Agricultural Service (FAS) issues a variety of regularly scheduled and special publications to assist agricultural exporters.

Foreign Agriculture is a monthly magazine for business firms selling U.S. farm products overseas. It offers news and background information useful in export marketing, feature articles reporting and analyzing conditions affecting U.S. agricultural trade, and details on programs to expand agricultural exports.

Cost

Annual subscription $16 in U.S.; $20 foreign. Single copies $2.75 in U.S.; $3.45 foreign. Order no.: S/N 001-009-80001-6.

Contact

Superintendent of Documents
U.S. Government Printing Office
Washington, DC 20402
(202) 783-3238

Foreign Agricultural Circulars include production, trade, and other specialized reports on major commodities and monthly statistical reports on commodities in world trade. Circulars are issued at irregular intervals during the year.

Cost
From $5 to $55, depending on commodity. Available in U.S. only.

Contact
Information Services Staff
Foreign Agricultural Service
U.S. Department of Agriculture
South Building, Room 5918
Washington, DC 20250
(202) 447-7937

Weekly Roundup of World Production and Trade is a bulletin presenting current news items and statistics on various commodities. It also summarizes recent developments in world production and trade.

Cost
Free.

Contact
Information Services Staff
Foreign Agricultural Service
U.S. Department of Agriculture
South Building, Room 5918
Washington, DC 20250
(202) 447-7937

Monthly World Crop Production provides the Agriculture Department's estimates on the production of wheat, rice, coarse grains, oilseeds, and cotton in major countries and selected regions of the world.

Cost
Annual subscription $30.

Contact
Information Services Staff
Foreign Agricultural Service
U.S. Department of Agriculture
South Building, Room 5918
Washington, DC 20250
(202) 447-7937

Special Reports and Backgrounders. Special Reports focus on foreign agricultural situations, particularly those relating to major commodities and trade policy developments, and provide detailed analyses of topics in world agricultural trade. *Backgrounders* are concise, single-sheet

OUTLOOK FOR U.S. AGRICULTURAL EXPORTS

Table 4—U.S. agricultural exports: Value by region, 1982-83

Region 1/	October-March 1981/82	October-March 1982/83	Fiscal year :Preliminary: 1982	Fiscal year Forecast 1983
	--------Billion dollars---------			
Western Europe	6.934	5.884	12.164	10.7
European Community 2/	5.135	4.422	8.894	8.1
Other Western Europe	1.799	1.462	3.270	2.6
Eastern Europe	.566	.363	.920	.8
USSR	1.783	.757	2.322	1.2
Asia	7.514	7.034	14.137	13.8
Middle East 3/	.837	.737	1.486	1.6
South Asia 4/	.342	.666	.711	1.3
Southeast & East Asia 5/	2.148	2.185	4.383	4.5
Japan	3.168	2.966	5.737	5.6
China	1.019	.478	1.819	.8
Canada	.945	.889	1.872	1.7
Africa	1.272	.985	2.447	2.6
North Africa 6/	.722	.603	1.389	1.6
Sub-Saharan Africa	.550	.382	1.058	1.0
Latin America	2.557	2.110	4.938	4.5
Mexico	.880	.714	1.493	1.6
Central America & Caribbean	.533	.537	1.112	1.1
South America	1.144	.859	2.333	1.8
Oceania	.183	.117	.294	.2
Total	21.754	18.139	39.094	35.5
Developed Countries 7/	11.230	9.856	20.067	18.2
Less Developed Countries	7.156	6.683	13.965	14.5
Centrally Planned Countries	3.368	1.598	5.061	2.8

1/ Annual data are adjusted for transshipments through Canada and Western Europe. Quarterly data are adjusted for Canadian transshipments.
2/ Includes Greece.
3/ Turkey, Cyprus, Syria, Lebanon, Iraq, Iran, Israel, Jordan, Gaza Strip, Kuwait, Saudi Arabia, Qatar, United Arab Emirates, Yemen (Sana), Yemen (Aden), Oman, and Bahrain.
4/ Afghanistan, India, Pakistan, Nepal, Bangladesh, and Sri Lanka.
5/ Mongolia, Burma, Thailand, Vietnam, Laos, Malaysia, Singapore, Indonesia, Brunei, Philippines, Macao, Korea, Hong Kong, Taiwan, and Cambodia.
6/ Morocco, Algeria, Tunisia, Libya, and Egypt.
7/ Western Europe, Japan, Canada, and Oceania.

Sample pages from quarterly *Outlook for U.S. Agricultural Exports,* which follows developments around the world affecting U.S. agricultural exports. Annual subscription cost is $8.

Developing Countries

U.S. agricultural exports to Africa are now projected to increase 6 to 7 percent from last year.

Exports to Sub-Saharan Africa are estimated at $1 billion, down about 5 percent from last year. Severe drought in southern Africa will result in larger corn and oilseed shipments, offsetting declines to Nigeria and other markets. A number of African countries are having or have had protracted negotiations with the IMF in efforts to obtain foreign exchange loans to continue essential imports of food, fuel, and raw materials. Most have a severe foreign exchange shortage, related in part to lower prices for their exports. Economic growth has been slow or negative, and many of these countries have had to devalue their currency drastically.

U.S. exports to Nigeria during fiscal 1983 are projected to fall 35 percent from last year's $523 million, because of sharp declines in shipments of wheat, rice, and corn. Thailand is replacing the United States as Nigeria's major supplier of rice, primarily because of the price differential. Thai rice is $150 to $200 a ton lower than the U.S. product. The U.S. share of the market has fallen from 61 percent in 1981 to 12 percent currently. The Nigerian Government has imposed import restrictions as part of an austerity package.

U.S. agricultural exports to North Africa are expected to rise to $1.6 billion in fiscal 1983, mainly due to an expansion in U.S. credit programs. Blended credit, GSM-102, and P.L.-480 Title I in Egypt and Morocco are expected to raise exports of wheat, wheat flour, and corn from 6.5 million to 8.0 million tons. However, U.S. exports of wheat to Algeria declined by 70 percent during the first half of fiscal 1983 as Algeria imported wheat from countries with which it signed trade agreements—Canada, France, and Argentina. If Algeria makes some purchases with blended credit, the U.S. share may increase during the rest of this year and into the next year.

U.S. agricultural exports to the Middle East in fiscal 1983 are estimated at $1.6 billion. Agricultural exports to Israel should remain about the same. The most dramatic rise will be in shipments to Iraq through blended credit. Total exports to Iraq may surpass $400 million. Exports to Iran were very small last year, and no change is expected in the foreseeable future. Exports to Saudi Arabia are expected to increase, and shipments of many U.S. processed foods expanded markedly in the first half of the year.

U.S. farm exports to South Asia are expected to climb to a record $1.3 billion, almost double fiscal 1982. The sharp increase stems primarily from larger purchases of U.S. wheat by all South Asian countries, particularly India. Increased purchases of U.S. soybean oil are also forecast. Recently, prospects have improved for larger wheat purchases by Bangladesh and increased Pakistani imports of soybean oil.

South Asian imports of U.S. wheat are sharply higher this year because of a poor 1982 monsoon that reduced 1982/83 harvests of rice and coarse grains. These shortfalls in cereal production are being alleviated by drawing on government-owned cereal stocks and importing wheat.

FAS REPORT

WEEKLY ROUNDUP OF WORLD PRODUCTION AND TRADE

United States
Department of
Agriculture

Foreign
Agricultural
Service

Washington, D.C. 20250

WR 21-83

WASHINGTON, May 25--The Foreign Agricultural Service of the U.S. Department of Agriculture today reported the following developments in world agriculture and trade:

EC TRADE NOTES

The EUROPEAN COMMUNITY (EC) agreed to raise agricultural farm support prices for the 1983/84 season (beginning August 1) by an average 4.2 percent. Last year's record increase was 10.5 percent. For grains, support prices will increase by an average of 3 percent compared to 8.5 percent last year. However, grain target prices, which are the basis for determining the prices of imported grains, will increase by 4.3 percent. This continuing divergence between target and support (intervention) prices means that imported grains (U.S. corn and wheat) will continue to be placed at a relatively greater price disadvantage compared to domestically produced grains.

*****

EC agricultural ministers have reportedly agreed to transfer some intervention wheat stocks from surplus countries like France and West Germany to deficit producers like Italy and Ireland. Officials have indicated that 400,000 tons of wheat would be transferred to Italian intervention stocks and 50,000 tons each to Ireland and Northern Ireland to ensure that the benefits of the feed scheme were shared equally by member states. This would be the first step in the EC plan to incorporate 2-3 million tons of wheat into feed channels. This tonnage would be in addition to the estimated 13 million tons of wheat being fed in 1982/83. Increased wheat feeding could mean reduced demand for imported corn or increased pressure to export EC barley displaced by the wheat in feed rations.

GRAIN AND FEED

ARGENTINA's FOB asking prices for wheat have been about $115 per ton in mid-May, falling almost $40 per ton since the beginning of the Argentine wheat marketing year in December. Argentine wheat prices have shown a rather steady decline through the season until recently when prices plunged about $10 per ton, actually falling $5 to $10 per ton below Argentine corn asking prices for the first time this season. Record wheat export availabilities and the need to attract additional sales have likely precipitated the falling prices.

-more-

EDWIN MOFFETT, Editor, Tel. (202) 382-9443. Additional copies may be obtained from FAS Information Services staff, 5918-South, Washington, D.C. 20250. Tel. (202) 447-7937.

Example of weekly *FAS Report*, which follows significant developments in world agriculture and trade. The publication is available free of charge.

summaries reporting current facts and statistics on issues related to U.S. agricultural trade.

Cost
Free.

Contact
Information Services Staff
Foreign Agricultural Service
U.S. Department of Agriculture
South Building, Room 5918
Washington, DC 20250
(202) 447-7937

FAS Commodity Circulars, which are published at irregular intervals, cover developments in world production and trade for many different commodities.

Cost
From $5 to $65 a year, depending on commodity.

Contact
Information Services Staff
Foreign Agricultural Service
U.S. Department of Agriculture
Room 5918
Washington, DC 20250
(202) 447-3448

FAS Attaché Commodity Reports are raw data reports providing information on unexpected changes in crop production prospects, weather damage, insect infestation, tariff decisions, major policy changes, and other foreign agricultural developments. Raw data reports are available on specific countries and commodities, covering 100 markets and over 125 commodities. These include approximately 1100 scheduled reports and an equal or greater number of voluntary-alert reports.

Cost
Raw data reports are available on a subscription basis or by special request. Costs vary.

Contact

H. Lee Schatz, Reports Officer
Foreign Agricultural Service
U.S. Department of Agriculture
Room 6058-S
Washington, DC 20250
(202) 382-8924

The Foreign Agricultural Service's International Agricultural Statistics (IAS) area has two specific divisions that provide analytical, international agricultural information.

1. The Trade and Economic Information Division develops, maintains, and analyzes trade, international financial, and macroeconomic data and information in support of expansion of U.S. export programs and trade policies.

Contact

Division Director	(202) 382-9017
Tariff and Economic Information Branch	(202) 382-9052
Trade and Marketing Information Branch	(202) 382-9051

2. The Foreign Production Estimates Division estimates world production for crops and livestock. Computer-generated statistical reports for production-related information are available upon request.

Contact

Division Director	(202) 382-8888
Crops Branch, Chief	(202) 382-8865
Livestock Branch, Chief	(202) 382-8868

3. The Foreign Crop Condition Assessment Division, located in Houston, Texas, works with the Foreign Production Estimates Division in developing estimates for world crop production.

Contact

Division Director	(713) 488-9780

USDA: ALERT REPORTS

A prolonged drought in Australia's wheatlands or a hurricane in Honduras can affect supply and price in the world's farm markets and change the competitive position in the United States. Consequently, accurate information on weather damage is vital to investors and the U.S. government as well. To keep the U.S. market posted, the Department of Agriculture maintains an international telex communication network in addition to a microcomputer system that allows instant contact between major U.S. embassies and the Department. The system issues about 5000 alert reports each year to keep the farm community and others abreast of unexpected changes in crop production prospects, weather damage, insect infestation and other developments that affect markets.

World Agricultural Transportation Report is a monthly newsletter that highlights the role of ocean and air transportation in the international marketing of agricultural products. Each issue includes an update on current events, legislation, and the ocean freight market. The editions also include feature articles that explore topical agricultural exports.

Cost
Annual subscription $8 (for residents of the United States, Canada, and Mexico).

Contact
Martin F. Fitzpatrick, Director
Office of Transportation
U.S. Department of Agriculture
Auditors Building, Room 1405
Washington, DC 20250
(202) 447-3963

Agricultural information is also available through AGNET, an on-line computer data base. AGNET offers several marketing information packages, including the following:

> MARKETS. A package that includes weekly USDA–FAS reports on world trade, world production roundups, and U.S. export highlights, as well as monthly USDA–FAS reports on U.S. crop exports and production estimates of corn, cotton, soybeans, and wheat for each major export country.
>
> NEWSRELEASE. A package providing information on a broad range of agriculture and consumer topics, including analyses of national and international factors affecting the grain or livestock market.

Cost
Annual membership fee is $50. Most users spend $20–30 per hour while linked to AGNET during weekday business hours (8 A.M.–5 P.M. Central Time). Rates are lower for evening and weekend use.

Contact
Patrick Ebmeier, User Services Supervisor
Agricultural Computer Network
105 Miller Hall
University of Nebraska-Lincoln
Lincoln, NE 68583
(402) 472-1892

INDUSTRY/COMMODITY INFORMATION

Foreign Trade Report

The Bureau of the Census' monthly *Foreign Trade Report, FT 410: U.S. Exports—Commodity by Country* provides a statistical record of shipments of all merchandise from the United States to foreign countries, including the quantity and dollar value of exports to each country. It also contains cumulative export statistics from the first of the calendar year. Sales of 4500 U.S. products to 160 countries are covered. Review of the reports for three to four years can reveal the countries that are the largest, most consistent markets for specific products.

Cost
Annual subscription $100 in U.S.; $125 foreign. Single copies $9.50 in U.S.; $11.90 foreign. Order no.: S/N 003-001-80010-1.

Contact
Superintendent of Documents
U.S. Government Printing Office
Washington, DC 20402
(202) 783-3238

Commodity Reports

The annual *Market Share Report*'s Commodity Series shows U.S. participation in foreign markets for manufactured products. These reports also provide basic data for exporters to evaluate overall trends in the size of import markets, measure changes in the import demand for specific products, compare the competitive position of U.S. and foreign exporters, select distribution centers for U.S. products abroad, and identify existing and potential markets for U.S. components, parts, and accessories.

Reports in the Commodity Series provide combined total exports from 14 major industrialized countries for particular products shipped to 100 countries. Each of the 1672 commodity reports also shows the value of exports from the United States and eight other major exporting countries as well as the U.S. percentage share. Commodity reports exhibit data for three years.

TABLE 2. SCHEDULE E COMMODITY BY COUNTRY-DOMESTIC MERCHANDISE-CONTINUED

(See "Explanation of Statistics" for information on coverage, definition of f.a.s. export value, security restrictions, sampling procedures, sources of error in the data, OTH CTY (other countries), and other definitions and features of the export statistics. The figure preceding Canada is the number in the sample for Canada. "SC" at the end of the alphabetic commodity description identifies "Special Category" commodities)

Column headers (repeated for each of the three panels):

Country of destination	Current month Net quantity	Current month Value (000 dollars)	Cumulative, January to date Net quantity	Cumulative, January to date Value (000 dollars)

Panel 1

Country	Cur. Net qty	Cur. Value	Cum. Net qty	Cum. Value
U KING	363	17	363	17
NETHLDS	304	13	304	13
S ARAB	2 074	183	2 074	183
SINGAPR	250	10	250	10
MACAO	453	105	453	105
OTH CTY	511	15	511	15
TOTAL	9 445	526	9 445	526

6353020 WOODEN DOORS, NSPF, WITH OR WITHOUT HARDWARE NO

Country	Cur. Net qty	Cur. Value	Cum. Net qty	Cum. Value
CANADA	6 876	211	6 876	211
MEXICO	382	19	382	19
BERMUDA	947	34	947	34
BAHAMAS	310	19	310	19
LW WW I	1 355	41	1 355	41
N ANTIL	207	6	207	6
SURINAM	431	18	431	18
F GUIAN	163	11	163	11
ICELAND	403	16	403	16
FINLAND	845	30	845	30
U KING	857	37	857	37
BELGIUM	700	42	700	42
FR GERM	587	35	587	35
ITALY	465	49	465	49
KUWAIT	2 044	57	2 044	57
S ARAB	1 313	104	1 313	104
JAPAN	2 307	161	2 307	161
AUSTRAL	39	6	39	6
OPAC IS	54	11	54	11
OTH CTY	392	29	392	29
TOTAL	20 677	934	20 677	934

6353030 WOOD BLINDS, SHUTTERS, SCREENS AND SHADES, WITH/WITHOUT HARDWARE

Country	Cur. Net qty	Cur. Value	Cum. Net qty	Cum. Value
1 CANADA	-	34	-	34
BERMUDA	-	9	-	9
LW WW I	-	22	-	22
VENEZ	-	24	-	24
FR GERM	-	18	-	18
ITALY	-	12	-	12
OTH CTY	-	7	-	7
TOTAL	-	126	-	126

6353040 COMPLETE WINDOW AND DOOR CASINGS, WOOD NO

Country	Cur. Net qty	Cur. Value	Cum. Net qty	Cum. Value
MEXICO	294	11	294	11
N ANTIL	2 060	66	2 060	66
JAPAN	690	36	690	36
OTH CTY	266	9	266	9
TOTAL	3 310	122	3 310	122

6353050 WOOD WINDOW UNITS AND SASHES, WHETHER OR NOT KNOCKDOWN, OPEN OR GLAZED NO

Country	Cur. Net qty	Cur. Value	Cum. Net qty	Cum. Value
CANADA	25 879	1 037	25 879	1 037
BERMUDA	525	9	525	9
TRINID	241	5	241	5
U KING	756	14	756	14
JAPAN	4 178	103	4 178	103
OTH CTY	735	6	735	6
TOTAL	32 314	1 174	32 314	1 174

6353060 FABRICATED STRUCTURAL WOOD MEMBERS

Country	Cur. Net qty	Cur. Value	Cum. Net qty	Cum. Value
2 CANADA	-	78	-	78
BAHAMAS	-	27	-	27
JAPAN	-	61	-	61
OTH CTY	-	7	-	7
TOTAL	-	172	-	172

6353070 PREFABRICATED BUILDINGS OF WOOD, WHETHER OR NOT ASSEMBLED

Country	Cur. Net qty	Cur. Value	Cum. Net qty	Cum. Value
CANADA	-	208	-	208
MEXICO	-	94	-	94
DOM REP	-	22	-	22
F W IND	-	18	-	18
VENEZ	-	13	-	13
CH E	-	190	-	190
FR GERM	-	5	-	5

Panel 2

Country	Cur. Net qty	Cur. Value	Cum. Net qty	Cum. Value
ITALY	-	18	-	18
ISRAEL	-	6	-	6
S ARAB	-	336	-	336
OMAN	-	48	-	48
JAPAN	-	17	-	17
OTH CTY	-	5	-	5
TOTAL	-	981	-	981

6353080 BUILDING COMPONENTS OF WOOD, NSPF

Country	Cur. Net qty	Cur. Value	Cum. Net qty	Cum. Value
CANADA	-	91	-	91
MEXICO	-	10	-	10
BERMUDA	-	122	-	122
BAHAMAS	-	124	-	124
LW WW I	-	153	-	153
TRINID	-	49	-	49
N ANTIL	-	13	-	13
VENEZ	-	129	-	129
ARGENT	-	17	-	17
NETHLDS	-	18	-	18
SPAIN	-	10	-	10
S ARAB	-	1 145	-	1 145
BAHRAIN	-	86	-	86
SINGAPR	-	33	-	33
HG KONG	-	26	-	26
JAPAN	-	153	-	153
GUINEA	-	9	-	9
REP SAF	-	18	-	18
OTH CTY	-	21	-	21
TOTAL	-	2 228	-	2 228

6354100 PICTURE AND MIRROR FRAMES, OF WOOD

Country	Cur. Net qty	Cur. Value	Cum. Net qty	Cum. Value
2 CANADA	-	51	-	51
MEXICO	-	5	-	5
BAHAMAS	-	13	-	13
CHILE	-	37	-	37
S ARAB	-	13	-	13
AUSTRAL	-	95	-	95
OTH CTY	-	8	-	8
TOTAL	-	222	-	222

6354220 WOOD HOUSEHOLD UTENSILS AND PARTS THEREOF, NSPF

Country	Cur. Net qty	Cur. Value	Cum. Net qty	Cum. Value
CANADA	-	35	-	35
MEXICO	-	19	-	19
GUATMAL	-	144	-	144
PANAMA	-	9	-	9
BARBADO	-	27	-	27
VENEZ	-	9	-	9
SURINAM	-	20	-	20
U KING	-	12	-	12
FR GERM	-	10	-	10
JAPAN	-	13	-	13
AUSTRAL	-	6	-	6
OTH CTY	-	21	-	21
TOTAL	-	326	-	326

6354240 CLOTHESPINS GR

Country	Cur. Net qty	Cur. Value	Cum. Net qty	Cum. Value
MEXICO	7 297	6	7 297	6
TOTAL	7 297	6	7 297	6

6354920 WOODEN JEWELRY BOXES, SILVERWARE CHESTS, CIGAR/CIGARETTE BOXES, TOOL CHESTS, ETC NO

Country	Cur. Net qty	Cur. Value	Cum. Net qty	Cum. Value
CANADA	10 503	21	10 503	21
DOM REP	2 600	9	2 600	9
U KING	464	11	464	11
KUWAIT	1 830	22	1 830	22
AUSTRAL	1 424	7	1 424	7
OTH CTY	3 097	14	3 097	14
TOTAL	19 918	85	19 918	85

6354940 WOOD CARVINGS

Country	Cur. Net qty	Cur. Value	Cum. Net qty	Cum. Value
N ANTIL	-	13	-	13
NIGERIA	-	16	-	16
OTH CTY	-	9	-	9
TOTAL	-	39	-	39

6359120 WOODEN TOOLS, TOOL BODIES, HANDLES; BACKS FOR BROOMS, MOPS AND BRUSHES

Country	Cur. Net qty	Cur. Value	Cum. Net qty	Cum. Value
CANADA	-	126	-	126

Panel 3

Country	Cur. Net qty	Cur. Value	Cum. Net qty	Cum. Value
MEXICO	-	18	-	18
DOM REP	-	107	-	107
COLOMB	-	9	-	9
DENMARK	-	12	-	12
U KING	-	17	-	17
IRELAND	-	12	-	12
BELGIUM	-	5	-	5
FR GERM	-	12	-	12
S ARAB	-	23	-	23
AUSTRAL	-	44	-	44
N ZEAL	-	50	-	50
LIBERIA	-	14	-	14
OTH CTY	-	15	-	15
TOTAL	-	464	-	464

6359140 WOODEN SHOE LASTS, TREES AND STRETCHERS NO

Country	Cur. Net qty	Cur. Value	Cum. Net qty	Cum. Value
AUSTRAL	7 702	15	7 702	15
N ZEAL	2 737	7	2 737	7
MOZAMBQ	3 109	11	3 109	11
TOTAL	13 548	32	13 548	32

6359200 SPOOLS, BOBBINS AND SIMILAR ARTICLES OF WOOD

Country	Cur. Net qty	Cur. Value	Cum. Net qty	Cum. Value
2 CANADA	-	21	-	21
MEXICO	-	14	-	14
PERU	-	17	-	17
OTH CTY	-	4	-	4
TOTAL	-	56	-	56

6359910 WOOD SHINGLES AND SHAKES SQ

Country	Cur. Net qty	Cur. Value	Cum. Net qty	Cum. Value
1 CANADA	2 622	96	2 622	96
MEXICO	331	9	331	9
BAHAMAS	114	6	114	6
JAMAICA	200	11	200	11
F W IND	2 430	97	2 430	97
FR P IS	204	8	204	8
TOTAL	5 901	228	5 901	228

6359920 WOOD DOWEL RODS AND PINS LFT

Country	Cur. Net qty	Cur. Value	Cum. Net qty	Cum. Value
CANADA	2 895 395	130	2 895 395	130
JAPAN	625 557	22	625 557	22
OTH CTY	96 751	19	96 751	19
TOTAL	3 617 703	171	3 617 703	171

6359930 WOODEN TOOTH PICKS, SKEWERS, CANDY STICKS, TONGUE DEPRESSORS, ETC

Country	Cur. Net qty	Cur. Value	Cum. Net qty	Cum. Value
1 CANADA	-	42	-	42
SALVADR	-	14	-	14
PANAMA	-	5	-	5
F W IND	-	14	-	14
ARGENT	-	11	-	11
NETHLDS	-	14	-	14
S ARAB	-	6	-	6
JAPAN	-	79	-	79
OTH CTY	-	11	-	11
TOTAL	-	196	-	196

6359940 WOODEN COAT AND GARMENT HANGERS

Country	Cur. Net qty	Cur. Value	Cum. Net qty	Cum. Value
1 CANADA	-	8	-	8
BAHAMAS	-	201	-	201
DOM REP	-	12	-	12
JAPAN	-	28	-	28
OTH CTY	-	6	-	6
TOTAL	-	255	-	255

6359950 PENCIL SLATS, WOOD PGR

Country	Cur. Net qty	Cur. Value	Cum. Net qty	Cum. Value
CANADA	51 091	113	51 091	113
MEXICO	106 172	243	106 172	243
DOM REP	16 744	38	16 744	38
COLOMB	36 441	99	36 441	99
VENEZ	39 995	100	39 995	100
PERU	33 800	78	33 800	78
ARGENT	20 861	45	20 861	45
U KING	76 031	218	76 031	218
NETHLDS	38 272	103	38 272	103
FRANCE	132 931	324	132 931	324
FR GERM	200 572	487	200 572	487

Cost
$6.50 per report; catalog free.

Contact
Trade Performance Division/OTIA/ITA
U.S. Department of Commerce
Room 2217
Washington, DC 20230
(202) 377-4211

Information on Foreign Industry Sectors

Additional trade information and assistance in identifying markets for specific industrial products can be obtained by contacting either a Commerce Department District Office or the appropriate industry officer at the Department of Commerce in Washington, D.C.

Contact
Nearest Commerce Department district office (see appendix) or appropriate Commerce officer in Washington, D.C.:

Industry Specialties	Officer	Telephone
High technology industries	Roy Gootenberg	(202) 377-2795
Utilities, construction, and production and processing machinery industries	William Walmsley	(202) 377-5455
Consumer goods, and transport and industrial components industries	Einar Olsen	(202) 377-5783
Information, and finance and management service industries	Fred Crupe	(202) 377-4781
Construction, and transport and tourism service industries	Albert Alexander	(202) 377-4581

(*Opposite page*) **Sample page from** *Foreign Trade Report FT 410: U.S. Exports—Schedule E, Commodity by Country,* **which provides statistical records of all merchandise shipped from the United States to foreign countries. An annual subscription is $115.**

Direct written inquiries to appropriate officer (see previous page) at:
Office of Service Industries
U.S. Department of Commerce
Room 2800A
Washington, DC 20230

Export Statistics Profiles

U.S. suppliers of medical equipment, telecommunications equipment, electronic components, computers, and peripheral equipment can benefit from a new market analysis publication offered by the Department of Commerce. The *Export Statistics Profile* has detailed statistics on industry exports for the last five years, plus a narrative analysis of the export potential.

The basic profile summarizes essential market data, including leading and fastest growing export items, leading and fastest growing foreign markets, major foreign competitors, and the ten best market prospects. In addition, statistical tables for 1978 to 1982 rank the industry's 75 top foreign markets. More detailed marketing information is contained in an expanded profile, which analyzes market data for specific product categories.

Cost
$20–50 (may be higher depending upon complexity of profile).

Contact
ITA/OTIS
U.S. Department of Commerce
Room 1837
Washington, DC 20230
(202) 377-4532

Agricultural Commodity Analysis

Commodity experts and economists at the Foreign Agricultural Service (FAS) analyze U.S. embassy reports on production and trade, combining them with accumulated background information and expertise. The Deputy Directors for Analysis can provide information on consumption, trade, and stocks for their specific commodity areas. Questions regarding marketing a specific commodity should be directed to the appropriate Deputy Director for Marketing. These individuals can provide commodity-specific information concerning competition, export financing, marketing opportunities, and cooperator programs. Commodity information compiled and analyzed by the FAS is available to anyone interested in foreign trade. Commodity experts also will research individual inquiries for specific commodity-related information.

Contact
Appropriate FAS specialists in Washington, DC:

Office	Specialist	Telephone
Dairy, Livestock, and Poultry Division		
Deputy Director for Marketing	Harold Sanden	(202) 447-3899
Deputy Director for Analysis	Carol Harvey	(202) 447-7217
Grain and Feed Division		
Deputy Director for Marketing	Frank Piason	(202) 447-4168
Deputy Director for Analysis	Lyle Sebranek	(202) 447-3179
Horticultural and Tropical Products Division		
Deputy Director for Marketing	Richard Schroeter	(202) 447-7931
Deputy Director for Analysis	Edmond Missiaen	(202) 382-8895
Oilseeds and Products Division		
Deputy Director for Marketing	Gerald W. Harvey	(202) 382-8219
Deputy Director for Analysis	Richard T. McDonnell	(202) 382-0142
Tobacco, Cotton, and Seeds Division		
Deputy Director for Marketing	Leon G. Mears	(202) 382-9516
Deputy Director for Analysis	Gordon Lloyd	(202) 382-9487

Agricultural Research and Technical Assistance

The Agricultural Research Service provides exporters with information on research, publications and consultations on transportation, packaging, storage, refrigeration, animal and plant diseases, insect control, and pesticide residues.

Contact

The appropriate Regional Administrator:

Northeastern Region
Dr. William Tallent
Acting Regional Administrator, ARS
Room 333, B-003, BARC-W
Beltsville, MD 20705
(301) 344-3418

Southern Region
Dr. Robert F. Barnes
Acting Regional Administrator, ARS
P.O. Box 53326
New Orleans, LA 70153
(504) 589-6753

North Central Region
Dr. Paul J. Fitzgerald
Regional Administrator, ARS
2000 West Pioneer Parkway
Peoria, IL 61615
(309) 671-7176

Western Region
Dr. H. C. Cox
Regional Administrator, ARS
1333 Broadway, Suite 400
Oakland, CA 94612
(415) 273-4191

Forest Products Information

The Forest Service prepares periodic analyses of U.S. timber supply and demand, which can be used by the U.S. timber industry to plot overseas investment strategies.

Cost
Free.

Contact
Director
Forest Resources and Economics Research
U.S. Department of Agriculture Forest Service
P.O. Box 2417, Room 3843 South
Washington, DC 20013
(202) 447-2747

The Forest Products Laboratory publishes technical papers, guidelines, and books on various aspects of engineering and applications for timber products. Free mailing lists can be requested by letter or telephone.

Contact
Publications Office
Forest Products Laboratory
Box 5130
Madison, WI 53705
(608) 264-5600

Solar Market Conditions and Potential

A Department of Energy study conducted from mid-1980 through late 1981 analyzed the market conditions and potential for solar energy equipment in 28 countries around the world. Copies of these reports are available at no cost.

Contact

Marci Schweda
Technical Information Branch
Solar Energy Research Institute
1617 Cole Boulevard
Golden, CO 80401
(303) 231-1158

COUNTRY INFORMATION

Foreign Economic Trends

Foreign Economic Trends and Their Implications for the United States is a series of country-specific reports that provides an in-depth review of business conditions and current and near-term prospects. The reports include most recent data on the gross national product, foreign trade, wage and price indexes, unemployment rates, and construction starts. This series analyzes current developments and their implications for future U.S. trade. Reports are prepared by U.S. embassies and consulates abroad. Approximately 150 reports are issued each year.

Cost
Annual subscription $90.00 in U.S.; $112.50 foreign. Order no.: S/N 003-009-81002-7.

Contact

Superintendent of Documents
U.S. Government Printing Office
Washington, DC 20402
(202) 783-3238

For single copies:
Publication Sales Branch
U.S. Department of Commerce
Room 1617
Washington, DC 20230

Country Analyses

Each of the State Department's *Background Notes* provides a survey of a nation's people, geography, economy, government and foreign policy pursuits. The publications provide economic information, including total and per capita gross domestic product, a country's annual growth rates, and percentage shares for natural resources by product, industry, and agriculture. The reports also include trade information on imports and exports, major trading partners, official exchange rates, and a country's membership in international organizations.

Background Notes are published for most countries.

Cost
Annual subscription $34 in U.S.; $42.50 foreign. Single copies $2 in U.S.; $2.50 foreign. Order no.: S/N 044-000-81001-8.

Contact
Superintendent of Documents
U.S. Government Printing Office
Washington, DC 20402
(202) 783-3238

background
notes

Turkey

United States Department of State
Bureau of Public Affairs

March 1983

Official Name:
Republic of Turkey

PROFILE

People

Nationality: *Noun*—Turk(s). *Adjective*—Turkish. **Population** (1982 est.): 46.6 million. **Annual growth rate:** 2.1%. **Ethnic groups:** 85% Turkish, 12% Kurdish, 3% other. **Religions:** Muslim (98%), Christian, Jewish. **Languages:** Turkish (official), Kurdish, Arabic. **Education:** *Years compulsory*—6. *Attendance*—95%. *Literacy*—70%. **Health:** *Infant mortality rate*—15.3/1,000. *Life expectancy*—57 yrs. **Work force** (18.1 million): *Agriculture*—61%. *Industry and commerce*—12%. *Services*—27%.

Geography

Area: 766,640 sq. km. (296,000 sq. mi.); slightly larger than Texas. **Cities:** *Capital*—Ankara (pop. 2.8 million). *Other cities*—Istanbul (4.7 million), Izmir (1.98 million), Adana (1.48 million). **Terrain:** Narrow coastal plain surrounds Anatolia; an inland plateau becomes increasingly rugged as it progresses eastward. **Climate:** Moderate in coastal areas, harsher temperatures inland.

Government

Type: Republic. **Independence:** 1923. **Constitution:** November 7, 1982.
Branches: The 1982 constitution envisages a unicameral 400-member parliament (the Grand National Assembly). Under the present martial law regime, parliamentary functions have been performed by a 160-member Consultative Assembly and the National Security Council. The judicial system has been left intact. The military government has announced that parliamentary elections will be held as early as October 1983. *Executive*—president (chief of state), prime minister. *Legislative*—Consultative Assembly and National Security Council. *Judicial*—Constitutional Court, Court of Cassation, Council of State, High Council of Judges and Prosecutors.
Political parties: None. **Suffrage:** Universal over 21.
Central government budget (1983): $12 billion (1,780 Turkish lira), or 17.6% of 1981 GNP or 17.6% of 1982 budget. **Defense:** 4.8% of 1981 GNP or 17.6% of 1982 budget.
National holiday: Republic Day, October 29.
Flag: White crescent and star on a red field.

Economy

GNP (1981): $59.7 billion. **Annual growth rate** (1970–79): 6%. **Per capita income:** $1,300. **Avg. annual inflation rate** (1982 est.): About 30% under present government's stabilization plan, which has reduced recent yearly rates of more than 100%.
Natural resources: Coal, chromite, copper, boron, oil.
Agriculture (21.8% of GNP): Cotton, tobacco, cereals, sugar beets, fruit, nuts.
Industry (31.4% of GNP): Textiles, processed foodstuffs, iron and steel, cement, leather goods.
Trade (1981): *Exports*—$4.7 billion: tobacco, cotton, textiles, cement, raisins, nuts, leather, glass, ceramics. *Imports*—$8.9 billion: (by value) petroleum, pharmaceuticals and dyes, iron and steel, machinery, plastics and rubber, transport vehicles. *Major partners*—Iraq, FRG, US, France, UK, Italy, Iran, Libya, and Eastern Europe.
Fiscal year: Calendar year.
Official exchange rate (Dec. 1982): 185 Turkish lira = US$1.
US economic aid received (FY 1946–82): $3.5 billion. **US military aid** (FY 1946–82): $5.2 billion.

Membership in International Organizations

UN, Organization for Economic Cooperation and Development (OECD), INTELSAT, NATO, Islamic Conference Organization, EC associate member, Council of Europe.

Example from a U.S. State Department series, *Background Notes,* **which is available for most countries. Single issues are $2, while an annual subscription is available for $34.**

Overseas Business Reports

The Commerce Department's *Overseas Business Report* series provides basic background data for business people who are evaluating export markets or considering entering new areas. The series discusses pertinent marketing factors in individual countries, presents economic and commercial profiles of countries and regions, issues semiannual outlooks for U.S. trade with countries and geographical regions, and publishes selected statistical reports on the direction, volume, and nature of U.S. foreign trade. Some 60 reports are issued each year for both developing and industrialized markets.

Cost

Annual subscription $44.00 in U.S.; $55.00 foreign. Single copies vary in price. Order no. S/N 003-000-81001-1.

Contact

Superintendent of Documents
U.S. Government Printing Office
Washington, DC 20402
(202) 783-3238

Business Risk Assessment

The State Department's Office of Business and Export Affairs provides information on which to base business risk assessments. The Office develops and reviews commercial action programs and strategies for 71 countries in which the Department of State has primary responsibility for business support.

Contact

James R. Tarrant, Director
Office of Business and Export Affairs
U.S. Department of State
Room 3638
Washington, DC 20520
(202) 632-0354

Market Share Reports

The Commerce Department's annual *Market Share Report* Country Series provides basic data to evaluate overall trends in the size of import markets; measure changes in the import demand for specific products; compare the competitive position of U.S. and foreign exporters; select distribution centers for U.S. products abroad; and identify existing and potential markets for U.S. components, parts, and accessories. The reports show U.S. participation in foreign markets for manufactured products. Reports in the Country Series provide a basis for examining the relative shifts in total imports from the United States and eight leading suppliers into each of 88 countries for approximately 1600 manufactured products. Most country reports show data for five years.

Cost
$9; catalog free.

Contact
Trade Performance Division/OTIA/ITA
U.S. Department of Commerce
Room 2217
Washington, DC 20230
(202) 377-4211

Market Research Reports

Two types of market research reports are produced by the Department of Commerce.

International Market Research Surveys are comprehensive studies covering a variety of industry and country subjects, generally performed in-country by private contractors. They provide detailed information on market prospects and range up to 400 pages in length. Each report contains statistics and analyzes the market for selected products, end users and their purchasing plans, marketing practices, and trade restrictions. These reports also list key potential buyers, government purchasing agencies, and similar relevant organizations.

Cost
From $50 to $100.

Country Market Surveys summarize the more detailed market research surveys. They are available for the following industries: agricultural machinery and equipment, communications equipment, computers and peripheral equipment, electric power systems, electronic components, equipment and materials for electronic components production, food processing and packaging equipment, graphic industries equipment, industrial process controls, laboratory instruments, machine tools, medical equipment, and sporting goods and recreational equipment.

Cost
$7.50 and up per copy, depending on title.

Contact
International Market Research, OTIS/ITA
U.S. Department of Commerce
Room 1322
Washington, DC 20230
(202) 377-2665

Country Seminars

The Commerce Department's district offices frequently sponsor seminars on conducting business in specific countries.

Contact
Sandy Necessary
U.S. Commercial Service, ITA
U.S. Department of Commerce
Washington, DC 20230
(202) 377-0727

or nearest Commerce district office (see appendix).

Country Demographic Profiles

The U.S. Bureau of the Census collects and analyzes worldwide demographic, social, and economic data that can assist companies in identifying potential markets. Thorough demographic analyses, along with data on education and economic activity, are published for selected countries in the *Country Demographic Profiles* series. Profiles currently available cover the countries listed below:

Country	Order No. (S/N)	Cost: U.S./Foreign
Colombia	003-024-02121-8	$4.75/$5.95
Malaysia	003-024-02123-4	4.50/ 5.65
Morocco	003-024-02124-2	4.50/ 5.65
Nepal	003-024-02122-6	4.50/ 5.65
Pakistan	003-024-02125-1	3.75/ 4.70
Turkey	003-024-02126-9	4.25/ 5.35

Contact
Superintendent of Documents
U.S. Government Printing Office
Washington, DC 20402
(202) 783-3238

Caribbean Basin Business Information

The Department of Commerce's Caribbean Basin Business Information Center assists U.S. companies seeking business opportunities in the Caribbean Basin. Country specialists provide counseling on the business environment in specific countries and sectors, collect and distribute information on trade and investment opportunities, prepare articles and publications on key topics, and organize seminars on conducting business in this region.

A *Caribbean Basin Business Information Starter Kit* is available free of charge. It includes a list of publications and U.S. and Caribbean government contacts and private-sector organizations, along with information on the Caribbean Basin Initiative and trade statistics. Business profiles on the individual countries of the Caribbean Basin are also available. They cover a country's development priorities, export prospects, investment incentives, regulatory environment, economic infrastructure, key economic indicators, and important business contacts.

Country specialists are:

Area	Specialist	Telephone
Guatemala, Costa Rica, Panama	Robert Bateman	(202) 377-5563
Haiti, Dominican Republic	George Fitch	(202) 377-3637
Guyana, Suriname, French Departments, Netherlands Antilles	Robert Dormitzer	(202) 377-2218
Bahamas, Bermuda, Caymans, British Virgin Islands	Libby Roper	(202) 377-2912
Barbados, Belize, Eastern Caribbean	Desmond Foynes	(202) 377-5563
Cuba, Honduras, Jamaica, Trinidad and Tobago, El Salvador, Nicaragua	Scott Wylie	(202) 377-3637

Contact
Caribbean Basin Business Information Center
U.S. Department of Commerce
Room 3027
Washington, DC 20230
(202) 377-2527

Caribbean Agribusiness Information

A special program of the Department of Agriculture promotes private-sector agribusiness investment in the countries of the Caribbean and Central America. The Agribusiness Investment Information Desk assists potential investors seeking technical agricultural expertise and data on the Caribbean Basin. The Desk provides information on plant and health inspection requirements, quality standards, and other country regulations. The staff also collects and distributes information on Caribbean investment opportunities.

The Agribusiness Promotion Council, a private-sector advisory committee, advises the Secretary of Agriculture and the Department on accelerating agricultural development through private-sector investment. The Council's six committees focus on Costa Rica, the Dominican Republic, Honduras, Guatemala, small-medium investor involvement/management training, and marketing and U.S. distribution outlets.

Contact
Beri Milburn, Agribusiness Specialist
OICD/Agribusiness Programs
U.S. Department of Agriculture
Auditors Building, Room 4102
Washington, DC 20250
(202) 447-4515

Egypt Sector Surveys

The Egyptian government, with support from the Agency for International Development and the Chase Trade Information Corporation, has prepared surveys of 10 industrial sectors. Each survey includes present participants in the market, estimates of local supply and demand, raw material availability, current production and distribution, and profiles of specific investment project opportunities. The following surveys are available:

Food Crop Production and Processing

Projects
Canning, freezing, dehydration, or other processing and packaging of fruits and vegetables for domestic and export markets; crushing oil seeds, refining oils, and utilizing oil residues to produce edible oils, soaps, detergents, and other related products; production of sweeteners and yeasts; manufacture of biscuits and confectionary items for domestic and export markets.

Meat, Poultry, and Fish Production and Processing

Projects
Integrated poultry processing and freezing; fish farming, processing, freezing, and canning; dairy production and dairy farms; precooked convenience packaging; cattle feeding and slaughtering; processing, freezing, and canning of meat products for domestic and export markets.

Health Care Products and Equipment

Projects
Preparation of medical, pharmaceutical, and other products subject to registration with the Ministry of Health; production of health care and personal hygiene supplies and equipment for use by physicians, hospitals, and clinics, or in the home.

Construction Materials, Components, and Systems

Projects
Production of construction materials, structural and mechanical components and equipment for use in industrial, commercial, residential, and civil works construction; establishment of contracting enterprises to operate and maintain specialized construction systems and equipment.

Nonelectrical Machinery

Projects
Production of mechanical industrial machinery, e.g., machine tools, pumps, valves, compressors; materials handling equipment for use in the manufacture of industrial and consumer products or provision of services to business and the public.

Integrated Agribusiness

Projects
Development of fully reclaimed lands for commercial food production, and processing activities, e.g., crops, meat, dairy.

Nonfood Chemical Process Industries

Projects
Continuous processing of chemicals, metallic and nonmetallic minerals, and nonagricultural crops.

Automotive Components

Projects
Production of parts, components, and other supplies for manufacture of cars, trucks, buses, and construction and farm machinery. Production of tires, wheels, brake linings, mufflers, upholstery, dashboard instruments, spark plugs, air filters, fan belts, and radiators for replacement, both for domestic use and export.

Electrical and Electronic Machinery

Projects
Production of electric power distribution and transmission equipment; electrical appliances; motors and other industrial apparatus and controls; lighting and wiring equipment; electronic communications equipment, components, and accessories.

Maintenance and Repair Facilities

Projects
Establishment of facilities for the production and supply of maintenance spare parts, components, and materials; provision of technical services for maintenance, rebuilding and repair of capital equipment, e.g., aircraft, construction machinery, motor vehicles, machine tools; provision of management and maintenance services for industrial, commercial, and residential buildings and civil works.

Cost
Free.

Contact
Ismail Kamel
General Authority for Investment and Free Zones
8 Adly Street
P.O. Box 1007
Cairo, Arab Republic of Egypt
Phone: 902645; 903776
Telex: 92235 INVEST

EGYPTIAN SECTOR SURVEY

Table 5-1

JOINT-VENTURE POSSIBILITIES DISCUSSED IN REPORT ON EGYPTIAN FOOD CROPS

Project	Egyptian Interest in Public Law 43 Joint Ventures	Page Reference
1. Corn syrups and starches	The Egyptian Starch, Yeast, and Detergent Company (100 percent government-owned)	66, Profile F-1
2. Biscuits and confectioneries	BISCOMISR (PL 43 company)	73-75, Profile F-2
3. Biscuits and confectioneries	BISCOMISR (PL 43 company)	76, Profile F-2
4. Biscuits and confectioneries	CHOCOROYAL (100 percent government-owned)	71, Profile F-2
5. Biscuits and confectioneries	National Bank for Development (PL 43 company)	76, Profile F-2
6. Ice cream	CHOCOROYAL (100 percent government-owned)	72, Profile F-2
7. Edible oils	The Nile Oil & Soap Company (100 percent government-owned)	88, Profile F-3
8. Toiletries	The Egyptian Salt & Soda Company (100 percent government-owned)	90
9. Toiletries	The Nile Oil & Soap Company (100 percent government-owned)	90
10. Detergents	Egyptian Salt & Soda Company (100 percent government-owned)	90
11. Seeds and tissue culture	CENTECH (private Egyptian company)	97-98
12. Bulk tomato paste	KAHA (100 percent government-owned)	101, Profile F-6

Sample page from a ten-volume survey of Egyptian industrial sectors published by the Egyptian government, with support from the Agency for International Development and the Chase Trade Information Corporation. The surveys are available at no charge.

CHAPTER
THREE

TARGETING
OPPORTUNITIES

After determining an area or industry of interest for an overseas enterprise, the next step is to identify specific business opportunities. A number of U.S. government programs provide trade and investment leads. Many of these programs are based on information and analyses transmitted to government offices in Washington by U.S. embassies and consulates overseas. This chapter reviews approximately two dozen federal services and programs for targeting overseas opportunities in four broad categories:

Publications. Magazines and bulletins providing specific trade leads on potential markets and new products.

Systems. Information systems containing data on potential business leads, including computer "match" and response programs.

Customized Services. Services that locate agents or distributors, provide background information on foreign trading companies and businesses, or identify investment opportunities in specific countries.

Special Programs for Small Business. Management assistance programs to help small businesses make a preliminary assessment of their export potential.

PUBLICATIONS

Business America

The Commerce Department's *Business America* is a biweekly magazine designed to help U.S. exporters penetrate overseas markets by providing timely information on opportunities for trade and methods of doing business in foreign countries. A typical issue includes an analytical piece on U.S. trade policy, a "how to" article for new exporters, a review of the nation's economic trends, and news of Congressional and government actions affecting trade. It also includes trade news generated by the Commerce Department, other U.S. government agencies, and foreign governments; trade and investment opportunities abroad; and a calendar of upcoming catalog shows, exhibitions, seminars, and international trade fairs.

Cost
Annual subscription $55 in U.S.; $68.75 foreign. Single copies $3.25 in U.S.; $4.10 foreign. Order no.: S/N 003-025-80002-7.

Contact
Superintendent of Documents
U.S. Government Printing Office
Washington, DC 20402
(202) 783-3238

Commerce Business Daily

The U.S. and Foreign Commercial Service publicizes foreign trade leads as well as commodity needs of foreign governments in *Commerce Business Daily*. Contact names and phone numbers are provided for the dozen or more opportunities listed daily.

Cost
Annual subscription $160 (first-class postage); $81 (second-class postage) in U.S. No single copies sold. Order no.: S/N 003-008-80006-8.

Contact
Superintendent of Documents
U.S. Government Printing Office
Washington, DC 20402
(202) 783-3238

April 18, 1983   THE MAGAZINE OF INTERNATIONAL TRADE

District Export Councils
Promote
Local Sales Abroad

Brought to you by the 50 DECs

A Publication of the U.S. Department of Commerce

Cover (*above*) and calendar of events (*opposite page*) from *Business America,* a biweekly magazine published by the Commerce Department for U.S. exporters and others interested in trade and investment opportunities abroad. Annual subscription cost is $55.

Calendar For World Traders

April 5—Portland, Ore.—An all-day seminar on barter and countertrade will be sponsored by the District Export Council. For additional information, call James Mied, 503-221-3001.

April 11-12—Atlantic City, N.J.—The Third Annual Mid-Atlantic Conference of the New Jersey District Export Council. Topics will include: international law, tax, finance, marketing, and distribution. Phone Tom Murray, 609-989-2100.

April 12-13—Dallas—The Center for International Business will host its Tenth Annual International Trade Conference. Theme: Global interdependence and economic nationalism. Lionel Olmer, Under Secretary of Commerce for International Trade, will speak. Phone 214-742-7301.

April 14—Los Angeles—An international round table conference on international finance, credit, collection, and exchange problems will be sponsored by FCIB-NACM Corporation. Participation fee is $80. For further information, call 212-578-4417.

April 15—New York City—A cabinet-level Moroccan delegation will be guest at a luncheon of the American-Arab Association for Commerce and Industry. For information and reservations, call 212-986-7229.

April 18-19—Chicago—The 46th Chicago World Trade Conference will explore attempts to reinvigorate the U.S. economy by removing artificial trade barriers. Commerce Secretary Malcolm Baldrige will deliver the keynote address. For information, phone 312-786-0111 (Ext. 215).

April 20—Boston—A workshop on ocean freight documentation will be held by the International Business Center of New England. The cost is $65. Phone 617-542-0426.

May 4—Boston—Insurance and export licensing are the themes of a workshop sponsored by the International Business Center of New England. The cost is $65. Phone 617-542-0426.

May 4—Washington, D.C.—The Association of Chambers of Commerce in Latin America will host its 13th corporate briefing. Twenty-one American Chamber presidents will give off-the-record analyses and forecasts for business conditions in their countries. Call Lynn Stevens, 202-463-5490.

May 5-6—London—A conference entitled "Successful Joint Ventures in Egypt" will be sponsored by the London management training firm, Monadnock International. The two-day event is designed to give a balanced assessment of the risks and rewards of doing business in Egypt. Call London 01-262-2732, telex 299180 MONINT G.

May 10 & 12—Santa Clara & Los Angeles, Calif.—A one-day workshop on "Export Licensing and Controls" will be sponsored by Unz & Co. Topics will include: Export Administration regulations, documentation requirements, commodity classifications. For further information, call 800-631-3098.

May 15-20—Chicago—"Credit—The Key in '83" is the theme of the 87th Annual NACM Credit Conference hosted by FCIB-NACM Corporation. For details, phone G.E. Lota, 212-578-4417.

June 1—Seattle—A workshop on "Marketing Service-Related Industries Abroad" will be hosted by the Seattle District Office of the International Trade Administration. Call Pat LeDonne, 206-442-5615.

WEDNESDAY JUNE 29, 1983
Issue No. PSA-8366

Commerce Business Daily

A daily list of U.S. Government procurement invitations, contract awards, subcontracting leads, sales of surplus property and foreign business opportunities

---

U.S. GOVERNMENT PROCUREMENTS

Services

A Experimental, Developmental, Test and Research Work (research includes both basic and applied research)

2750 ABW/PMR, Specialized Contracting Branch, Area C, Bldg 1, Rm 1W, Wright-Patterson AFB, OH 45433. Attn: G L King, 513/257-4343
A — MANAGEMENT SCIENTIFIC STUDY: STRATEGIC AND TACTICAL MISSILE SPARES REQUIREMENTS, funding levels and operational capability assessment to develop models of computational methodology and algorithms. Only acceptable technical proposals will be considered for negs. See notes 49 & 64. Reference RFP F33600-83-R-0442. (174)

Ballistic Missile Defense Systems Command, Contracts Office, BMDSC-CRR, Attn: Mr W F Fitzpatrick, 205/895-3000, PO Box 1500, Huntsville, AL 25807
★ **A — BMD SYSTEMS ANALYSIS**—An 18 month R&D effort for the Ballistic Missile Defense Systems Command, Huntsville, AL, RFQ DASG60-83-Q-0204—Negs conducted with Science Applications Inc, 2109 W Clinton Ave, Huntsville, AL 35805. See note 46. (175)

Naval Air Development Center, (Code 84563), Warminster, PA 18974
A — DESIGN, FABRICATION, TEST AND DELIVERY OF 60 EACH CPU-60/P QUICK DONNING ANTI-EXPOSURE COVERALLS, stowage bags and interface components—RFP N62269-83-R-0289—Closing date o/a 9 Aug 83. Tel 215/441-2683. (174)

NOAA, Western Administrative Support Center (WASC), Attn: AT/WC3, 7600 Sand Point Way, NE, Bin C15700, Seattle, WA 98115
❶ **A — DEVELOP ESTIMATES OF POLLUTANT DISCHARGES INTO THE MARINE WATERS OF THE EAST AND WEST COAST REGIONS** of the U.S.; and a cost-effective and operational framework for manipulating these estimates. The framework is to provide NOAA with the capability to make revisions to these estimates as new data becomes available as well as analyze the effects of alternative policies and factors which affect pollutant discharges. The project will build upon previous work already completed in the Gulf of Mexico region. The estimates for the east and west coast will be incorporated into NOAA's National Coastal Pollutant Discharge Inventory. This inventory will contain estimates of pollutant discharges from all land-based and ocean-based sources in the ocean coastal areas of the contiguous United States. The inventory for each regional data base is comprised of three separate, but closely related components: (1) an inventory of all land-based and ocean-based point sources and their pollutant discharges, including disposal of dredged materials and operational discharges of oil from marine transportation activities; (2) an inventory of all land-based nonpoint sources and their pollutant discharges; and (3) an inventory of pollutant inflows from upstream sources into surface waters of coastal counties, some portion of which eventually is transported to coastal and ocean waters. RFP WASC-83-00259 closes Aug 9, 1983. Notes 42, 64, 80. (175)

Commander, Naval Ocean Systems Center, San Diego, CA 92152, Attn: M.E. Taylor, Code 422B, 619/225-7873
★ **A — DESIGN AND CONSTRUCTION OF A MICROPROCESSOR-BASED DATA**

CBD ON-LINE

An electronic edition of the COMMERCE BUSINESS DAILY will be available from the following contractors to the Department of Commerce effective immediately. Interested parties may contact them for full commercial and competitive details. Dialog Information Services, Inc., 3460 Hillview Ave., Palo Alto, CA 94304; toll free 800/227-1927 (outside CA) or 800/982-5838 (in CA) DMS/On-Line. 100 Northfield St., Greenwich, CT 06830; toll free 1-800/243-3852 or 203/661-7800. United Communications Group, 8701 Georgia Ave., Silver Spring, MD 20910; toll free 800/638-7728 (Joanne Gionnola) or 301/589-8875 collect.

BUSINESS NEWS

FEDERAL PROCUREMENT CONFERENCE—MACON, GEORGIA

Senator Samuel Nunn, in cooperation with the U.S. Departments of Commerce and Defense, is sponsoring a Federal Procurement Conference on 23 August 1983, at Macon Coliseum, 200 Coliseum Dr., Macon, GA 31201. The purpose of the conference is to provide the business community with an opportunity to meet on a person-to-person basis with procurement specialists from Federal military and civilian agencies and Federal prime contractors. Attendees will be counseled on sales opportunities to the Federal Government, Federal procurement and contracting procedures, and export opportunities. For further information contact: Hazel Winfield, or Alen Chootkin, ℅ Senator Nunn, 335 Dirksen SOB, Washington, D.C. 20510, Tel: 202/224-3521.

COLLECTION AND PROCESSING UNIT EMPLOYING OFF-THE-SHELF, commercially available circuit boards. Negotiations to be conducted on a sole source basis with Varian Microwave Tube Div, 611 Hansen Way, Palo Alto, CA 94303 as a result of an unsolicited proposal received from that company. N66001-83-R-0306. See note 46. (175)

ETD/HV Contracts Branch, Fort Monmouth Contracts Office, U.S. Army Electronics Research and Development Command, Attn: DRDEL-AQ-MC(APP), Fort Monmouth, NJ 07703, Buyer Bill Applegate, 201/532-5486
★ **A — 3.2MM TRANSMITTER WAVE TUBE.** Under Sol DAAK20-83-Q-0330 an award is in process to Hughes Aircraft Company. (175)

Defense Supply Services-Washington, Rm 1D245, The Pentagon, Washington, DC 20310, Attn: Mrs. Edna Clark
★ **A — IMPLEMENTATION OF THE MOBILIZATION BASE REQUIREMENTS MODEL (MOBREM).** Negotiation conducted with Presearch Incorporated, 2361 S. Jefferson Davis Highway, Arlington, VA, on a sole source basis. The work to be performed will be to provide a model through which time-phased CONUS base mobilization requirements for manpower and equipment can be derived, analyzed and utilized in mobilization planning and programming. See note 46. (175)

U.S. Department of Energy, Albuquerque Operations Office, Contract and Industrial Relations Division, PO Box 5400, Albuquerque, NM 87115
★ **A — STUDY OF SOLAR THERMAL INDUSTRY TECHNOLOGY TRANSFER.** Negotiations conducted on a sole source basis with Solar Energy Industries Association, 1001 Connecticut Avenue, NW, Washington, DC 20036. See note 46. (175)

U.S. Department of Energy, Office of Procurement Operations, Washington, DC 20585
★ **A — REVIEW AND ANALYSIS OF SITE AND DESIGN CRITERIA FOR THE WASTE ISOLATION PILOT PLANT.** DE-AC01-83DP48015. Negotiations are being conducted with National Academy of Sciences, Washington, DC 20418. Use note 46.

U.S. Department of Energy, Oak Ridge Operations Office, Procurement and Contracts Division, PO Box E, Oak Ridge, TN 37830
★ **A — PLD/SET IV UPPER SUSPENSION ASSEMBLY SUSTAINING ENGINEERING FOR THE ADVANCED GAS CENTRIFUGE PROGRAM.** Negotiating with Boeing Engineering and Construction Southeast, Inc, 767 Mitchell Road, Oak Ridge, TN 37830. See note 46. (175)

Contracting Officer, Naval Research Laboratory, Washington, DC 20375
★ **A — RESEARCH FOR CARBON DIOXIDE REMOVAL OR REDUCTION.** Negotiations are being conducted with General Electric Corp, 50 Fordman Rd, Wilmington, MA 01887. See note 46.
★ **A — CONTINUATION OF "RESEARCH ON THEORETICAL INVESTIGATIONS OF DENSE PLASMA X-RAY CONCEPTS".** Negotiations are being conducted with Berkeley Research Associates, PO Box 241, Berkeley, CA 94701. See note 46. (175)

U.S. Department of Energy, Morgantown Energy Technology Center, PO Box 880, Morgantown, WV 26505, Attn: Danette L. Hardman, Contract Specialist, 304/291-4241
❶ **A — A RESEARCH STUDY OF PARTICULATE COLLECTION DEVICES DEVELOPED FOR PRESSURIZED FLUIDIZED-BED COMBUSTORS AS APPLIED**

TO COAL GASIFICATION PROCESSES. The study will involve identification problems, limitations, and applicability of ten specific particle collection devices which used for hot-gas cleanup for coal gasification processes. These ten devices were originally developed for hot-gas cleanup of gas streams from pressurized fluidized-bed combustors. addition, the study will develop a priority listing of the particle collection devices as their potential use for coal gasification and will identify future research needs. Sol DH RP-21-83MC20035 issued o/a Jun 28, 1983. A cost reimbursement of CPFF type contract contemplated for a period of 8 months. Source selection will be based primarily on the te merits of proposals with secondary emphasis on cost and other factors. Requests for copi of the RFP must be submitted in writing to the Attn: Danette L. Hardman. (175)

National Cancer Institute, Carcinogenesis & Field Studies, Contrac Section, Research Contracts Branch, Blair Building, Rm 114, Nti Behtesda, MD 20205
A — AMENDMENT. SUPPORT SERVICES FOR CLINICAL EPIDEMIOLOGIC STUDIES. Due date RFP NCI-CP-FS-31034-77, which was listed in the May 13, 1983 iss of the CBD, is hereby reset for Jul 22, 1983. (175)

National Heart, Lung & Blood Institute of Health, Federal Bldg, P 5C14, Bethesda, MD 20205
★ **A — CONTINUATION OF SUPPORT SERVICES FOR THE TEN YEAR UPDA OF THE NATIONAL PLAN.** Negotiations are being conducted with JRB Associate Division of Science Application Inc, 8400 Westpark Drive, McLean, VA 22102, Contract HO-1-3003, Modification No. 11 for the continuation of work in process. The final stages the Ninth Report of the Director, NHLBI, the Tenth Report, and the Interagency Techni Committee Summary Report remain to be finished. See note 46. (175)

AFOSR-PKO, Bldg 410, Bolling AFB, Washington, DC 20332
★ **A — STUDY OF SUBMICRON PARTICLE SIZE DISTRIBUTIONS BY LASE DOPPLER MEASUREMENT OF BROWNIAN MOTION.** Negotiations are to be cond with Aerodyne Research Inc, Billerica, MA 01821. See note 40. Unsolicited.
★ **A — NEAR-SOURCE STRUCTURAL EFFECTS ON UNDERGROUND EXPLI SIONS** at Shagan River. Unsolicited. Negotiations are to be conducted with Sie Geophysics Inc, Redmond, WA 98052. See note 40. (175)

NASA Headquarters, Contracts and Grants Division, Code HWD Washington, DC 20546, Attn: Laurance A. Milov
★ **A — RESEARCH IN THE AREA OF "DEGRADATION OF PCB".** Negotiati with Analytical Labs and Services, Inc, Huntsville, AL 35801. See note 46. (175)

EPA, Contracts Management Division (MD-33), Office of Administra tion, Attn: NCCM-7, Research Triangle Pk, NC 27711
A — INTEGRATED DOSIMETRIC BIOLOGICAL MODEL FOR USE IN REVIE ING THE PRIMARY NATIONAL AMBIENT AIR QUALITY STANDARD FOR OZON

Content

New Product Publicity

The Commerce Department's New Product Information Service (NPIS) provides worldwide publicity for new U.S. products available for immediate export. This service enables foreign firms to identify and contact U.S. exporters of specific products, thereby giving the U.S. company a direct indication of market interest and often generating sales, agent contacts, and other benefits.

NPIS information is distributed in two ways. The monthly *Commercial News USA* contains short, promotional descriptions of some 100 to 150 new products, together with the names and addresses of the exporters and (on a selected basis) black and white product photographs. This magazine is distributed to 240 U.S. embassies and consulates, 50 American Chambers of Commerce abroad, and Commerce Department district offices. Product data in *Commercial News USA* ultimately reach approximately 200,000 business and government leaders worldwide. Information on selected NPIS products is also broadcast overseas by the U.S. Information Agency's "Voice of America" radio programs.

To qualify for the NPIS, products must have been sold on the U.S. market for no more than two years, must be currently exported to no more than three countries on a regular basis, and must meet other guidelines.

Cost
$40 per product listing.

Contact
Commercial News USA
Office of Event Management and Support Services
U.S. Department of Commerce
Room 2106
Washington, DC 20230
(202) 377-4918

or nearest Commerce Department district office (see appendix).

(*Opposite page*) Cover page from sample issue of *Commerce Business Daily*, a listing of foreign business opportunities and trade leads, as well as U.S. government contract invitations and awards. Annual subscription is $81 by second-class postage, $160 by first-class postage.

International Market Search

The Commerce Department also selects six industries each year for promotion through the International Market Search program. This program provides worldwide publicity for U.S. products and technology for each industry. Jewelry, food equipment for catering, hotels and restaurants, mining and heavy construction equipment, telecommunications, and renewable energy were selected for promotion in 1983. In 1984 the program will focus on water resources; household consumer goods; automotive parts and accessories; computers, peripherals, and business equipment; plastics machinery and raw materials; and safety and security equipment. Through publication in *Commercial News USA* magazine, information on these products ultimately reaches approximately 200,000 business and government leaders worldwide.

To qualify for this service, products must conform to the definition of the industry being highlighted, must be currently exported to no more than 15 countries on a regular basis, and must meet other requirements.

Cost
$40 per product listing.

Contact
Commercial News USA
Office of Event Management and Support Services
U.S. Department of Commerce
Room 2106
Washington, DC 20230
(202) 377-4918

or nearest Commerce Department district office (see appendix).

COMMERCIAL NEWS USA

U.S. PRODUCTS FOR EXPORT

NPIS

The following products have been selected by the U.S. Department of Commerce for promotion through the New Product Information Service (NPIS) and meet the NPIS criteria (not on the U.S. market for more than two years, not currently exported to more than three countries on a regular basis, etc.). This information is also made available by Commerce on a selected basis to VOA for worldwide broadcasting. While the information listed in Commercial News USA is believed to be reliable, no responsibility can be assumed by the U.S. Government or its representatives for the accuracy of the new product descriptions which are based on data supplied by the listed U.S. firms. Both technical and non-technical products are included to ensure worldwide market applicability. A Glossary of the most frequently used scientific or technical terms is included in this issue. Text is prepared in camera-ready copy. Please reprint as many new product descriptions as possible.

AGRICULTURAL MACHINERY AND EQUIPMENT
(Including Animal Husbandry and Veterinary Sciences)

AIRTIGHT GRAIN STORAGE FACILITIES — According to the company, the "Agristore System" provides airtight, moisture free, and rodentproof grain storage. It can do so, explains the firm, by using ancient principles of controlled atmosphere and highly effective components treated with PVC. The facilities are tailored to specifications on site and result in grain of the highest marketable quality. It is priced from $5,000 to $2 million. WRITE: Thurman L. Boykin, Pres., The Boykin Co., Dept. CN, 1800 N. Kent St., Suite 901, Arlington, Virginia 22209 U.S.A.

TOTALLY ORGANIC SOIL FERTILIZER — The firm says that farmers and horticulturists can produce superior crops without chemicals at a low cost with C.B.S.E. - Crop Booster - Soil Enricher." This new 100-percent organic fertilizer consists of a beneficial strain of soil bacteria plus enzymes said to increase crop yields, build humus, and conserve water through proper penetration and retention. Easy to apply, this product can be either sprayed or dripped. WRITE: Bob Friedman, Gen. Mgr., Creative Sales West, Dept. CN, Bio Science Div., P.O. Box 2581, Sepulveda, California 91343 U.S.A.

CLEAR, EASY-TO-MAINTAIN FLOW FILTERS — "Vu Flow Filters" are made of noncorrosive PVC and clear Lexan plastic to allow a visual inspection. Used for low volume irrigation systems, models are available to handle from 228 to 3,800 l/min. Because there is no mineral buildup, these filters are easy to clean and no tools are needed. All models are 200 PSI rated with low pressure drop, says the firm. Distributors and agents are actively sought for these $39-$125 filters. WRITE: Gardner Russell, Vice Pres., Vu Flow Filters Co., Dept. CN, 645 Cinnamon Court, Satellite Beach, Florida 32937 U.S.A.

Page from the New Product Information Service section of *Commercial News USA,* a monthly publication that describes new U.S. products as a means of fostering exports. The publication is distributed to all U.S. embassy and consulate libraries around the world.

SYSTEMS

Foreign Firm Information

The Commerce Department receives information on foreign firms from overseas posts and stores the data in a master computer file called the Foreign Traders Index (FTI). The FTI lists firms that import from the United States, have a high potential to purchase U.S. goods and services, and are interested in representing U.S. exporters. This file covers 143 countries and contains information on more than 150,000 importing firms, agents, representatives, distributors, manufacturers, service organizations, wholesalers, retailers, and potential end users of U.S. products and services. Newly identified firms are continually added to the FTI file and information on listed firms is updated frequently. Firms can be retrieved singly or by product, product group, industry, and country.

This information is available to U.S. companies in three forms:

Export Mailing List Service

The EMLS provides foreign firm data to individuals requesting lists according to specific criteria. EMLS lists can be provided on gummed mailing labels or as printouts. The following data are available: the name and address of the firm, name and title of the chief executive officer, year established, relative size, number of employees, telephone and telex number, cable address, and product or service code or type of business (e.g., manufacturer, wholesaler, distributor).

Cost
For 500 firms within 5 SIC codes, $35 for the first country, $10 for each additional country (labels or printout). For more than 500 firms or more than 5 SIC codes, see contact on page 51.

FTI Data Tape Service

Information on all firms in the FTI for all or selected countries is available on magnetic tape through this service. Users can retrieve data segments in various combinations through their own computer facilities.

Cost

Data for 15 or more countries or the entire file is $5000 (prepaid). Users can also request selected, customized retrievals based on product, country, or other data items listed above for a fee of $400 plus 12 cents for every name over 1000. Tapes containing all information for a particular country can be purchased for $300 per country.

Trade Lists

FTI information also is available in booklet form for selected countries and industry or product groups. These lists contain the same information as the computer tapes and printouts, but they are sold off the shelf. *Country Trade Lists* contain information on all firms in the FTI for a particular country and are currently available for Bahrain, Egypt, Ivory Coast, Japan, Mexico, Nigeria, Romania, Saudi Arabia, United Arab Emirates, and Venezuela. *Industry Trade Lists* contain worldwide or regional information on firms in a particular industry. Most recently published industry trade lists are for the computer, apparel, and medical and communications equipment industries. An index of country and industry trade lists and their costs is available free of charge.

Cost

From $3 to $40, depending on content and date of information.

Contact

Export Contact List Services
Office of Trade Information Services
U.S. Department of Commerce
Room 1837
Washington, DC 20230

or nearest Commerce Department district office (see appendix).

Trade Opportunities Information

U.S. firms can receive active trade leads from overseas companies in their product categories through the Commerce Department's Trade Opportunities Program (TOP). U.S. company subscribers indicate their products or services, countries of interest, and type of overseas business opportunity being sought (e.g., direct sales, overseas representation, or foreign government tenders). Subscribers then are sent a trade opportunity notice with the names of foreign company "matches." Notices include descriptions of the products and services needed, their end uses, and the quantities required; foreign buyer information; transaction requirements and preferences; trade and credit references; bid deadline dates; and other pertinent information.

Cost
$30 and up, depending on client profile.

As an alternative, U.S. companies can subscribe to the *TOP Bulletin* or the *TOP Datatape Service*. The weekly *TOP Bulletin,* a compilation of all export leads received and processed by TOP, is designed for firms with broad product lines or service interests. The *TOP Datatape Service* provides the same information on computer tape on a weekly or biweekly basis.

Cost
Annual *TOP Bulletin* subscription $175; annual *Datatape Service* subscription $4200 (weekly) or $2100 (biweekly).

Contact
Trade Opportunities Program
Office of Trade Information Services
U.S. Department of Commerce
Room 1324
Washington, DC 20230
(202) 377-2988
or nearest Commerce Department district office (see appendix).

Major Project Contracts Information

The Commerce Department's Office of Major Projects helps U.S. firms compete for major planning, engineering, and construction contracts on large foreign construction projects, including equipment and "turnkey" installations. The Office identifies foreign capital projects with export potential of $5 million and over and distributes this information to engineering and construction firms and equipment manufacturers. It assists U.S. firms on a case-by-case basis in competing for these projects and coordinates support when needed from other areas of the Commerce Department and other federal agencies.

A monthly listing of major new overseas engineering and construction projects requiring procurement of products and services of more than $5 million is available to firms and associations interested in obtaining early, limited information on overseas projects.

KENTRON INTERNATIONAL

For many American businesses, it is important to learn early of bidding opportunities overseas and then to obtain the necessary information to effectively compete for sales. The Commerce Department's Office of Major Projects has assisted scores of small and medium-sized U.S. firms in gaining such information. Take the case of Kentron International of Dallas.

In late 1978 the Office of Major Projects learned that a contract worth $30 million would be let to upgrade the Pakistan Railway's communication system. The Office alerted a variety of U.S. firms to the upcoming tender. When Kentron notified the Commerce Department office of its interest in the contract, Kentron was provided with a World Bank loan appraisal report that outlined the project's scope.

Over the next two years, the Office of Major Projects continued to work with Kentron, coordinating action with the U.S. Embassy in Islamabad on visits by Pakistani officials to the United States, and on using the Embassy's resources to verify information received by Kentron on the project's status. In late 1980 Kentron was awarded a contract valued at approximately $50 million.

FORM ITA-412 (REV. 6-80)

NOTICE NO.	DATE	LOCATION OF OPPORTUNITY	TYPE OF OPPORTUNITY
407933	11/04/80	BURMA	FOREIGN GOVERNMENT TENDER

DESCRIPTION OF OPPORTUNITY

SUPPLY ONE 8 TON LATTICE GRINDER TYPE ELECTRIC OVERHEAD TRAVELLING CRANE WITH CABLE CONTROL GRAB BUCKET 2.5M3, 1 SET GEAR REDUCER COMPLETE WITH ELECTRIC MOTOR TO BE USED FOR EXISTING RAW GRINDING MILL HAVING 2.4 METER DIA. X 13 METER LENGTH WITH 3 COMPARTMENTS TO PRODUCE CEMENT SLURRY 32 TON/HOUR % 1 LOT COMPLETE LIMESTONE CRUSHING PLANT WITH RATED CAP. 200 TONS/HOUR CONSISTS 30 TON STRUCK CAP. REINFORCED CONCRETE HOPPER, 200 TONS/HOUR CAP. HEAVY DUTY STEEL APRON FEEDER, SINGLE ROTOR HAMMER CRUSHER % 300 TONS/HOUR MAX. BELT CONVEYOR. FINANCED WITH ADB CREDIT. INTERESTED U.S. FIRMS SHOULD WRITE DIRECTLY TO BELOW ADDRESS CITING BID NO.; ENCLOSING CHECK FOR #30.00 PER SET FOR BID DOCS., WHICH MUST BE OBTAINED PRIOR TO SUBMITTING OFFERS.

OBTAIN BID DOCS. FROM--
MANAGING DIR.: CERAMIC INDUSTRIES CORP.
196 KABA AYE PAGODA ROAD
RANGOON, BURMA
CABLE" ;CERAMICS, RANGOON;

REF. BID NO. 3/80/GMT-CIC/ADB

BID DEADLINE 12/15/80
666666

PLEASE SEND COPY YOUR RESPONSE TO--
EMBASSY OF THE UNITED STATES
RANGOON, BURMA
DEPT. OF STATE
WASHINGTON, D.C. 20521

THE A & CO
ATTN MR B J ABLE
9 SINCLAIR AVE
SUITE 19
BALTIMORE   MD   21202

	PRODUCT CLASS-IFICATION	ACCT. BAL.

U.S. GOVT. REFERENCE	ACCOUNT NO.	TYPE NOTICE	
546/01/T0001	700001	CHARGE	

IMPORTANT INFORMATION ON THE REVERSE. NOTE ESPECIALLY: REGULATIONS APPLICABLE TO BOYCOTTS, RESTRICTIVE TRADE PRACTICES AND EXPORT LICENSING REQUIREMENTS.

TRADE OPPORTUNITIES PROGRAM
A joint activity of the
U.S. DEPARTMENT OF COMMERCE
and the
U.S. FOREIGN SERVICE-U.S. DEPARTMENT OF STATE

Contact

James R. Phillips, Director
Office of Major Projects
U.S. Department of Commerce
Room 2007
Washington, DC 20230
(202) 377-5225

or nearest Commerce Department district office (see appendix).

Export Opportunities

The Agency for International Development (AID) operates two types of program in which U.S. companies can benefit as exporters. AID's commodity import programs finance the procurement of basic commodities needed in developing countries. Under this program, funds are allocated by the recipient government to its ministries and to the private sector to provide foreign exchange needed to purchase machinery, industrial chemicals, farm equipment, medical supplies, and other products. Another opportunity for U.S. businesses to export to the developing world is created by AID-financed infrastructure projects, such as construction of irrigation facilities, rural health networks, and disease control programs.

Foreign government requirements for U.S. commodities are advertised in the *Export Opportunity Bulletin,* which is sent to companies registered with AID's Office of Business Relations.

Cost

Free.

Contact

Office of Business Relations
Agency for International Development
Plaza West, Room 648
Washington, DC 20523
(703) 235-1720

(*Opposite page*) Example of a notice giving the name of a potential foreign company "match" for an American company subscribing to the Commerce Department's Trade Opportunities Program. U.S. firms can receive active trade leads from overseas companies in their product categories.

Investment Opportunities Search

The Overseas Private Investment Corporation offers an investment information network supported by a data base called the Opportunity Bank. A U.S. firm seeking investment in the developing world can submit a profile of the firm, listing type of investment sought, intended product lines, and countries of interest. This information is then matched with corresponding submissions of project opportunities by foreign governments and businesses. The data base contains more than 4000 U.S. companies that have engaged in or are seriously considering overseas investment and more than 1000 overseas projects for which U.S. business participation is being sought.

Cost
No charge to register a company or project profile. The cost for up to 10 company or 10 project profiles is $50.

Contact
Opportunity Bank
Overseas Private Investment Corporation
1129 20th Street, N.W.
Washington, DC 20527
(202) 653-2800

Agricultural Trade Leads

AGNET, the on-line computer data base for agricultural information, offers trade leads and commodity reports directly from the Foreign Agricultural Service. Trade leads on potential buyers of U.S. agricultural products are made available to subscribers on the day they are received.

Cost
Annual membership fee is $50. Most users spend $20–30 per hour while linked to AGNET during weekday business hours (8 A.M.–5 P.M. Central Time). Rates are lower for evening and weekend use.

OPIC Overseas
Private
Investment
Corporation

1129 20th Street, N.W.
Washington, D.C. 20527
(202) 653-2920
Telex: 440227 OPIC UI

OPIC Opportunity Bank

Investment Project Opportunity

Country: Philippines

Keywords:
FISH PROC   FISH PACK   CATFISH   FROGS LEG

Project Description:
Production and processing of catfish and frogs legs.
Assistance sought in marketing and supply of technology.

Standard industrial classification codes:
0279 0921 2091 2092

Date of submission: 04/01/83

Type of project:
Management Assistance
Technical Assistance
Technology Transfer

Markets: Domestic.

New Project: Yes.

Project cost: Undetermined.

Source of project:
Mr. George E. Paine
International Trade Specialist
International Economic Policy
U.S. Department of Commerce
Room 2310
Washington, D.C. 20230
(202) 377-3875

Name of project contact:
Mr. Thomas Moore, Commercial Counselor
U.S. Embassy, Manila, Philippines
Can provide contact with Governor Zayco,
Board of Investment, Manila, Philippines
who is proposing this project.

**Type of profile information on a foreign investment project
seeking American business participation that is provided
upon request by the Opportunity Bank service of OPIC. Up to
ten profiles matching a specified U.S. investor interest can
be provided for $50.**

57

Contact
Patrick Ebmeier, User Services Supervisor
AGNET
105 Miller Hall
University of Nebraska-Lincoln
Lincoln, NE 68583
(402) 472-1892

Seafood Export Opportunities

The Commerce Department's National Marine Fisheries Service helps U.S. companies locate foreign market opportunities as part of its services to increase the sale of U.S. seafood abroad. The Office of Industry Services provides computerized listings of U.S. seafood products and producers for export use and multilingual promotional information for several species of U.S. food fish. The Office also identifies foreign market opportunities, analyzes tariffs and other trade barriers, sponsors sales missions, and helps U.S. participants in trade shows in foreign countries.

Cost
Free.

Contact
Bruce Morehead
Industry Development Division
National Marine Fisheries Service
Office of Industry Services
3300 Whitehaven Street, N.W.
Washington, DC 20235
(202) 634-7451

Caribbean Basin Opportunities

The Caribbean Basin Business Information Center assists U.S. companies seeking business opportunities in the Caribbean region through its computer data base of trade and investment information. The Center publicizes the capabilities of U.S. firms interested in doing business in the Caribbean and offers information to U.S. firms on specific Caribbean business opportunities.

AGNET

Concerning CORN   06/03 TORS/SIC Number: 01131020
Issued From GREECE   U.S.D.A. Ref Num: 1111-820602-484B0084
Corn, barley (Greece). Wants corn (Maize) and barley, approx. 60,000-100
mt. corn, amount will be decided after negotiations for barley. U.S. or
equivalent No. 2 or better max. moisture 15% USDA standards. Packed in
bulk. Delivery Port of Piraeus. Quotations CIF Piraeus. Bank ref:
Commercial Bank of Greece, Voulis St. Branch, Athens. CONTACT: D.
Galiatsatos, AlCyon-D.K. Galiatsatos Ltd., 9, Kolokotroni St., Athens,
Greece. TELEX: 215452 GR. Phone: 322-6016. (EB 881-882).

Concerning CORN OIL   06/03 TORS/SIC Number: 20460035
Issued From SPAIN   U.S.D.A. Ref Num: 1113-820602-469B0158
Corn oil and Corn germ (Spain). Wants corn germ for crushing and raw corn
oil, 500-1,000 mt. each, high oil content. Quotations CIF Barcelona.
Koipe, S.A. would like to receive quotations directly from U.S. exporters
(No Agents) for direct shipments to Spain. CONTACT: Koipe S.A., Koipe
S.A., Jorge Juan, 19, Madrid, Spain. TELEX: 42147 E. Cable: KOIPE. Phone:
91/431 51 42. (EB 883).

Concerning CORN SEED   06/03 TORS/SIC Number: 01193050
Issued From COLOMBIA   U.S.D.A. Ref Num: 1110-820602-301A0104
Yellow onion seed (Colombia). Wants Hybrid yellow onion seed, wishes to
expand into other kinds of seeds, 500 lbs to begin, high quality, for
export. Delivery ASAP. Phytosanitary certificate required. Quotations FOB
Miami, Florida. Bank ref: Banco De Bogota and Banco De Colombia (both in
Bogota). CONTACT: Jose Antonio Avello R., Ferrango Ltda., Calle 10 No.
17-26, Bogota, Colombia. Phone: 241-3126 Bogota. (EB:880)

Concerning BERRIES, EX STRAWBERRIES   06/03 TORS/SIC Number: 0122301C
Issued From JAPAN   U.S.D.A. Ref Num: 1105-820528-588B0406
Cowberries and partridge berries (Japan). Wants frozen cowberries and
partridge berries, 50 mt. Products must be individually quick-frozen.
Packed in poly-lined carton box - 10 to 20 kg. or 30 to 40 lbs. to a box.
Delivery Sept. '82 - Nov. '82. Quotations: CIF Japan. Bank ref: Daiichi
Kansyd Bank, Showadori Branch, Tokyo. CONTACT: Toyotsusu Arisaka, J.A.M.
Incorporated, 4th Floor, Chiyoda Kaikan Bldg., 16-16, Nihonbashi,
Chuo-Ku, Tokyo 103, Japan. Telex: 252-4134 JAMINC J. Phone: (03)
668-3021. Cable: TYOJAMINC. (EB: 0875)

Sample printout page from AGNET, the on-line computer
data base for agricultural information, including potential
foreign buyers of U.S. agricultural products.

Cost

No charge to register in the system.

Contact

Tom Moore
Caribbean Basin Business Information Center
U.S. Department of Commerce
Room 3027
Washington, DC 20230
(202) 377-2527

CUSTOMIZED SERVICES

World Traders Information

The World Traders Data Reports service of the Department of Commerce provides U.S. companies with information on foreign companies with which they might be interested in doing business. Reports contain information on foreign companies such as the type of organization, year established, relative size, number of employees, general reputation, territory covered, language preferred, product lines handled, principal owners, and financial and trade references. Each report also contains a general comment on the foreign firm's reliability by the U.S. Commercial Officer who conducted the investigation.

Reports are prepared upon request by a U.S. company, which must submit the complete name and address of the foreign firm. Reports are not available on firms located in the United States, Puerto Rico, U.S. Trust Territories, the Soviet Union or Soviet bloc countries, or in countries where credit reports are available only from private sources.

Cost
$40 per search.

Contact
World Traders Data Reports
Office of Trade Information Services
U.S. Department of Commerce
Room 1315
Washington, DC 20230
(202) 377-4203

or nearest Commerce Department district office (see appendix).

Agent/Distributor Information

The Agent/Distributor Service, administered by the Department of Commerce, helps U.S. companies find interested and qualified overseas agents or distributors for their products or services. On request, U.S. foreign commercial specialists will seek a foreign representative specifically for a U.S. company's product line. The report sent to the requesting company provides information on up to six qualified representatives

World Traders Data Report

This report, submitted to the U.S. Department of Commerce by the U.S. Foreign Service—U.S. Department of State, and the Foreign Commercial Service—U.S. Department of Commerce, is transmitted in confidence No responsibility can be assumed by the Government or its officers for any transactions had with any persons or firms herein mentioned The report is not for publication All correspondence relating to information in this report should be addressed to the

U.S. Department of Commerce International Trade Administration World Traders Data Reports, Room 1837 Washington, D.C. 20230

R 1008202 JAN 83
FR AMEMBASSY LONDON
TO USDOC WASHDC
BT
UNCLAS LONDON 0128
EO 12356: N/A
TAGS: BBSR, UK
SUBJ: WTDR/FTI: FRANKLIN, CLAYTON-WRIGHT LTD. (REQUESTED AS: F.C. WRIGHT)
REF: USDOC 18269

1. United Kingdom
   Office use: 2. 412 3. 0705400 4. 01
5. Franklin, Clayton-Wright Ltd.
6. P.O. Box 189; 56 Oxford St.
7. London WC2H 8BA
8. *CONTACT:* Robert Peterson
9. *TITLE:* Managing Director
   Other officials are: Arthur Smythe, President and John S. Carlyle, Foreign Sales Manager.

10. *PHONE:* 01/9924321 11. *TELEX:* 889352
12. *CABLE:* Claytonite London
13. *ESTABL:* 1952 14. Empl: 1300 15. Size: very large
16. *REPUTATION:* Y-Satisfactory 17. *RPT DATE:* Jan 83.
    Office use: 18. K 19. X 20. X 21. N/A 22. A3582

23A.	20650/M04	Mfr, dist, exp, of confectionery products and
23B.	20665/OM4	Chocolate and cocoa products
23C.	20231/5G	Imp. of dry milk products; interested in license to produce
23D.	35514/F	Interested in purchasing confectionery packaging equip

24. *FOREIGN SALES:* France 35%, Spain 28%, Germany and USA (by value).

25. *FINANCIAL REFS:* International Bank, 739 Park Ave., New York, Morrison Bank Ltd., 17 Northrup CT., London W1VOE, England.

26. *TRADE REFS:* Johnson Machinery, Inc., 862 S. Los Angeles St., Los Angeles, CA 96102; Tedenson Co., Inc., 125 South Street, Boston, MA 02111.

27. *FOREIGN FIRMS REPRESENTED:* Agency Rep. of North-Am Chicle Co., Inc., P.O. Box 245, Washington, DC 20001 for chewing gum, acquired 1954; licensee of Hobart Candy Co., 1215 N Eads St., Atlanta, GA 37259 for peanut brittle & choc. covered peanut butter.

28. *POST EVALUATION:* This firm is one of the leading manufacturers of all types of confectionery in the United Kingdom. The firm has a basic capital of 3 million pounds and fixed assets valued at 1.5 million pounds. Its center of operations, including manufacturing facility, is in London. It has distribution facilities in Glasgow, Liverpool and London. The firm's major stockholder is Burton's Ltd., a holding company. Local credit sources report satisfactory experience on loans in the low five figures: the firm's finances appear sound and obligations are promptly met: it has, however, recently encountered cash flow problems. The Embassy considers company a satisfactory trade contact for U.S. firms.

with interest in the U.S. company's proposal, including the name and address of the foreign firm, name and title of contact person, telephone number, cable address and telex number, and brief comments about the firm or its stated interest in the proposal. A search usually requires 30 days.

Cost
$90 per search.

Contact
> Agent/Distributor Service
> Office of Trade Information Services
> U.S. Department of Commerce
> Room 1837
> Washington, DC 20230

or nearest Commerce Department district office (see appendix).

Business Consultation

Minority entrepreneurs can receive advice and assistance in entering the international marketplace from the Commerce Department's Minority Business Development Agency. The Agency has created a nationwide network of Minority Export Development Consultant organizations to help minority firms develop export marketing plans, identify potential markets and trade leads, and complete international transactions. In addition, the Agency's six regional offices can provide guidance on other minority assistance programs and refer minority firms to a locally funded Minority Business Development Center in their area for further specialized help at a nominal fee. The Minority Business Development Agency has six regional offices.

Contact
The appropriate regional office (see page 66).

(*Opposite page*) **Example of the information provided by the World Traders Data Reports service of the Commerce Department. U.S. firms can, upon request, receive information on foreign companies with which they are interested in doing business. The cost is $40 per search.**

AGENT DISTRIBUTOR SERVICE

```
R 211622Z SEPT 80
FM AMEMBASSY LONDON
TO USDOC WASHDC
BT
UNCLAS LONDON 1224

E. O. 11652: N/A
TAGS: BEXP, UK
SUBJECT: ADS REQUEST FOR COMPUSCALES, INC., SOUTHMOORE, MI.

REF: COMMERCE CD-144, AUG. 1, 1980

THE FOLLOWING FIRMS HAVE BEEN CONTACTED INDIVIDUALLY AND HAVE EXPRESSED
AN INTEREST IN REPRESENTING COMPUSCALES AS COMMISSION SALES AGENTS FOR
ELECTRONIC SCALES.

1. DWIGHT ALDERSON    (PTY) LTD.
CROFTON LANE 122
LONDON 2Y3 C5D, UNITED KINGDOM
CONTACT: MR. DWIGHT ALDERSON, OWNER & MANAGER
PHONE: AREA-012 LOCAL- 574-2953
TELEX: ITT 2559753
COMMENT: MR. ALDERSON STATED THAT COMPUSCALE'S LINE FITS IN PERFECTLY
WITH SIMILAR EQUIPMENT HANDLED. FIRM CALLS REGULARLY ON POTENTIAL END-
USERS THROUGHOUT UK. SOME, MR. ALDERSON SAID, HAVE EXPRESSED NEED FOR
ELECTRONIC SCALES. FIRM IS SMALL BUT HIGHLY CAPABLE: CAN UNDERTAKE
SERVICING. MR. ALDERSON HAS WRITTEN DIRECTLY TO COMPUSCALES EXPRESSING
INTEREST.

2. ASHFORD & BENSON LTD., ELECTRONIC DIVISION
CROMWELL RD. 222, KNIGHTSBRIDGE
LONDON KN1 A2B, UNITED KINGDOM
CONTACT: MR. DAVID SMITH, CHIEF
PHONE: AREA- 012 LOCAL-733-4516
CABLE: ASHBEN, LONDON
TELEX: 662595, LONDON
COMMENT: THIS IS A LARGE AGENCY REPRESENTING A LONG LIST OF BRITISH,
EUROPEAN AND AMERICAN FIRMS THROUGH ITS VARIOUS PRODUCT DIVISIONS. IT
DOES NOT NOW HANDLE ELECTRONIC SCALES AND IS VERY INTERESTED IN COMPUSCALE'S
PRODUCTS. MR. SMITH IS INTERESTED IN SCALES MADE FOR METRIC STANDARDS.

3. GUILFORD'S LTD.
#2 BENNINGTON ST.
CAMBRIDGE CAI A2A, UNITED KINGDOM
CONTACT: SIR MICHAEL CARTER, VICE PRESIDENT
PHONE: AREA- 077 LOCAL- 55323
CABLE: GUILFORD
COMMENT: THIS IS AN OLD, ESTABLISHED FIRM WITH CAPABLE SALES FORCE CALLING
ON INDUSTRY THROUGHOUT THE UK. FIRM PRIMARILY HANDLES ELECTRONIC EQUIP-
MENT: WISHES TO EXPAND INTO OTHER FIELDS. LORD GUILFORD, CHAIRMAN AND
PRESIDENT, FEELS COMPUSCALES PRODUCTS WOULD BE COMPATIBLE WITH HIS PRESENT
PRODUCT LINES.

APPROVED: JOHN MACKENZIE                  PREPARED: IAN WATERFORD
```

Sample report from the Agent/Distributor Service, which can provide an American firm with information on a potential foreign representative for a certain product or service. Search reports such as this one are available for $90 per search.

Form Approved: OMB No. 41-R2710

FORM ITA-424P (FORMERLY OIB-424P) (REV. 4-80)	U.S. DEPARTMENT OF COMMERCE INTERNATIONAL TRADE ADMINISTRATION	"No request for the Agent/Distributor Service may be processed unless a completed application form has been received. (15 U.S.C. 171-197; 15 U.S.C. 1525-1527)"

AGENT/DISTRIBUTOR SERVICE APPLICATION

GUIDELINE: For each territory for which an ADS search is to be made, submit four (4) copies of this form to the District Office nearest you.

Requestors Name/Title and Firm Name/Address:	District Office Address:
•George K. Jones Export Manager Compuscales, Inc. 1281 Poplar Road Southmoore, Michigan 48870	445 Federal Building 231 West Lafayette Detroit, Michigan 48226

Signature:	TELEPHONE			Telex Number: 2-53471		Date Submitted:
	Area Code 313	Number 223-2112	Extension 3341	Cable Address: CSCALE, Michigan		7-15-80

SECTION A

1. Your Firm's Activity

(a) [X] Manufacturer or Export Dept. (b) [ ] EMC./Manufacturer's Representative (c) [ ] Other — (Describe) _____
                                           Distributor-Wholesaler

2. Export Sales:

(a) [ ] Product New to Export (b) [X] Product New to Market

3. Number of Employees:

(a) [X] Less than 100 (b) [ ] 100 – 500 (c) [ ] Over 500

4. If you are presently represented for this product/service in this market, please list the representative's name and address.

Name:	Address:
Wells International Ltd.	P. O. Box 21, Lye, Stourbridge

(a) Does this firm handle your product/service on an exclusive basis? [ ] Yes [X] No

(a) Has the firm been notified of your desire to obtain new representation? [X] Yes [ ] No

(An ADS cannot be undertaken without assurance that your present representative has been informed.)

5. If you have corresponded with any firm in this market regarding this proposal, please list their name and address and their reaction.

Name of Firm:	Reaction:
John Davies, Ltd.	Has indicated preliminary interest. Continuing to negotiate.
Address: 128 Crofton Square London	

SECTION B

1. Type of Business Connection Desired:

(a) [X] Agent (b) [ ] Distributor

Market: (City or Country)

United Kingdom

3. Product/service to be exported: Electronic scales for weighing railroad cars and automotive vehicles, etc. Scales can be made available for metric standards. Readouts are displayed in lighted liquid crystal diodes, in various sizes, up to 10 cm. The smaller scales in our line are applicable to super-markets, etc. use. (See details in brochure)

4. List special technical or other qualifications appropriate agents/distributors should have.

Agencies handling electronic testing instruments, with servicing capabilities, and selling preferably to both private industry and to the government, are likely candidates.

5. Additional Comments:

Agency should have servicing capability within the electronic field but does not need to have skills in servicing scales. We are willing to train the firm's personnel, bringing them to the U.S.A., if need be.

65

Atlanta Region

Stanley Tate, Regional Director
Minority Business Development Agency
U.S. Department of Commerce
1371 Peachtree Street, N.E., Suite 505
Atlanta, GA 30309
(404) 881-4091

Chicago Region

Richard Sewing, Acting Regional Director
Minority Business Development Agency
U.S. Department of Commerce
55 E. Monroe Street, Suite 1440
Chicago, IL 60603
(312) 353-0182

San Francisco Region

Powell McDaniel, Acting Regional
  Director
Minority Business Development Agency
U.S. Department of Commerce
Federal Building, Room 15045
450 Golden Gate Avenue
P.O. Box 36114
San Francisco, CA 94102
(415) 556-7234

Dallas Region

Ruben Porras, Acting Regional Director
Minority Business Development Agency
U.S. Department of Commerce
1100 Commerce Street, Room 7B19
Dallas, TX 75242
(214) 767-8001

New York Region

Joseph Korpsak, Acting Regional Director
Minority Business Development Agency
U.S. Department of Commerce
Federal Office Building
26 Federal Plaza, Room 36-116
New York, NY 10278
(212) 264-3262

Washington, D.C. Region

Roy Mixon, Acting Regional Director
Minority Business Development Agency
U.S. Department of Commerce
1730 K Street, N.W., Suite 420
Washington, DC 20006
(202) 634-7897

Joint Agricultural Consultative Corporation

The Joint Agricultural Consultative Corporation, a private not-for-profit organization, was created by the Agency for International Development to help facilitate the flow of capital and technology from the private U.S. agribusiness sector to the private agribusiness sectors of selected developing countries. The Corporation is currently active in the Caribbean, Sri Lanka, Nigeria, Indonesia, and Thailand.

The Corporation operates through country-specific committees of U.S. and foreign agribusiness companies. A U.S. company that becomes a member of a country committee receives general information on the country, monthly reports covering country committee activities, and special reports on country developments. Member companies also receive notices of opportunities for meetings with foreign committee counterparts, access to a Washington office for business use, and notification of foreign business opportunities.

Cost

To join one committee $500; two, $750; three or more committees, $1000.

Contact

James E. Thorton, President
Joint Agricultural Consultative Corporation
815 Connecticut Avenue, N.W., Suite 208
Washington, DC 20006
(202) 429-1985

Eastern Caribbean Project Opportunities

The Agency for International Development has engaged the firm of Coopers & Lybrand to promote private-sector business development in the Eastern Caribbean countries of Antigua and Barbuda, Barbados, Belize, Dominica, Montserrat, St. Kitts–Nevis, St. Lucia, and St. Vincent and the Grenadines. Program staff provides a variety of services to U.S. businesses interested in opportunities for investment and contract production in these countries. Services include advice on how these countries might fit into a company's overall business planning, general information about the economies and investment climates of the countries, help in costing out potential investment, and assistance in arranging an exploratory trip to the region. In-country staff arranges meetings with local government officials and private-sector leaders, helps find suitable local partners, conducts tours of factory sites, and describes local transportation services and labor practices.

Cost

Free.

Contact

Robert E. Brown
Investor Service Program
Coopers & Lybrand
1800 M Street, N.W.
Washington, DC 20036
(202) 822-4265

AID: Country Market Information

The Agency for International Development (AID) in late 1982 contracted with a New York publisher to prepare a study of the investment climate in five developing nations. The countries—Zimbabwe, Jamaica, Haiti, the Ivory Coast, and Sri Lanka—were selected because of low per capita income and their importance to the United States. Sri Lanka, for example, receives about $45 million in bilateral aid from the development agency each year. But AID also sees a need to strengthen Sri Lanka's economy through private U.S. investment. The $72,000 AID-sponsored study is designed to augment investment knowledge about the political and labor climate, taxes, incentives, and import tariffs in these countries.

Thailand, Indonesia, and Sri Lanka Investment Opportunities

The Agency for International Development has awarded contracts to several U.S. consulting firms to provide information and assistance to U.S. companies interested in exploring business opportunities in Thailand, Indonesia, and Sri Lanka. Information on specific project opportunities, potential local joint-venture partners, and investment incentives and policies are among the services offered.

Cost
Free.

Contact
Agency for International Development
Bureau for Asia
Washington, DC 20523

For Thailand: Bill Nance, (202) 632-9086
For Indonesia: Steven Singer, (202) 632-9842
For Sri Lanka: John Gunning, (202) 632-8226

Videotaped Investment Opportunities

A two-hour satellite Telemission program includes prerecorded segments on a specific country or region and its investment climate, along with live discussions among business experts and leaders from the United States and the developing country or countries. The Overseas Private Investment Corporation initiated the Telemission concept in 1982. To date, an Egyptian and a Caribbean Telemission have been conducted.

Cost
Videotapes of the Egypt and Caribbean Telemissions are available for $150 each.

Contact
Marketing Services
Overseas Private Investment Corporation
1129 20th Street, N.W.
Washington, DC 20527
(202) 653-2800

TELEMISSION

New York Moderator . . . . Walter Cronkite
Cairo Moderator . . . . Bill Beutel

WELCOME TO TELEMISSION
Greeting from Hosni Mubarak,
President of the Arab Republic of Egypt

INVESTMENT CLIMATE IN EGYPT
Investment Opportunities in Egypt
A pre-recorded program introduced by Deputy Prime Minister for
Economic and Financial Affairs, Muhammad 'Abd Al-Fattah Ibrahim

Message from Prime Minister of Egypt,
Dr. Ahmad Foad Muhieddin

Questions and Answers
In New York:
Richard A. Debs, Managing Director, Morgan Stanley and
Company, Inc., and President, Morgan Stanley International, Inc.

In Cairo:
Deputy Prime Minister Ibrahim
Muhammad Salah El-Din Hamed, Minister of Finance
Dr. Foad Hashem, Minister of Economy
Dr. Kamal Ahmad El-Ganzouri, Minister of Planning

HEALTH AND MEDICAL PRODUCTS
Investment Opportunities
A pre-recorded program introduced by Minister of Health,
Dr. Muhammad Sabri Zaki

Questions and Answers
In New York:
Barry MacTaggart, Chairman and Chief Executive Officer,
Pfizer International, Inc.

In Cairo:
Dr. Zaki
Dr. Abdel Moniem Khazbak, Chairman, Al Gomhouria Company
Dr. Ahmed Fouad Hetta, Managing Director, Chemilab

FOOD PRODUCTION AND FOOD PROCESSING
Investment Opportunities
A pre-recorded program introduced by Minister of Agriculture, Dr.
Yousif Amin Wali and Minister of Industry Eng. Foad Ibrahim Abu
Zaghla

Questions and Answers
In New York:
Frank W. Considine, President and Chief Executive Officer,
National Can Corporation and Chairman, U.S. Section, Egypt-
U.S. Business Council

In Cairo:
Dr. Wali
Eng. Abu Zaghla
Eng. Saad Hagrass, Deputy Minister of Agriculture
Eng. Niazi Mostafa, Chairman, Nimos Engineering Company and
Chairman, Egypt Section, Egypt-U.S. Business Council

CONSTRUCTION MATERIALS
Investment Opportunities
A pre-recorded program introduced by Minister of Housing and
Land Reclamation, Eng. Hasaballah El-Kafrawi

Questions and Answers
In New York:
Harry Holiday Jr., Chief Executive Officer, ARMCO, Inc.

In Cairo:
Eng. El-Kafrawi
Eng. Mohamed Sami Beheri, Consultant, Ministry of Development
Eng. Adly Ayoub, Chairman, Ayoubco S.A.E.

CLOSING REMARKS
Ismail Helmy Ghanem, Deputy Chairman, The General Authority
for Investment & Free Zones

Ronald Reagan, President of the United States

Craig A. Nalen, President, Overseas Private Investment
Corporation

The Honorable Alfred L. Atherton Jr.,
U.S. Ambassador to the Arab Republic of Egypt

His Excellency, Dr. Ashraf A. Ghorbal,
Ambassador of the Arab Republic of Egypt

Dr. Abd-El Rahman Khane, Executive Director,
United Nations Industrial Development Organization

The Honorable Bradford Morse, Administrator,
United Nations Development Program

Sample program from an Egyptian Telemission sponsored by OPIC. Telemissions are live-by-satellite, televised investment conferences with foreign countries or regions.

SPECIAL PROGRAMS FOR SMALL BUSINESS

Advice on Overseas Contracts

The Office of Business Relations in the Agency for International Development (AID) is the principal distribution point for information on AID programs. The Office provides information to U.S. suppliers, particularly small, independent enterprises, regarding purchases to be financed with AID funds. The Office also notifies prospective purchasers in AID-recipient countries about commodities and services provided by some 12,000 small, independent enterprises in the United States.

The Office maintains a Contractor's Index of approximately 4000 firms and consultants interested in providing professional and technical services under AID programs.

U.S. small businesses can obtain special counseling and related services in order to furnish equipment, materials, and services to AID-financed projects.

SOLIO RANCH, LTD.

A Colorado mining engineer revolutionized the cattle industry in Kenya with a ranch insured by a U.S. government agency. In 1966 Courtland Parfet established the Solio Ranch, Ltd. near Mt. Kenya. There he built a modern breeding operation in which he cross-bred a native breed of cattle with French Charolais bulls. The ranch now has approximately 20,000 head of top-grade cattle and is one of the largest suppliers of beef in Kenya. What's more, Kenyan beef is now exported to Switzerland and other countries. The Solio Ranch enterprise employs more than 200 Kenyans and is an important exporter for the country.

Cost

Free.

Contact

Barbara Otis
Director of Office Business Relations
Agency for International Development
State Annex 14, Room 648
Washington, DC 20523
(703) 235-2333

Initial Trade Consultation

Under an agreement signed between the SBA and the Federal Bar Association, qualified attorneys from the International Law Council of the FBA will provide free initial consultations to small companies in an effort to answer some of their basic legal questions concerning international trade and investment. Interested small businesses will be referred by local SBA offices to nearby attorneys through program coordinators of the FBA local chapters around the country.

Cost

Free.

Contact

Nearest Small Business Administration district office (see appendix).

Export Marketing Assistance

The Department of Commerce offers export marketing services to small- and medium-sized manufacturers throughout the United States. Student interns prepare reports that provide selected manufacturers with information to identify the most promising export opportunities and appropriate marketing techniques. The program is operated by District Export Councils in cooperation with local universities.

Contact

Donald W. Fry, Director
Phoenix District Office
U.S. Department of Commerce
2750 Valley Bank Center
Phoenix, AZ 85073
(602) 261-3285

Consulting Opportunities

The Agency for International Development (AID) provides loans and grants to finance consultant services that support project activities related to agriculture, rural development, nutrition, health, population planning, education, human resources, and housing. At times, AID acts on behalf of the foreign country and serves as the prime contractor for the procurement of technical experts. In such cases, AID frequently restricts competition for technical services through small business set-asides and the Small Business Administration's 8(a) Program.

Contact
Office of Business Relations
Agency for International Development
State Annex 14, Room 648
Washington, DC 20523
(202) 235-1720

Orientation on Overseas Private Investment Corporation Services

Domestic offices of Deloitte Haskins & Sells (DH&S), an international accounting and consulting firm, offer to companies considering investments in the developing world the opportunity to learn more about the programs of the Overseas Private Investment Corporation (OPIC) and the chance to view an orientation film on OPIC. The film describes OPIC services and the benefits of investing in the developing world.

Contact
Robert P. Wynn, Partner
Deloitte Haskins & Sells
655 Fifteenth Street, N.W.
Suite 700
Washington, DC 20005
(202) 626-1946

CHAPTER
FOUR

THE
FIRST
TRIP

After identifying trade leads and opportunities in individual countries, most firms want to determine the general climate for doing business or investing in these countries. Several services are available to help American businesses plan and pay for a first trip, as well as provide a temporary base of operations for business people visiting the country. This chapter is organized in four subsections:

Pretrip Preparation. Obtaining business counseling and commercial information from regional desk officers and country and commodity specialists.

Planning the Trip. Coordinating and planning the trip to take advantage of investment missions, trade fairs, shows, and exhibits. Special programs for small businesses include management assistance and minority business development.

Financing the Trip. Obtaining funds to undertake a preliminary reconnaissance trip to assess a country's investment climate.

People to See. Listing of people to see during a first trip, including overseas commercial officers in the U.S. embassies; provision of temporary base of operations.

PRETRIP PREPARATION

Country Officers

Several U.S. government agencies have country desk officers located in Washington. These officers provide general and specific country information to U.S. businesses involved in overseas business activities.

Department of Commerce

The Department of Commerce offers professional business counseling and commercial information on a geographical basis for major overseas markets. Country specialists provide the following services:

Statistical data on production, exports and imports, market share, and third-country competition.

Analyses of industrial sector reports and growth projections.

Listings of overseas market research firms that assist companies in preparing marketing strategies.

Advice on selecting agents or distributors.

Contacts with Foreign Commercial Service officers at U.S. embassies and consulates and with U.S. companies successfully operating in the country.

Contact
See appendix for listing of Department of Commerce country officers.

Department of State

Country officers at the Department of State can provide information on their assigned country's political, economic, and investment climate.

Contact
See appendix for listing of State Department country officers.

Agency for International Development

Country officers at the Agency for International Development (AID) can provide information on development programs in the countries for which they are responsible.

Contact
See appendix for listing of AID country officers.

Department of Agriculture

Foreign Agricultural Service (FAS) officers stationed in Washington provide agricultural information on specific blocs of countries:

Contact

Region	Officer	Telephone
Europe (non-EC countries)	Gordon Nicks	(202) 447-2144
Europe (EC countries)	Norman Pettipaw	(202) 447-6083
Western Hemisphere	Shackford Pitcher	(202) 475-4066
East Asia and Pacific	Lyle Moe	(202) 447-7053
Near East, South Asia, Africa	Cline Warren	(202) 447-7053

Analysts in the Department of Agriculture's Economic Research Service provide information on the current agricultural situation and forecast future market trends.

Contact

Region	Officer	Telephone
Africa/Middle East	Cheryl Christiansen	(202) 447-9160
Asia	Carmen Nohre	(202) 447-8860
Latin America	Oswald Blaich	(202) 447-9110
Western Europe	Reed Friend	(202) 447-6809
Eastern Europe/U.S.S.R.	Anton Malish	(202) 447-8380
North America/Oceania	Donald Seaborg	(202) 447-8376

USDA: China Trade Show

Since the start of the 1980s, the People's Republic of China has become a large and fast-growing market for U.S. leather. Trade shows, such as one held in China in 1982, helped develop this market. Participating at the International Leather and Equipment Show in Canton, for example, were the Tanner's Council of America and representatives of six U.S. tanning companies. To assist them, the Department of Agriculture's Foreign Agricultural Service gave financial and logistical support through its Washington headquarters and its field officers in China. Through this help, the tanners were able to take along a large assortment of U.S. leather products to show Chinese leather executives, some of whom had come 3000 miles to see the exhibit. This trade show helped ease the American business executives' entry into China's leather market. Sales of U.S. leather increased to $65 million in 1982 from $49 million two years earlier.

Peace Corps

Country officers at the Peace Corps can provide information on host-country contacts familiar with small-scale enterprises.

Contact
The appropriate country officer:

Region	Officer	Telephone
Africa		
Benin/Ghana/Togo	Gary Laidig	(202) 254-5644
Botswana/Lesotho/Swaziland	David Browne	(202) 254-6046
Cameroon/Central African Republic/Gabon	Susan Baity	(202) 254-8397

Region	Officer	Telephone
Mali/Niger/Upper Volta	Jerry Brown	(202) 254-7004
Gambia/Liberia	Theresa Joiner	(202) 254-8003
Rwanda/Zaire	Colleen K.	
	Kennedy-Roberts	(202) 254-8694
Kenya/Malawi/Seychelles		
Tanzania	Anika McGee	(202) 254-5634
Sierra Leone/Mauritania/		
Senegal	Elena Hughes	(202) 254-3185
Central and South America		
Costa Rica/Eastern		
Caribbean	Eugene Rigler	(202) 254-6322
Dominican Republic/Haiti/		
Jamaica	Noreen O'Meara	(202) 254-6375
Guatemala/Honduras/Belize	Katie Wheatley	(202) 254-6320
Paraguay/Ecuador	Marie Lameiro	(202) 254-6298
North Africa, Near East, and the Pacific		
Cook Islands/Fiji/Tuvalu/		
Western Samoa	Steven Prieto	(202) 254-3227
Philippines	Rebecca Mushingi	(202) 254-3290
Malaysia/Papua New		
Guinea/Thailand	Edward Geibel	(202) 254-3040
Kiribati/Micronesia/Solomon		
Islands/Tonga	Lisbeth Thompson	(202) 254-3231
Nepal/Sri Lanka/Yemen	Susan Belmont	(202) 254-3118
Morocco/Tunisia	Robert Philipson	(202) 254-3196

Department of Commerce District Offices

The Department of Commerce's 48 district offices throughout the United States are staffed by trade specialists who provide trade-related information, business advice, and counseling. Each district office maintains an extensive business library containing the Department's latest reports and statistical data. District offices are linked by direct telex communication to the commercial sections of U.S. embassies around the world, enabling U.S. companies to obtain specific market information, assistance with export-related problems, or help in planning a business trip itinerary. A fee ranging from $25 to $50 is charged for most customized services, depending on the number of countries involved and the nature of the request.

Trade specialists in the U.S. district offices can furnish information on trade and investment opportunities abroad, foreign markets for U.S. products and services, financing and insurance, tax advantages of exporting, international trade exhibitions, export documentation requirements, foreign exchange regulations, economic facts on foreign countries, and export licensing and import requirements. To encourage U.S. businesses to enter the international marketplace, trade specialists draw on the Commerce Department's many export marketing aids and services, including assistance in promoting U.S. products in special markets, computerized trade and investment opportunities, locating overseas agents or distributors, promoting U.S. products through Export Development Offices abroad, introducing foreign buyers to U.S. firms, sponsoring export seminars and conferences, organizing trade missions and promoting international trade fairs, and assisting in establishing relationships with—and forming—export trading companies.

The district offices work closely with U.S. business people experienced in all aspects of export trade through the District Export Councils (DECs). Volunteer DEC members counsel prospective exporters on getting started in international trade, co-sponsor export seminars and workshops with the district offices, address business groups on exporting, and promote awareness of the export-assistance programs of the Department of Commerce. A council has been established in every city that has a Department of Commerce district office.

Contact
Nearest Commerce Department district office (see appendix).

Small Business Administration District Offices

The Small Business Administration's district offices are located throughout the country. Each district office is staffed by a team of experts in the lending, procurement, and assistance areas, who consider loan applications, offer individual management assistance, and coordinate other small business services. District offices are the contact point for small businesses needing information or assistance concerning SBA programs.

Contact
Nearest SBA district office (see appendix).

PLANNING THE TRIP

Overseas Trade Promotion Events

The Commerce Department's Overseas Export Promotion Calendar lists U.S. trade promotion events held abroad, such as exhibitions, missions, and seminars featuring U.S. products and services. The Calendar is indexed by product and gives the location and date of each event.

Cost
Free.

Contact
Export Awareness Division
International Trade Administration
U.S. Department of Commerce
Room 2106
Washington, DC 20230
(202) 377-5367

International Trade Fairs and Exhibitions

The Department of Commerce sponsors official U.S. participation in selected major international trade fairs and exhibitions to promote the sale of U.S. goods and services overseas. When research reveals promising sales potential in areas where no suitable international trade fairs are planned, the Department sponsors, conducts, and manages its own exhibitions of U.S. products organized along an industry sector.

Participating U.S. firms receive a full range of promotional and display assistance. Companies make a financial contribution to offset the cost of the services provided. In addition to preshow promotional services, the Department of Commerce provides exhibit space, lounge or meeting rooms for exhibitor-customer conferences, market counseling, design and construction of the exhibit area, advice on shipment of products to the site, unpacking and positioning of displays, and basic utilities and housekeeping services.

CALENDAR ─────────────────

September 1982 – September 1983

The activities described below are listed by industry and include the following: Date of event, name of event, location and contact person for each event. For an update on activities listed in the Calendar, contact the Washington D.C. telephone number included as part of the activity description.

AGRICULTURAL CHEMICALS ───────────────────────────

March 1983	David International Fair Agricultural Chemicals Trade Fair	Panama	Mary Weining (202) 377-4708

AGRICULTURAL MACHINERY AND EQUIPMENT ─────────────────

Sept. 13-28, 1982	Agri. Business Trade Mission	Nigeria Ivory Coast Cameroon	Mary Wiening (202) 377-4708
Nov. 15-18, 1982	Australian National Field Days Trade Fair	Orange N.S.W.	Mary Wiening (202) 377-4708
Jan. 25-30, 1982	Agrotek Solo Fair	Thailand	Mary Wiening (202) 377-4708
April 1983	National Agri. and Trade Show Trade Fair	Belize	Mary Wiening (202) 377-4708
June 1983	U.S. Agri. Implements and Machinery Exhibition Trade Fair	Paraguay	Mary Wiening (202) 377-4708

AIR CONDITIONING AND REFRIGERATION EQUIPMENT ──────────

Aug. 23, – Sept. 10, 1982	Food Refrigeration and Freezing Equipment Trade Mission	China	G. Strausbaugh (202) 377-3786
August 1983	Air-Conditioning and Refrigeration Equipment Trade Mission	Peru Chile	Walter Fausel (202) 377-4065

AIRCRAFT AND PARTS ──────────────────────────────

May 26, – June 5, 1983	Salon International for Aircraft and Aerospace Trade Fair	France	Robert Baddy (202) 377-4704
September 1983	Aircraft Parts and Accessories Trade Mission	Japan	Robert Baddy (202) 377-4704

Contact

Nearest Commerce Department district office (see appendix).

The Commerce Department's new trade fair certification program recognizes and supports international trade shows that are organized and operated by private fair organizers, trade associations, and exhibition management companies in the U.S. and overseas.

Contact

Office of Event Management and Support Services
U.S. Department of Commerce
Room 2806
Washington, DC 20230
(202) 377-2525

Catalog Shows and Video/Catalog Exhibitions

The Department of Commerce annually schedules 20 to 30 catalog shows and video/catalog exhibitions worldwide. These shows allow U.S. firms to test product interest in foreign markets, develop sales leads, and locate agents or distributors. These exhibitions, held at U.S. embassies and consulates, feature displays of U.S. product catalogs, sales brochures, and other graphic sales aids at American embassy and consulate trade shows.

Exhibitions are supported by the Foreign Commercial Service and an industry expert selected by the Department. Participating companies make a contribution to offset the Department's costs.

Contact

Office of Event Management and Support Services
U.S. Department of Commerce
Washington, DC 20230
(202) 377-2525

or nearest Commerce Department district office (see appendix).

(Opposite page) **Sample page from the Overseas Export Promotion Calendar, which lists U.S. trade promotion events that will be held overseas. The publication is provided, upon request, at no charge.**

Agricultural Shows and Exhibits

National Food and Agricultural Exposition

The National Association of State Departments of Agriculture (NASDA), in cooperation with the Foreign Agricultural Service, sponsors expositions for foreign food buyers.

Contact
J. B. Grant, Director
NASDA National Food and Agricultural Exhibit
National Association of State Departments of Agriculture
1616 H Street, N.W.
Room 710
Washington, DC 20006
(202) 628-1566

Trade Fair Exhibits

The Foreign Agricultural Service (FAS) conducts trade fair exhibits to attract buyers for U.S. agricultural products. These exhibits are an effective means for U.S. companies to introduce and promote their food products overseas. A fee covers exhibit space, facilities, and trade relations services. Exhibitors are responsible for providing the products and full-time representation at their displays.

Hotel-restaurant institutional exhibits are held in several countries each year for all segments of the foreign food service trade. Usually, 25 to 50 U.S. firms exhibit institutional-size packs of products. Professional demonstrators are used. Exhibits run two to three days.

International food shows are held annually in some of the leading foreign markets. Exhibits sponsored by FAS are generally consumer-trade-oriented food and beverage expositions attracting exhibitors and buyers from many foreign countries.

Agent food exhibits are organized and managed by representatives of the Foreign Agricultural Service overseas, in cooperation with foreign agents of U.S. food companies.

Agricultural attaché product displays offer an opportunity to show U.S. food products to key officials in controlled economies where the consumer is unable to influence imports.

Point-of-purchase promotion is utilized in leading foreign markets for drawing consumer attention to U.S. food products. Foreign Agricultural Service representatives contact the chain and/or department stores and foreign agents of U.S. food manufacturers to make arrangements for these promotions.

Livestock shows are held in a number of countries to promote the sale of U.S. breeding stock and feedstuffs.

Sales teams are arranged through the FAS to put U.S. suppliers and foreign buyers together. The FAS selects a market with export potential and invites five or six U.S. firms handling food products to participate in a coordinated sales mission.

Contact
William L. Scholz, Director
Export Programs Division
Foreign Agricultural Service
U.S. Department of Agriculture
4945 South Agriculture Building
Washington, DC 20250
(202) 447-6343

USDA: SEMINARS TO OPEN MARKETS

Evans Browne, the Department of Agriculture's trade officer in Seoul, Korea, was the diplomatic point man in persuading the Korean government to allow American Holstein dairy cows to be brought into the country. In 1982 Browne helped set up a well-attended series of seminars to explain how Korea could improve its dairy industry with American stock. Because of his efforts and those of American dairymen, the Korean government in 1982 allowed dairy cattle imports of registered, high-quality cows, a major source of which is the United States.

COMMERCE: TRADE MISSIONS

For more than 15 years, Gerhardt's Inc. of Louisiana and Texas has sold engines and turbine accessories to the oil and gas industry abroad. In 1981 its international division won a Presidential E award for export success in Latin America. But until the company took part in a trade mission organized by the Commerce Department in 1983, it was unfamiliar with the oil and gas market in the Gulf States of the Middle East. Bruce Gerhardt, the firm's Houston assistant general manager and trade mission participant, not only had the chance to locate potential sales representatives during the mission to Kuwait, the United Arab Emirates, and Saudi Arabia, but was able to learn about the market potential and the necessary ways to sell in these Gulf countries. As a result of the mission, Gerhardt's International Inc. expects to sign several new sales representatives. Bruce Gerhardt anticipates that the sales developing from the Middle East will help offset the present lag in the Latin American oil markets.

Trade Missions

The Commerce Department sponsors and supports several types of trade missions to promote the sale of U.S. goods and services abroad and to help establish sales agents and other foreign representatives for U.S. exporters.

Seminar missions are multicountry business trips designed to facilitate the sale of sophisticated products and technology. During a mission, a team of U.S. high-technology industry representatives presents papers of interest to potential foreign buyers, agents, and distributors. Mission members also participate in private appointments arranged by the overseas post.

Specialized trade missions are planned, organized, and led by officers of the Department of Commerce. The mission itinerary may involve three or four stops within a country or region. The Department plans the details, publicizes the event, and arranges appointments for mission members with government officials and potential agents and distributors. Missions usually are limited to representatives of eight U.S. companies. Participants pay their own travel expenses and reimburse the Department for its costs in supporting the mission.

Industry-organized, government-approved trade missions are organized by trade associations, chambers of commerce, state development agencies, and similar groups with the advice and support of the Department of Commerce. The Department assists in planning these missions and in coordinating arrangements and support through its Export Development Offices, the Foreign Commercial Service, and Foreign Service posts.

Contact
Nearest Commerce Department district office (see appendix).

Investment Missions

The Overseas Private Investment Corporation annually conducts six to eight investment missions to introduce U.S. corporate executives to overseas investment opportunities. An investment mission usually visits one country for seven to ten days. During the mission, participants meet with host-country officials, U.S. government officials, and private-sector representatives for briefings on the country's investment climate. Mission members hold private business meetings with potential joint-venture partners to discuss specific projects. They may also meet with local bankers, accountants, and lawyers to discuss structuring their investment.

Cost
Participants pay round-trip air travel between their home city and the mission country, lodging, meals, and a share of mission expenses.

Contact
Mike McKone, Missions Manager
Overseas Private Investment Corporation
1129 20th Street, N.W.
Washington, DC 20527
(202) 653-2911

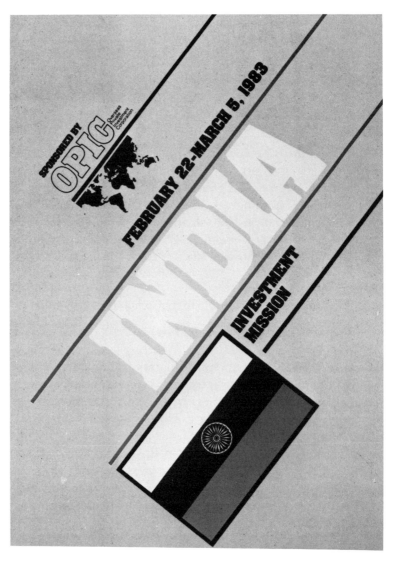

Portions of a pamphlet describing an investment mission to India sponsored by OPIC.

INVESTMENT POTENTIAL

TENTATIVE INDIA MISSION SCHEDULE

Opportunities exist in a wide range of industries including those listed below. Projects involving technologies new to India, with or without equity participation by the U.S. partner, and those involving exports or import substitution, are given the highest priority by the Indian government.

Agriculture/Agribusiness
- Fertilizer (based on natural gas)
- Food processing, packaging and distribution
- Pesticides production
- Poultry production

Chemicals and Materials
- Coal chemicals
- Industrial explosives (slurry and nitroglycerine types)
- Organic and inorganic chemicals

Electrical Industries
- Electronics production
- Test equipment manufacturing

Energy
- Power generation and transmission systems
- Oil and gas exploration and development equipment and technology
- Solar systems technology and components
- Synthetic fuel technology

Fisheries

Industrial Machinery Manufacturing
- Air pollution control equipment
- Boilers and steam generating equipment
- Packaging machinery and technology
- Specialized machine tool manufacturing
- Textile machinery

Light Industries
- Dyes
- Housing construction materials
- Minicomputers/software development
- Process control equipment
- Rubber products
- Telecontrol and data logging interface systems

Medical Industry
- Dental x-ray equipment
- Medical electronic equipment
- Instrument manufacturing

Mining
- Coal mining machinery
- Other equipment
- Processing

Petroleum-Related Industries
- Downstream petrochemical products

Telecommunications

Tourism

Transportation

Tuesday, February 22 NY/London

8:25 p.m. Depart JFK/New York via Air India 108 to London.

Wednesday, February 23 London/New Delhi

8:05 a.m. Arrive London Heathrow.

9:30 a.m. Depart London via Air India 108 to New Delhi.

11:55 p.m. Arrive New Delhi. Transfer to Maurya Sheraton.

Thursday, February 24 New Delhi

a.m. OPIC Breakfast Briefing.

a.m. Briefing by U.S. Ambassador Barnes and staff.

Afternoon and Evening free.

Friday, February 25 New Delhi

a.m. Briefing by Government of India Ministers.

p.m. Courtesy call on Prime Minister Gandhi.

p.m. Reception hosted by Ambassador Barnes.

Saturday, February 26 New Delhi/Agra

a.m. Depart New Delhi for overnight excursion to Agra, site of the Taj Mahal.

Sightseeing at Taj Mahal/Red Fort.

8:00 p.m. Business dinner with selected executives from Indo-American Chamber of Commerce.

Sunday, February 27 Agra/New Delhi

a.m. Sightseeing at Taj Mahal/Red Fort.

Luncheon and briefing on individual appointment schedules.

p.m. Depart Agra for New Delhi.

8:00 p.m. Dinner hosted by Federation Indian Chamber of Commerce and Industry (FICCI).

Monday, February 28 through New Delhi, Bombay, Bangalore, Calcutta,
Thursday, March 3 Madras, or other locations as necessary.

Pre-arranged individual appointment schedules begin. Participants depart for appropriate locations according to pre-established business interests.

Friday, March 4 Bombay

Noon Luncheon and debriefing hosted by Indo-American Chamber of Commerce.

Evening Farewell reception for Indian hosts, hosted by OPIC mission.

Saturday, March 5 Bombay/London/NY

5:00 a.m. Depart Bombay via Air India III for London.

1:00 p.m. Depart London via Air India III for New York.

3:45 p.m. Arrive New York (JFK).

Alternative travel arrangements may be made with the mission's travel agent, Ann Bavender of Travel World, either to remain in India or to book different routings back to the U.S. Ms. Bavender will also be happy to book delegates into London prior to Tuesday, February, 22. Costs incurred as a result of early arrival in London, or extended stay in India must be borne by the delegate. The travel agent will be available on the mission to make any desired changes.

HAWAIIAN HOLIDAY MACADAMIA NUT COMPANY

Having moved into a strong competitive position in the early 1980s, the Hawaiian Holiday Macadamia Nut Company began to think in terms of expansion.

Initially, the firm focused its attention on further growth on the Hawaiian Islands and Guam. But in June 1982 Hawaiian Holiday was one of several U.S. business firms participating in an Overseas Private Investment Corporation mission to Egypt. By the end of the visit, the company entered into a joint-venture agreement to establish a pilot project for the cultivation of 200 macadamia trees there.

Just a month later, in July 1982, Hawaiian Holiday joined another OPIC mission to Thailand. There the firm found a promising possibility for macadamia nut production. During the ten-day mission to Thailand, Hawaiian Holiday reached an agreement with a local partner for cultivation of 500 to 1500 acres, a project expected to gross an estimated $3 to $9 million annually, and with potential for future expansion.

Fisheries Products Sales Missions

The National Marine Fisheries Service organizes sales missions and sponsors industry participation in trade shows in foreign countries. It also provides export services for fisheries products.

Contact

Bruce Morehead
Industry Development Division
National Marine Fisheries Services
U.S. Department of Commerce
Washington, DC 20235
(202) 634-7451

Textile and Apparel Export Development Program

This is a joint industry and Commerce Department program to promote exports of textiles and apparel. The program assists textile and apparel industry participation in overseas trade shows and trade missions, encourages foreign buyers to attend U.S. trade shows, and holds seminars on exporting. In addition, it provides global market surveys on potential export markets.

Contact
Ferenc Molnar, Director
Market Expansion Division
Office of Textiles and Apparel
U.S. Department of Commerce
Washington, DC 20230
(202) 377-2043

FINANCING THE TRIP

Reconnaissance Trip Grants

The Overseas Private Investment Corporation funds reconnaissance trips to developing countries in connection with specific project opportunities. Companies with revenue or net worth less than the smallest firm listed on the "Fortune 1000" are eligible for grants of up to $5000 to cover travel costs and per diem expenses.

INTERMARK TRADING COMPANY

The Overseas Private Investment Corporation in late 1982 approved a reconnaissance survey grant to Intermark Trading Company of Yakima, Washington, to visit India. Intermark's president, Eugene Andruchowicz, was interested in forming a joint venture to build a dehydration plant and wanted to assess the investment climate with his partner, the Jahkar Investment Group of Delhi. OPIC provided $5000 toward the survey.

Based on the results of the survey trip, OPIC in early 1983 agreed to fund part of the costs of a feasibility study of Intermark's $4 million proposed plant. In the course of the study Intermark will examine specific financial and technical aspects of the project. At the study's conclusion it will decide whether to proceed with the undertaking.

The $4 million dehydration plant will be located at some central point between the three major apple-growing states of India. The plant will process locally grown fruit and vegetables, turning them into juices and food snacks. If completed, the project will hire between 60 and 100 employees, who will be trained to work in the factory. Most of the plant's output will be exported to Europe and the Middle East. Preliminary estimates indicate that $1.5 million worth of U.S. equipment will be needed to build the food-processing plant.

Contact
Burton Bostwick or Jeffrey Shafer
Overseas Private Investment Corporation
1129 20th Street, N.W.
Washington, DC 20527
(202) 653-2881

Export Revolving Line of Credit

The Small Business Administration (SBA) is authorized to provide revolving lines of credit to small businesses for export purposes. Funding is available to conduct foreign business travel, participate in trade shows, obtain professional export marketing services, and finance the acquisition of labor and materials necessary to produce products or services for export.

Terms
The SBA can guarantee up to 90 percent of a bank line of credit, up to $500,000.

Eligibility
The borrower must have been in business (though not necessarily exporting) one year. The request for financing must come from the applicant's bank or lending institution. Applicants must demonstrate that they have explored all private sources of funds before requesting SBA help. The SBA cannot provide financial assistance to establish overseas joint ventures.

Contact
Nearest Small Business Administration district office (see appendix).

Egypt Reconnaissance Trip Grant

Small- and medium-sized U.S. companies contemplating an investment in Egypt can investigate potential business opportunities using funds that the Agency for International Development has awarded to the government of Egypt. A company can be reimbursed up to a maximum of $6000 for the direct costs of short reconnaissance visits to Egypt, including two round-trip economy airfares between its home office and Egypt, per diem allowance, and other out-of-pocket expenses.

Contact

Commercial Representation Bureau
Embassy of the Arab Republic of Egypt
2232 Massachusetts Avenue, N.W.
Washington, DC 20008
(202) 265-9111
Telex: 64251 COMRAU

or

Deputy Chairman
General Authority for Investment and Free Zones
8 Adly Street
P.O. Box 1007
Cairo, Arab Republic of Egypt
Phone: 902645; 903776
Telex: 92235 INVEST

PEOPLE TO SEE

Overseas Officers

U.S. embassies and most consulates overseas are staffed with commercial, agricultural, development, and political officers to assist U.S. firms in their business activities. Overseas officers promote U.S. trade and investment by assisting U.S. companies in bidding on major contracts and identifying potential joint-venture partners, buyers, and representatives. Officers gather data on country trends affecting trade and investment and analyze industry sector prospects. They also monitor and analyze local laws, regulations, and practices that affect market access and business conditions, including local standards, licensing, import and investment restrictions, subsidies, taxes, patents and trademarks, and investment codes.

USDA: MARKET STUDIES

In 1979 Malaysia lowered the customs duty for fresh fruits by 50 percent and to 45 percent for fresh oranges shipped directly to Malaysia rather than through Singapore.

Sunkist Growers, Inc. of California, seizing the opportunity to promote U.S. products in this market, conducted a survey to explore the structure and distribution system for perishables in Malaysia's three largest markets. The Sunkist survey team, with the help of the Foreign Agricultural Service's Horticulture and Tropical Products Division, interviewed local importers, wholesalers, and retailers to determine produce distribution in that market.

In 1981/82, Malaysia bought approximately $2 million of Sunkist fresh valencia and navel oranges. Two years earlier, the California grower's cooperative had sales of a little over $200,000 in the Malaysian market.

Contact
U.S. embassies overseas (see appendix).

Agricultural Trade Offices

Agricultural trade offices, located in established overseas markets, offer assistance to U.S. companies interested in selling and investing overseas. The agricultural trade officer at each office can help establish government and business contacts, provide leads on potential buyers and joint-venture investors, and assist in setting up product displays. Overseas cooperators with U.S. trade associations also provide assistance at some trade offices. Offices are fully equipped to provide a full range of support services and to accommodate small product displays for visiting exporters. Visiting executives are expected to pay long-distance telephone and other similar charges they incur at the trade office.

Contact
Jimmy D. Minyard, Assistant Administrator for
Commodity and Marketing Programs
Foreign Agricultural Service
U.S. Department of Agriculture
Washington, DC 20250
(202) 447-4761

or the following agricultural trade officers:

Location and Telephone	Mailing Address and Telex
Bahrain	
Theodore Horoschak	American Embassy
Shalkh Isa Road	FPO New York, NY 09526
P.O. Box 26431	Telex: 9398 USATO BN
Manama	
Phone: 714-151	
People's Republic of China	
Robert D. Bagley	American Embassy
Xiu Shui Dong Jie 2	Box 50
Beijing	FPO San Francisco, CA 96659
Phone: 523-589	Telex: None

Location and Telephone	Mailing Address and Telex

Germany, Federal Republic of

Jon E. Falck
Gr. Theaterstrasse 42
D2 Hamburg 36
Phone: 341-207

c/o AmConGen
APO New York, NY 09215
Telex: 2163970 ATO D

Korea

LaVerne E. Brabant
63, 1-Ka Eulchi-Ro
Chung-Ku, Seoul
Phone: 778-9115, Ext. 4188

American Embassy
APO San Francisco, CA 96301
Telex: K25823 SOLATO

Nigeria

John H. Davenport
No. 1 King's College Road
Lagos
Phone: (01) 634-864

Lagos
Department of State
Washington, DC 20520
Telex: 21670 USEMLA NG

Poland

Ul Wiejska 19
00-480
Warsaw
Phone: 21-46-19; 29-82-54

Warsaw
Department of State
Washington, DC 20520
Telex: 816131 USATO PL

Saudi Arabia

Jerome M. Kuhl
Palestine and Hayel Streets
Jidda
Phone: 661-2408

American Embassy
APO New York, NY 09697
Telex: 404683 USATO SJ

Singapore

James Y. Iso
541 Orchard Road, No. 15-001
Singapore 0923
Phone: 737-1233; 737-1729

American Embassy
FPO San Francisco, CA 96699
Telex: RS 33229 USATO

Tunisia

Dale Good
149 Avenue de la Liberte
Tunis
Phone: 282-566

Tunis
Department of State
Washington, DC 20520
Telex: 13379 AMB TUN

United Kingdom

W. Lynn Abbott
101 Wigmore Street
(01) London, W1X 9PG
Phone: 499-0024

American Embassy
Box 40
FPO New York, NY 09510
Telex: 296009 USA GOF

Location and Telephone	Mailing Address and Telex
Venezuela	
Charles J. Larson	American Embassy
Centro Plaza Torre C	APO Miami, FL 34037
Piso 19, Los Palos Grandes	Telex: 29119 USATO VC
P.O. Box 62291	
Caracas 1060-A	
Phone: 282-2599; 282-2353	

Export Development Offices

Through its network of overseas Export Development Offices, the Commerce Department is able to make available exhibition or conference space to individual U.S. firms, their agents, or trade associations on a first-come, first-served basis. When no regular exhibitions are scheduled, facilities can be used for sales meetings, conferences, seminars, or one-company product promotions, or they can be used as a temporary "base of operation" for U.S. business travelers. Arrangements for use of exhibition or conference space must be made at least 30 days in advance.

Export Development Offices with exhibition and/or meeting facilities are located in London, Mexico City, Milan, São Paulo, Singapore, Sydney, and Tokyo. Charges for use of these facilities are based on specific services requested.

Contact
Far East: Barbara Brown, (202) 377-3741
Europe: Wanda Moore, (202) 377-4511
Latin America: Marlene Ruffin, (202) 377-4756

CHAPTER FIVE

JUDGING THE FEASIBILITY

After making a first trip and determining the general climate for doing business in a particular country, detailed information and an assessment of the commercial viability of the proposed operation are then required. These may involve a business plan, projections for cash flow and demand, materials and construction costs, and an estimate of operating expenses. There are several types of federal programs to provide funding and assistance for such feasibility studies. This chapter describes these programs, categorized into four broad areas:

Technology Transfer. A program to provide funding to transfer technology to foreign countries.

Major Projects. Various federal programs to help U.S. firms compete for major overseas contracts. These projects are typically government-to-government and involve infrastructure activity.

Specific Investor Projects. Programs for funding feasibility studies on specific investments. These projects typically involve private partners.

Special Programs for Small Business. Government programs to help small businesses determine the feasibility of export operations.

TECHNOLOGY TRANSFER

Research and Development Funding

The Bureau of Science and Technology, within the Agency for International Development (AID), identifies ideas for productive technology transfer to developing countries. The Bureau and overseas AID missions will help companies identify developing country markets for their technologies, profitably adapt the technologies using local materials and labor, and train the local labor force.

Terms
The terms are determined on a project-by-project basis by the overseas mission in the developing country for which the technology is targeted. The grants may range from several thousand to several million dollars.

Eligibility
Eligibility is determined by the respective AID overseas mission. The U.S. company must be committed to helping institutions in less developed countries develop and adapt technology.

Contact
John Eriksson, Deputy Assistant Administrator for Science and Technology
Agency for International Development
Washington, DC 20523
(202) 632-4322

and the AID country officer in Washington (see appendix) to determine the appropriate contact in the overseas AID mission.

TELECONSULT COMPANY

One objective of the U.S. Trade and Development Program (TDP) is to help developing countries utilize American high technology. West Germany and Japan are competing against U.S. firms to provide equipment and services to upgrade the Philippine telecommunications system. TDP has helped finance a feasibility study that will recommend standards for the Philippine government's Ministry of Telecommunications and Transportation to adopt. The U.S. firm conducting the feasibility study, the Teleconsult Company, will also prepare the standards for the tender documents associated with procuring goods and services for the project.

MAJOR PROJECTS

Feasibility Study Funding

The U.S. Trade and Development Program (TDP) funds project planning to help U.S. companies compete for, and participate in, major public-sector projects in developing countries. TDP also provides reimbursable grants to U.S. companies considering an equity investment in a project. These grants enable a company to analyze the technical, economic, and financial aspects of a proposed investment project and to develop data for planning.

EBASCO SERVICES, INC.

Ebasco Services Incorporated and TDP in 1982 entered into a reimbursable agreement for the feasibility study of a $4.5 billion coal gasification/methanol complex in Panama. The study project, to which TDP and the U.S. Department of Energy will contribute $2.5 million, will perform the project development for the conversion to methanol of 6.6 million tons annually of U.S. high-sulfur coal from the Illinois basin. The methanol is targeted to be used in Japan's new combined cycle electric-generating plants and co-generation facilities, or it will be blended with gasoline as a transport fuel.

By upgrading coal to methanol, the project will enable U.S. coal producers to compete in the Pacific rim markets against foreign coal supplies. If successful, it would improve the U.S. trade balance with Japan and create jobs in Midwestern mines, river barge companies, and at U.S. firms that manufacture equipment for methanol coal gasification. Ebasco estimates that U.S. exports from this project could run as high as $1 billion in equipment and services.

Terms

TDP will provide a grant to a host country to finance planning services for a public-sector project on the condition that a U.S. firm is selected to perform the study. For investor projects, TDP will provide up to 50 percent of the cost of the feasibility study, which must be reimbursed if the investment proceeds. TDP's participation usually ranges up to $500,000 for public-sector projects, and from $50,000 to $150,000 for investor projects.

Eligibility

1. The project must have the potential to generate substantial U.S. exports, usually equal to 75 to 100 times the value of the U.S. government's expenditure.
2. The project must have high priority for the host country.
3. The project must be consistent with U.S. foreign policy goals.
4. U.S. government aid must be critical to the project going forward.
5. The investor, if there is one, must be able to finance at least 40 percent of the project cost.

TDP: FEASIBILITY STUDIES

The Bechtel Power Corporation of San Francisco in 1982 was hired to study the possibility of converting Jamaica's public power generating plants from oil to coal. Bechtel's $456,000 study, commissioned by TDP, found that conversion to coal could initially save Jamaica some $50 million a year in scarce foreign exchange—and more in succeeding years. If Jamaica's alumina plants also converted to coal, the benefits would be even larger. The study, to be completed in 1983, estimates that the U.S. could export $122 million worth of equipment and services to convert the plants, in addition to coal exports of $100 million a year. Jamaica can use the Bechtel study as the basis for a loan application for funding the conversion to the Export-Import Bank, the World Bank, or the Inter-American Development Bank.

Contact
Director
U.S. Trade and Development Program
International Development Cooperation Agency
Washington, DC 20523
(703) 235-3663

LEMCO ENGINEERS, INC.

Through a TDP grant of $434,000 to the Royal Thai Government, LEMCO Engineers, Inc. of St. Louis, Missouri was hired in 1980 to perform a feasibility study on a high-voltage transmission line supplying Bangkok with much of its electricity. LEMCO also was awarded follow-on contracts of $9 million for engineering, design, equipment specifications, and construction supervision of the project. The project is now moving toward the stage of equipment purchase and installation. U.S. firms are well positioned to win contracts for more than $200 million worth of materials, equipment, and supplies.

SPECIFIC INVESTOR PROJECTS

Feasibility Study Funding

Bureau for Private Enterprise

The Bureau for Private Enterprise (PRE), within the Agency for International Development, provides reimbursable grants for feasibility studies intended to provide the basis for investment and financing decisions. The availability of this financing permits PRE to encourage investment in selected joint ventures in developing countries that have a high agency priority.

Terms

PRE will provide 50 percent of the total study cost, up to a maximum of $50,000. The project sponsor finances the original cost and is reimbursed after submitting a completed feasibility study. If the project goes forward, the sponsor must reimburse all PRE funds. In addition, PRE retains the right to finance up to 25 percent of the total investment.

RURAL VENTURES, INC.

After taking part in an investment mission to Jamaica in late 1981, Rural Ventures, Inc. of Bloomington, Minnesota was awarded a U.S. government feasibility study grant to examine ways of aiding small farmers in Jamaica. The company, a consortium of farmer cooperatives, foundations, and religious groups, is interested in increasing the productivity of smaller Jamaican farms by introducing advanced farming and marketing techniques. In its study, Rural Ventures concluded that its project has the potential for a successful commercial enterprise. The company now is negotiating with the Jamaican National Investment Corporation to take an equity position in the project and to secure start-up funds and grants for technical assistance from the Ministry of Agriculture.

Eligibility

PRE will consider only ventures with substantial ownership by a company in the host country. Project sponsors must be host-country firms or citizens. Priority consideration will be given to businesses within the agricultural, health, and medical products/services sectors. Projects must show potential for substantial developmental impact in the host country by generating net employment; earning net foreign exchange; developing managerial, technical, or other skills; or transferring technologies.

Application Procedure

A business plan containing a project description, financing requirements, and a technical plan should be submitted to PRE. A detailed listing of points to be covered in the application is available.

Contact

Bruce Bouchard
Bureau for Private Enterprise
Agency for International Development
New State Building
State Annex 14, Room 633
Washington, DC 20523
(703) 235-2274

Export-Import Bank

The Export-Import Bank (Eximbank) finances an average of three to four feasibility studies each year through its Direct Loan Program and its Exporter Credits, Guarantees and Insurance Programs. Under the latter program, feasibility studies can be assisted through export credit insurance provided by the Foreign Credit Insurance Association, the Commercial Bank Guarantee Program, the Small Manufacturers' Discount Loan Program, the Export Trading Company Loan Guarantee Program, and the Medium-Term Credit Program. The export value of a feasibility study may range up to $6 million, with the average around $3 million. Projects that would involve the purchase of U.S. goods and services are encouraged.

Terms and Eligibility
Refer to Eximbank's loan programs in Chapter 7 of this book.

Contact
Vice President for Engineering
Export-Import Bank of the United States
811 Vermont Avenue, N.W.
Washington, DC 20571
(202) 566-8802

Overseas Private Investment Corporation

The Overseas Private Investment Corporation (OPIC) will enter into a cost-sharing arrangement with a U.S. firm to study the feasibility of an investment the firm has identified through its own reconnaissance in a country. Small businesses are eligible for feasibility study assistance in all countries in which OPIC operates; feasibility study funds are available to larger firms only if the per capita income of the host country is less than $680 (in 1979 dollars).

Terms
The maximum OPIC participation in such a study is $100,000, which represents up to 50 percent of the total cost (60 percent if the project is sponsored by a small business).

For small businesses, funding for feasibility studies is provided through an interest-free, reimbursable grant. Repayment (over two years) is required only if the investor moves forward with the study-related project; repayment can be reduced if the investor insures or finances the project through OPIC.

For larger firms, feasibility financing assistance is provided through a two-year loan at a rate generally equivalent to two-thirds of the prime rate. Repayment may be reduced if the investment moves forward and the investor elects to obtain OPIC insurance or financing.

Eligibility
A U.S. company must have an appropriate operating and technical background in the industry for which the investment will be under-

taken. It must also demonstrate the financial capability and intention to undertake a long-term investment should the project prove feasible. A senior executive from the investing company must be a member of the feasibility study team. Investments relating to oil or gas extraction are not eligible for this program.

Application Procedure

Firms interested in obtaining feasibility study financing must provide the following preliminary information:

1. Location and business of the proposed project.
2. Identity, background, and financial statements of the principals sufficient to establish their financial and managerial ability.
3. Nature and results of preliminary or reconnaissance studies.
4. Scope of the survey, outlining in detail the factors to be studied.
5. Preliminary budget for the survey, indicating the members of the study team.
6. Tentative estimate of total project costs and the applicant's expected equity investment in the project.
7. Brief statement of the contribution the project will make to local economic and social development.
8. Résumés of the study participants.
9. Two bank references and two business references for the investing company.

OPIC will discuss the proposed survey and project with the sponsor and assist in preparation of a final workplan and budget, including the amount of OPIC participation and terms.

Contact

Burton Bostwick or Jeffrey Shafer
Overseas Private Investment Corporation
1129 20th Street, N.W.
Washington, DC 20527
(202) 653-7134

GRAVELY TRACTORS

When E. Peter Janke, president of Gravely International in Clemmons, North Carolina, first heard about the programs of the Overseas Private Investment Corporation, his thoughts turned to the Caribbean.

"For years we had been exporting some of our agricultural and grounds maintenance machinery to Jamaica and had reached the point where we were thinking in terms of establishing a base of operations in the Caribbean market," he reflected.

OPIC's feasibility study program, Mr. Janke decided, could provide him with the necessary information to make a final decision on whether to manufacture tractors in Jamaica for the Caribbean market. Early in 1983, OPIC agreed to provide feasibility study assistance to Gravely to explore the market for its products in the Caricom countries over the next five to ten years. If it appears the market will support a venture, Gravely wants to examine ways of establishing facilities in Jamaica. The study will also look at how items could best be marketed to other countries from Jamaica.

Gravely was considered an excellent candidate for OPIC feasibility study financing because of its 20-year history of sales experience in Jamaica. The company's identification of a joint-venture partner for product distribution, the potential for increasing food output by small farmers, and increased foreign exchange were other factors in Gravely's favor. The project would also lead to a demand for more U.S.-made equipment.

Agricultural Export Marketing Assistance

Market Development Cooperators, which are agricultural nonprofit associations, work with the Foreign Agricultural Service to promote and expand overseas markets for U.S. products. More than 50 foreign agricultural associations, 7000 processors and handlers, and 1500 farm cooperatives representing several million farmers participate in this program. U.S. companies can receive assistance in expanding overseas markets for their food products by contacting the Market Development Cooperator for their respective industry.

Contact

Jimmy D. Minyard, Assistant Administrator
Foreign Agricultural Service
U.S. Department of Agriculture
Washington, DC 20250
(202) 447-4761

USDA: COOPERATOR PROGRAMS

Thanks to the Department of Agriculture's Cooperator programs, Japan has become the largest market for U.S. farm exports. Demonstrations, marketing trips, and educational programs by American farm groups, sponsored by the Agriculture Department's Cooperator programs, have helped build a large poultry program that depends primarily on U.S. technology, feed grains, and soybeans.

The Cooperator programs have also helped promote the use of U.S. feed grains and soybeans for Japanese swine as well as dairy and beef cattle. In addition, these programs have opened Japan as a major market for U.S. beef, chicken parts, turkeys, and egg solids as well as for wheat, fruit, and vegetables.

Caribbean Project Assistance

The Agency for International Development has awarded $1 million to the Caribbean Project Development Facility. The Facility was created to generate employment, improve balance of payments, and encourage self-sustained growth and economic development in the Caribbean region through new, privately sponsored investment projects. It identifies promising small- and medium-sized projects in the $500,000 to 5,000,000 range and prepares them for financing. Staff members provide a full range of technical assistance, including helping sponsors of prospective projects find an appropriate Caribbean business partner, obtain equity and loan financing, and identify appropriate technology and export markets.

Contact
P. B. Quan, Manager
Caribbean Project Development Facility
1818 H Street, N.W.
Room I10/136
Washington, DC 20433
(202) 676-0482

Caribbean Agribusiness Grants

The Peace Corps offers feasibility study grants to assist local businesses and farmers in determining the viability of small and medium-sized agribusiness projects in the Caribbean. Trained in-country volunteers work with local counterparts and outside experts to provide market, technical, and financial analyses as well as strategy planning for promising agribusiness ventures. The program operates in Antigua, Belize, Barbados, Costa Rica, Dominica, Dominican Republic, Guatemala, Haiti, Honduras, Jamaica, Montserrat, St. Lucia, St. Kitts–Nevis, and St. Vincent.

Terms
The Peace Corps pays for the cost of volunteers and outside commercial experts.

Eligibility
U.S. companies are eligible for this service if they are working to establish a joint-venture project with a local company or farm group. The project must create local jobs and a host-country agency must request assistance through the Peace Corps country director.

Contact
Bill Gschwend
Inter-American Operations
U.S. Peace Corps
806 Connecticut Avenue, N.W.
Washington, DC 20526
(202) 254-9616

Egyptian Feasibility Study Funding

The Agency for International Development has awarded funding to the government of Egypt to enable U.S. businesses to investigate potential investment opportunities in Egypt.

Terms
For small or medium-sized companies, the funding covers 75 percent of the direct costs (up to a maximum of $200,000) for conducting a feasibility study on a specific joint-venture project. For Fortune 1000 companies, funding is limited to 50 percent of the direct costs of the feasibility study.

Eligibility
The applicant must be a U.S. company or a majority-owned subsidiary of a U.S. corporation. The company will supply the technology or management expertise to bring the proposed project on stream. New ventures established under the investment incentive regulations of Egyptian Law 43 are also eligible.

Contact
Commercial Representation Bureau
Embassy of the Arab Republic of Egypt
2232 Massachusetts Avenue, N.W.
Washington, DC 20008
(202) 265-9111
Telex: 64251 COMRAU

or

Deputy Chairman
General Authority for Investment and Free Zones
8 Adly Street
P.O. Box 1007
Cairo, Arab Republic of Egypt
Telephone: 902645; 903776
Telex: 92235 INVEST

SPECIAL PROGRAMS FOR SMALL BUSINESS

Management Assistance Programs

The following programs sponsored by the Small Business Administration (SBA) are available to U.S. businesses. In addition, SBA district offices offer free export counseling and co-sponsor export training programs.

The *Service Corps of Retired Executives (SCORE)* is an organization of retired business executives with many years of practical experience. Members with international trade expertise help small businesses assess their export potential and develop a basic export marketing plan. SCORE volunteers work in each SBA district office and their services are free (see appendix).

The *Active Corps of Executives (ACE)*, which augments SCORE's services, consists of more than 2600 active executives from all major industries, professional and trade associations, educational institutions, and many other professions. ACE members volunteer their expertise whenever needed by a U.S. small business.

The *Small Business Institute* makes senior and graduate-level students of international business available to small companies to provide overseas marketing information and to develop export marketing feasibility studies. Students from more than 450 U.S. colleges and universities participate in this program.

Small Business Development Centers based at U.S. universities assist new exporters by providing counseling, market information, and training programs in international trade.

Export Workshops and Training Programs are conducted periodically by seasoned exporters and knowledgeable international traders under the cosponsorship of SBA district offices, the U.S. Department of Commerce, and other agencies and institutions concerned with international trade development. The workshops discuss procedures and techniques involved in exporting, from identifying overseas markets to insuring the receipt of payment for exported goods and services.

The *Call Contract Program* utilizes professional management and technical consultants who can provide to eligible small and minority businesses marketing and production technology information and assistance. Specialized export assistance may be provided at no cost to an eligible client through this program.

Contact
Nearest Small Business Administration district office (see appendix).

SBA: SMALL BUSINESS INSTITUTE PROGRAM

When a Sweet Home, Oregon electronics firm wanted advice on how to enter South American markets, it turned to a Small Business Administration-supported research program at Oregon State University. After Jim McCrary, president of McCrary Electronics, explained his needs, a team of Oregon State business students spent a semester working out a market plan that was financed by the university's Small Business Institute program. Working under a faculty adviser, the graduate and undergraduate team developed information—political and cultural background, trade and economic facts—on three Latin American countries. The plan also set out marketing strategies that McCrary might follow, as well as names of banks, export firms, and freight forwarders to help him execute the plan. McCrary Electronics expects to begin testing the targeted markets in late 1983.

CHAPTER SIX

REGULATIONS AND REQUIREMENTS

Before undertaking an overseas venture, American firms should be aware of foreign country agreements that must first be obtained, host-country regulations regarding certain types of business, tax incentives and requirements, and general regulations affecting trade between the United States and foreign countries. These subjects are reviewed in this chapter, which is organized into four major subgroupings:

Overseas Agreements. How to locate information on investment treaties, trade barriers, and foreign government approvals.

Export-Import Regulations and Restrictions. Programs for assisting U.S. firms with trade disputes and product standards, and information on customs and export restrictions.

Taxation. Information on the taxation of U.S. individuals and companies abroad and on U.S. government incentives for operating overseas.

Host-Country Incentives. Existing investment incentives available in foreign countries for American businesses willing to invest in those countries, including import duty exemptions, tax holidays, and training grants.

OVERSEAS AGREEMENTS

Bilateral Investment Treaties

A Bilateral Investment Treaty (BIT) is a reciprocal agreement between the U.S. government and a foreign government, which outlines the treatment of investors in the two countries. For the U.S. investor abroad, such treaties are valuable. They assure increased stability of the investment climate in the foreign country, provide a legal framework for settling disputes, and guarantee that investors will receive treatment no less favorable than that required by international law.

The U.S. government seeks to negotiate BITs that contain the following major elements:

Most-favored-nation or national treatment (with limited exceptions), whichever is better, for the U.S. investor abroad.

Guarantees of prompt, adequate, and effective compensation for expropriation, as well as the right to transfer such compensation at the prevailing exchange rate.

The right of investors to make free transfers of currency in connection with the investment at the prevailing exchange rate.

A legal framework for the settlement of disputes between a firm and host country and between governments, based on prevailing standards of international law.

A treaty of at least ten years' duration.

The Office of the United States Trade Representative can provide copies of all BITs in force and a list of countries that have entered into BIT negotiations with the United States. Information on performance requirements and other investment restrictions in major host countries is also available.

Contact
Phyllis O. Bonanno, Director
Office of Private Sector Liaison
Office of the U.S. Trade Representative
600 17th Street, N.W.
Washington, DC 20506
(202) 395-6120

USTR: NEGOTIATING ENTRY

Negotiating entry for a U.S. firm into a country that restricts foreign investment is a major duty of the Office of the United States Trade Representative (USTR). For example, the USTR recently assisted a Washington, D.C. high-technology company in investing in a neighboring country. For three years, meetings and negotiations had taken place between the company and the host government, but without success. If the firm's products were to be marketed successfully, an actual presence in the neighboring country was needed. The Trade Representative met with the other country's officials to clarify the nature of the proposed investment and to persuade the neighbor that the investment met its economic objectives. In early 1983 the investment was finally approved.

Foreign Government Approvals

Before a U.S. overseas investment can receive political risk insurance from OPIC, the investor must secure a Foreign Government Approval (FGA) from the host country covering the total amount of the investment. Most bilateral agreements between OPIC and countries in which OPIC programs are offered require that the foreign government approve each project that is seeking OPIC insurance. The U.S. embassy in the host country can assist the investor in obtaining such FGAs. (*Caution:* A project must be registered with OPIC before the investor makes an irrevocable commitment to invest. See description of OPIC programs in Chapter 8.)

Contact
Elizabeth A. Burton, Country Agreements Officer
Overseas Private Investment Corporation
1129 20th Street, N.W.
Washington, DC 20527
(202) 653-2949

Business Counseling and Advice

The International Business Practices Division of the Commerce Department provides counseling and advice on U.S. and foreign country laws, regulations, and practices affecting international trade and investment. Staff members offer information and help U.S. firms research laws on taxation; antitrust, patent, and trademark rights; licensing patents; foreign agents, distributors, and joint ventures; product liability; and other issues related to exporting and overseas investment.

Contact

Ovidio Giberga
International Business Practices Division
U.S. Department of Commerce, Room 1128
Washington, DC 20230
(202) 377-2828

Business Assistance

The Office of Business and Export Affairs is a point of contact in the State Department for U.S. companies requiring assistance with international business negotiations and foreign investments.

Contact

James R. Tarrant, Director
Office of Business and Export Affairs
U.S. Department of State
Room 3638
Washington, DC 20520
(202) 632-0354

Patents and Trademarks

The Patent and Trademark Office can provide information on the Patent Cooperation Treaty, which enables individuals and companies to file a patent application in several countries simultaneously. The Patent Office's Legislation and International Affairs Office provides information on treaties covering patents and trademarks, along with countries participating in these treaties.

Contact
Office of Legislation and International Affairs
Patent and Trademark Office, Box 4
Washington, DC 20231
(703) 557-3065

Lowering Agricultural Trade Barriers

The Foreign Agricultural Service (FAS) identifies and works to reduce foreign trade barriers and practices that discourage the export of U.S. farm products. Agricultural representatives play a major role in trying to remove tariff or nontariff barriers affecting market access. FAS has offices at the headquarters of the European Community in Brussels and at the international negotiations center in Geneva. FAS also maintains contact with the Food and Agricultural Organization of the United Nations in Rome.

A company that has identified a barrier to exporting its products to a foreign country should contact its Market Development Cooperator group (see Chapter 4, Agricultural Trade Offices). The Cooperator and the Department of Agriculture will work together to have the barrier removed. A company that believes it has been treated unfairly by a foreign government in a trade issue, such as losing a tender to a higher bidder, should also contact the Cooperator.

AGRITRADE INTERNATIONAL

When Agritrade International (ATI) of Portland, Oregon faced restrictions on the import of U.S. potatoes into Korea, ATI's president, Donald Hutchinson, contacted the Department of Agriculture's trade office in Seoul. Through the trade office, the firm made contact with Korean government agricultural officials. Today, the Portland company exports frozen baked potatoes to Korea. As the first potato exporter to Korea, the ATI company has opened the door to a new market for the United States.

Contact
Rolland E. Anderson, Assistant Administrator for International Trade Policy
Foreign Agricultural Service
South Building, Room 5057
U.S. Department of Agriculture
Washington, DC 20250
(202) 447-6887

EXPORT-IMPORT REGULATIONS AND RESTRICTIONS

Trade Agreements

The International Trade Commission's annual report, the Operation of Trade Agreements Program, includes information on the General Agreement on Tariffs and Trade (GATT), the Export-Import Bank, U.S. actions on imports, revisions of trade laws, and other information.

Cost
Free.

Contact
Office of Publications
International Trade Commission
701 E Street, N.W.
Washington, DC 20436
(202) 523-5178

Trade Dispute Assistance

The Department of Commerce assists in settling trade disputes between U.S. and foreign traders. Assistance is limited to informal, conciliatory efforts directed toward removing misunderstandings between the two parties.

Only disputes related to a commercial transaction should be directed to the Commerce Department. The following types of case should *not* be referred for investigation: disputes involving less than $500; collection cases; and disputes that the complainant has made no effort to settle.

Contact
Nearest Commerce Department district office (see appendix).

Customs Requirements

Goods imported to the United States must be cleared by the U.S. Customs Service. The Service, with headquarters in Washington, has seven geographical regions that are further divided into districts with ports of entry. The Service is also responsible for administering the customs laws of the U.S. Virgin Islands and Puerto Rico.

The following free publications provide information on customs requirements for imports and exports:

U.S. Import Requirements: General information on U.S. Customs requirements for imported merchandise.

Customs Rulings on Imports: How to obtain a binding U.S. Customs duty ruling on items before they are imported.

Importing into the United States: Customs and other requirements for importing merchandise into the United States.

Marking of Country of Origin: Customs requirements for marking imported merchandise with the name of the country of origin.

Import Quota: Summary of import quotas administered by the Customs Service.

Notice to Masters of Vessels: Precautions that masters or owners of vessels should take to avoid penalties and forfeitures.

Notice to Carriers of Bonded Merchandise: Precautions that carriers and customhouse brokers should take to safeguard merchandise moving in-bond.

Drawback: How to obtain a duty refund on certain exports.

ATA Carnets: Use of ATA carnets, which simplify customs formalities for the temporary admission of certain goods.

Foreign Trade Zones: Advantages, use, and customs requirements of foreign trade zones.

807 Guide: Details use of Item 807.00 in the U.S. Tariff Schedule, which permits a reduction in duty to reflect the value of components manufactured in the United States and assembled abroad.

Contact
The appropriate U.S. Customs Service office:

Headquarters
U.S. Customs Service
1301 Constitution Avenue, N.W.
P.O. Box 7407
Washington, DC 20229
(202) 566-8195

New York Region
6 World Trade Center
Room 201
New York, NY 10048
(212) 466-4547

North Central Region
55 East Monroe Street
Chicago, IL 60603
(312) 353-8831

Northeast Region
100 Summer Street
Boston, MA 02110
(617) 223-7548

Pacific Region
300 North Los Angeles Street
Los Angeles, CA 90053
(213) 688-5939

South Central Region
423 Canal Street
New Orleans, LA 70130
(504) 589-2917

Southeast Region
99 Southeast 5th Street
Miami, FL 33131
(305) 350-4126

Southwest Region
5850 San Felipe Street, Suite 500
Houston, TX 77057
(713) 953-6905

The following publications are for sale:

Tariff Schedules of the United States Annotated: For use in classification of imported merchandise, for rates of duty, and for statistical purposes.

Cost

$37 for first class in U.S.; $46.25 foreign. Order no.: S/N 049-000-81001-6.

Customs Regulations of the United States: Looseleaf volume of regulations interpreting many of the customs, navigation, and other laws administered by the U. S. Customs Service.

Cost

$65 in U.S.; $81.25 foreign. Includes supplements issued during the subscription year. Order no.: S/N 048-002-81001-5.

Customs Bulletin: Weekly pamphlet containing proposed and final amendments to Customs Regulations, notices and administrative decisions of interest to the international trading community, and pertinent decisions of the U.S. Court of International Trade and the U.S. Court of Appeals for the Federal Circuit.

Cost

Annual subscription $95 in U.S.; $118.75 foreign. Single copies $3.75 in U.S.; $4.70 foreign. Order no.: S/N 048-000-80001-7.

Contact

Superintendent of Documents
U.S. Government Printing Office
Washington, DC 20402
(202) 783-3238

Binding Rates of Duty

U.S. companies may obtain from the U.S. Customs Service a decision on the tariff classification and rate of duty of specific merchandise before it is shipped to the United States. To obtain a decision, the following information must be provided:

1. Complete description of the goods, including samples, sketches, diagrams, and other illustrative material if the goods cannot be described adequately in writing.
2. Method of manufacture or fabrication.
3. Specifications and analyses.
4. Quantities and costs of the component materials.
5. Commercial designation and chief use in the United States.

Contact
Area Director of Customs
New York Seaport
6 World Trade Center, Room 423
New York, NY 10048
(212) 466-5817

or the U.S. Customs Service regional offices listed on pages 127 and 128.

Export-Import and Sales Restrictions

Any venture involving coffee, tea, cocoa, sugar, jute, cotton, bananas, or hard fibers could be affected by restrictions in international commodities agreements. The Office of International Commodities provides information on these restrictions.

Contact
John A. Barcas, Chief
Office of Food Policy
Tropical Products Division
U.S. Department of State
Room 3527
Washington, DC 20520
(202) 632-3059

Regulations Affecting Sensitive Exports

The staff of the Commerce Department's Office of Export Administration helps firms to meet the requirements of the Export Administration Act. The Act lists the licensing requirements for sensitive, high-technology equipment and data. For each listed commodity, it identifies the countries for which export license documents are required. The Export Administration Regulations are published in the *Federal Register* (codified in the *Code of Federal Regulations* [15 CFR Parts 368–395]). The following publications are available free of charge:

Exports by Mail—Export License Requirements for Exports by Mail.

Denial Orders Currently Affecting Export Privileges (reprint from Regulations, Supp. Nos. 1 and 2 to Part 388).

Export Administration Act of 1979 (reprint from Regulations).

Export Control of Technical Data (reprint from Regulations, Part 379).

Overview of the Export Administration Program.

A Summary of U.S. Export Administration Regulations.

Enforcement and Administrative Proceedings (reprint from Regulations, Part 387–388).

Contact
Office of Export Administration
U.S. Department of Commerce
Room 2602
Washington, DC 20230
(202) 377-4811

Introductory Course to Export Administration Regulations: Information on how to complete and submit export license applications.

Contact
Office of Export Administration
U.S. Department of Commerce
Room 1099D
Washington, DC 20230
(202) 377-5247

The following publications are for sale:

The Export Administration Regulations: A comprehensive list of the rules controlling exports of U.S. products and requirements for export licensing. An annual subscription includes Export Administration Bulletins, which explain recent policy changes and include updated regulations.

Cost
$105 in U.S.; $131.25 foreign. Order no.: S/N 003-009-81001-9.

Contact
Superintendent of Documents
U.S. Government Printing Office
Washington, DC 20402
(202) 783-3238

Export Licenses Approved and Re-exports Authorized: A list of all licenses by general commodity description, dollar value, and country of destination. Issued daily.

Cost
Annual subscription $37.50.

Contact
Operations Division
Office of Export Administration
U.S. Department of Commerce
Room 2626
Washington, DC 20230
(202) 377-3000

Agricultural Product Standards

The Department of Agriculture's Foreign Agriculture Service (FAS) identifies, collects, and analyzes foreign proposals concerning agricultural product standards. Notifications of proposed foreign standards are published in *Export Briefs,* a weekly newsletter.

Cost
$50 per year.

Contact
Foreign Agricultural Service
Export Promotion Division
U.S. Department of Agriculture
South Building, Room 4945
Washington, DC 20250
(202) 447-2423

FAS also solicits comments on proposed foreign standards from individuals and companies, U.S. government agencies, state departments of agriculture, exporter associations, and farm organizations. These comments are relayed to foreign countries.

USDA: GOING TO BAT FOR U.S. GROWERS

The Department of Agriculture makes a firm promise to farm product exporters: If your product meets U.S. health and safety standards, the Department will go to bat for you, should you meet trouble in a foreign market. For instance, consider the case of Pioneer Overseas Corporation of Johnston, Iowa. Due to an oversight, four containers of a total shipment of 48 containers of hybrid corn seed bound for Greece were released without inspection or cleaning by customs officials in Houston, Texas. All were loaded aboard a vessel en route to Europe when the USDA alerted Pioneer of the threat of Khapra beetle infestation in the four containers. The USDA has the responsibility to notify any foreign country of prohibited pests that may be in products shipped from the United States. However, instead of immediately cabling the Greek authorities and running the risk of a misunderstanding on the severity of the possible contamination, Dr. Al Chock, USDA Animal and Plant Health Inspection Service Regional Director for Greece, flew to Athens. With Dr. Chock's assistance, only the four containers were detained for inspection and finally released with a clean bill of health.

Contact

Technical Office
U.S. Department of Agriculture
South Building, Room 5530
Washington, DC 20250
(202) 382-1333

Agricultural Products Inspection Services

The Department of Agriculture provides inspecting, certifying, weighing, and grading services for agricultural, meat, and poultry products. These services help assure U.S. exporters that exports comply with the requirements of the importing country.

If a food quality standard imposed by a foreign importing country appears to be an unnecessary barrier to international trade, the Standards Code encourages the countries involved to resolve the problem informally. The Foreign Agricultural Service's agricultural counselors and attachés stationed in U.S. embassies overseas can be of help in settling these disputes (see appendix).

In addition, USDA's Food Safety and Inspection Service inspects meat and poultry products intended for export to assure that the product is sound, properly labeled, U.S.-inspected and passed, and meets all special requirements of the intended importing country at the time of export certification. To protect U.S. consumers, the Service is responsible for the following:

Evaluation of laws and regulations governing the meat inspection systems in foreign countries that export meat and meat products to the United States, to assure that they are comparable with U.S. requirements.

On-site reviews of certified foreign systems and plants preparing meat and meat products for export to the United States.

Inspection of an imported product at the time it is offered for entry at U.S. ports.

Routine inspection of both imported and exported products is provided free of charge through the Service's Meat and Poultry Inspection Operations.

Contact

Inquiries regarding routine inspection service should be directed to the appropriate Agricultural Department regional office.

North Central Region
Dr. K. O. McDougall, Director
607 East 2nd Street
Des Moines, IA 50316
(515) 284-4042

Northeastern Region
Dr. M. C. McNay, Director
1421 Cherry Street, 7th Floor
Philadelphia, PA 19102
(215) 597-4217

Southeastern Region
Dr. J. D. Willis, Director
1718 Peachtree Street, N.W., Room 216
Atlanta, GA 30309
(404) 881-3911

Southwestern Region
Dr. N. B. Isom, Director
1100 Commerce Street, Room 5-F41
Dallas, TX 75242
(214) 767-9116

Western Region
Dr. D. C. Breeden, Director
620 Central Avenue
Building 2C, Room 102
Alameda, CA 94501
(415) 273-7402

Meat and Poultry Export Information
Wallace I. Leary, Director, Export Coordination Division
International Programs
Food Safety and Inspection Service
U.S. Department of Agriculture
South Building, Room 4332
Washington, DC 20250
(202) 447-9051

Meat and Poultry Import Information
Grace Clark, Director, Foreign Programs Division
International Programs
Food Safety and Inspection Service
U.S. Department of Agriculture
South Building, Room 4346
Washington, DC 20250
(202) 447-7610

Live Animal and Plant Product Health Inspection

The Animal and Plant Health Inspection Service inspects and certifies that animals, plants, and agricultural products conform with health and sanitation requirements for import or export as prescribed by the United States and the country of destination. There is no charge for this service during working hours.

Contact

For information regarding inspection of live animals and poultry for export and import:

Import-Export, Animals and Products
Veterinary Services
Animal and Plant Health Inspection Service
U.S. Department of Agriculture
6505 Belcrest Road
Hyattsville, MD 20782
(301) 436-8383

For information regarding inspection of live plants for export and import:

Plant, Protection and Quarantine
Animal and Plant Health Inspection Service
U.S. Department of Agriculture
6505 Belcrest Road
Hyattsville, MD 20782
(301) 436-8537 (for exports)
(301) 436-8645 (for imports)

Export Grain Inspection

U.S. grain for export must be officially inspected and weighed, except for land shipments to Canada and Mexico. The Federal Grain In-

---

USDA: PROTECTING MARKETS

In the case of the recent Mediterranean fruit fly scare in California, the Foreign Agricultural Service and the Health Inspection Service worked together to keep open the important Japanese market for U.S. citrus fruit. Department experts flew to Japan to convince the government that U.S. inspections were being strictly enforced to prevent the export of the Medfly infestation. The mission was successful: the $40 million market for California oranges, lemons, and grapefruit remained open.

spection Service, or one of the eight qualified delegated states, performs these inspection and weighing services. Fees for these services vary.

Cost

For services performed under contract:

6 A.M.–6 P.M.: $21.80 per hour, per service representative.
6 P.M.–6 A.M.: $25.20 per hour, per service representative.

For services performed without a contract:

6 A.M.–6 P.M.: $24.20 per hour, per service representative.
6 P.M.–6 A.M.: $28.00 per hour, per service representative.

In addition to inspecting grain, the Service conducts other tests, such as testing protein content in wheat and aflatoxin levels in corn. It also tests processed grain products such as flour and cornmeal, and inspects certain related commodities such as rice, dry beans, peas, and lentils. The fees for these services vary.

Contact

To determine the appropriate person to contact in your area for the weighing and inspection of grain, processed grain products, and related commodities:

John Marshall, Acting Director
Field Management Division
Federal Grain Inspection Service
U.S. Department of Agriculture
South Building, Room 1641
Washington, DC 20250
(202) 382-0228

The Service also maintains an international monitoring staff to handle foreign buyer complaints about U.S. grain and provides technical information about U.S. grain quality standards and inspection and weighing procedures. There is no fee for this service. All companies exporting grain regularly must register with the Federal Grain Inspection Service. The annual registration fee ranges from $135 to $270.

Contact

To obtain a registration certificate for the export of grain:

J. T. Abshier, Director
Compliance Division
Federal Grain Inspection Service
U.S. Department of Agriculture
South Building, Room 1647
Washington, DC 20250
(202) 447-8262

Agricultural Grading and Standardization Services

The Agriculture Department's Agricultural Marketing Service develops grade standards and carries out grading services for meat, cattle, swine, wool, poultry, eggs, dairy products, fruits, vegetables, cotton, and tobacco. Upon request, the Service will evaluate samples of seed for export shipment. Standards for exported cotton are covered by the U.S. Cotton Standards Act.

The Service also provides food quality certification to foreign buyers to assure that any product shipped overseas meets contract specifications. Buyers must submit the specification or contract in advance. The Service reviews the contract and works with the buyers to write a contract or specification that can be certified. Requirements for Department of Agriculture certification can be made a part of the purchase agreement.

Cost

Based on usage.

Contact

William T. Manley, Deputy Administrator
Marketing Program Operations
Agricultural Marketing Service
U.S. Department of Agriculture
South Building, Room 3069
Washington, DC 20250
(202) 447-4276

For the grading of fresh agricultural products:
Mike Cannon
Fresh Products
Agricultural Marketing Service
U.S. Department of Agriculture
South Building, Room 2052
Washington, DC 20250
(202) 447-5870; direct line (202) 447-2185

For the grading of processed products (canned, frozen, or dry):
W. Howard Schutz
Processed Products
U.S. Department of Agriculture
South Building, Room 0717
Washington, DC 20250
(202) 447-4693

Technical Assistance on Transportation of Agricultural Commodities

The Office of Transportation (OT) is the center within the Department of Agriculture for all domestic and international transportation matters. OT develops transportation policies and programs and represents the interests of agriculture and rural communities with other government agencies. In addition, the Office supplies technical assistance and information, identifies barriers, and estimates adverse effects on transport systems in agriculture. It also offers economic assistance and technical research and development.

The International Transportation Service Branch is concerned with aiding the development of new international markets and the expansion of existing ones.

Contact
Thomas M. Poerstel, Chief
International Transportation Services Branch
Office of Transportation
Transportation Services Division
U.S. Department of Agriculture
Auditors Building, Room 1405
Washington, DC 20250
(202) 447-7481

The Transportation and Packaging Research Branch is concerned with preventing or solving problems experienced by the transportation industry through research, development of national and international standards, consultation, and personal assistance. The staff will assist exporters and shippers in transporting agricultural products.

Contact
Robert F. Guilfoy, Chief
Transportation and Packaging Research Branch
Office of Transportation
Research and Economic Analysis Division
Building 006, BARC/W
Beltsville, MD 20705
(301) 344-2815

In addition, a European Marketing Research Center in Rotterdam, the Netherlands, provides technical assistance to U.S. exporters, including help with lost and damaged exports shipped to the European market. The Center also provides information on foreign requirements for packaging and labeling and spoilage tolerances.

Contact
Gordon K. Rasmussen
European Marketing Research Center
ARS, USDA
386 Marconistraat
Rotterdam, The Netherlands
Phone: 765-538

Contract Procedures in the Near East and North Africa

An Introduction to Contract Procedures in the Near East and North Africa is published for business representatives who are involved in major projects and equipment sales in the Near East and North Africa. It describes contract conditions, regulations, and procedures in each of the countries and gives tips on bargaining and negotiating contracts. Each country is covered separately. Of special interest are the introduction, containing an overview of the region, and the chapter on Islamic law and its commercial use.

Cost

$4.50 in U.S.; $5.65 foreign. Order no. S/N 003-009-00336-9.

Contact

Superintendent of Documents
U.S. Government Printing Office
Washington, DC 20402
(202) 783-3238

TAXATION

Taxation and U.S. Corporations Operating Overseas

U.S. corporations are taxed on worldwide income. To assist international taxpayers, the Department of the Treasury's Internal Revenue Service (IRS) provides four publications:

No. 54, *Tax Guide for U.S. Citizens Abroad.*

No. 514, *Foreign Tax Credits for U.S. Citizens and Resident Aliens.*

No. 901, *Tax Treaties and Rates.*

No. 686, *Certification Required to Reduce Rates under Tax Treaties.*

Your state's IRS Forms Distribution Center can provide these publications.

New businesses may benefit from IRS Publication 454, *Your Business Tax Kit.* When requesting this publication, specify the nature of your business to receive additional specific information.

The IRS provides service to U.S. citizens through Revenue Service representatives attached to U.S. embassies and consulates in Bonn, Caracas, Jidda, Johannesburg, London, Manila, Mexico City, Nassau, Ottawa, Paris, Rome, São Paulo, Singapore, Sydney, and Tokyo. The IRS also maintains offices in San Juan, Guam, and the Virgin Islands.

If your firm's accounting is done internally, you may want to purchase tax references developed by major publishers. Internal accountants should be fully aware of the regulations passed by the Financial Accounting Standards Board (FASB). Accountants with international interest should review FASB 52, a publication that describes the legally binding regulations affecting financial reporting of most companies operating abroad.

Contact
Order Department
Financial Accounting Standards Board
High Ridge Park
Stamford, CT 06905
Main Office: (203) 329-8401
Order Department: (203) 356-1990

Taxation of U.S. Citizens Abroad

U.S. citizens and resident aliens who work or live abroad or receive income from external sources or U.S. possessions fall under special categories for tax purposes and are granted special exclusions or deductions under certain circumstances. It is recommended that individuals consult a tax attorney or accountant to determine whether modifications to the rules have been enacted and their effect, if any, on taxes. See publications listed on page 141.

Contact

For more information on taxes and exclusions, write or call your state's IRS Forms Distribution Center. Individuals in residence abroad should contact:

Director, Foreign Operations District
Internal Revenue Service
1325 K Street, N.W.
Washington, DC 20225

Operating Abroad: U.S. Income Tax Incentives

Major U.S. accounting firms offer comprehensive tax information for U.S. corporations, small businesses, and individuals engaged in international commercial transactions. They can provide detailed information on taxation of foreign operations, controlled foreign corporations, sale or liquidation of controlled foreign corporations, foreign tax credits, tax treaties, and special U.S. trade incentives, as well as tax incentives offered by host countries. The following summary was provided by the international accounting and consulting firm of Deloitte Haskins & Sells. All case studies in this section are hypothetical. This is an introduction to some of the more important tax aspects of foreign trade and investment. Because the tax subjects are complex, you are well advised to consult a knowledgeable tax advisor.

Domestic International Sales Corporation: Aid to Exporting*

A U.S. business may establish a special U.S. corporation called a DISC (Domestic International Sales Corporation) that allows an ongoing tax

*Copyright © by Deloitte Haskins & Sells.

deferral on income derived from exporting. To qualify as a DISC, a domestic corporation must derive at least 95 percent of its gross receipts from exporting activities and 95 percent of its assets must be export related. If the corporation meets these and other technical requirements, the DISC provisions of the tax code will allow the deferral of U.S. income taxes on up to 42.5 percent of profits from exporting. The DISC itself is not subject to U.S. tax. Its shareholders, however, are taxed on dividends the DISC actually pays from export profits previously deferred from U.S. income tax and on 57.5 percent of its current export profits, whether distributed to the shareholders or not. The DISC rules also provide special pricing and income-allocation techniques that help exporters to get maximum benefit from the DISC tax deferral.

EXPORTCO

EXPORTCO is a DISC, and its 1983 taxable income that qualifies for tax deferral is $100,000. Although none of this is distributed to its U.S. parent corporation, USCO, $57,500 is deemed distributed, and USCO is subject to federal income taxes on this deemed distribution at the normal corporate rates. Tax on the remaining $42,500 is deferred.

Because some of the U.S. trading partners who are parties to the General Agreement on Tariffs and Trade (GATT) believe that use of the DISC violates GATT rules, the U.S. government has proposed to meet these objections by substituting a "Foreign Export Sales Corporation" (FESC) for the DISC. The primary difference between a FESC and a DISC is that the FESC would require some actual foreign presence, whereas a DISC requires no real presence in a foreign country. The tax benefits of the FESC would be essentially the same as those currently available from a DISC.

Licensing Technology to a Foreign User

If a U.S. business decides not to operate abroad but to make its technology available to a foreign user, royalties or other fees received for the use of the technology may be subject to withholding by the foreign country on the gross amount of the fee. Generally, when such a withholding is made, it is creditable against the U.S. income tax payable upon the fee. An income tax treaty between the U.S. and the foreign country may reduce or eliminate this withholding.

FORCO

Assume that FORCO, a foreign corporation, pays a $100 fee for the use of USCO's patents or technology. FORCO must withhold $20, which is the foreign income tax imposed on such fees. FORCO pays the $20 to the foreign tax authorities and $80 to USCO. USCO increases the net it receives by the $20 withheld and reports a fee of $100 on its U.S. tax return. The U.S. tax of $46 on this $100 fee is reduced to $26 because a credit is allowed for the $20 foreign tax withheld.

For some U.S. businesses that have neither the desire nor the capacity to set up operations overseas, licensing technology may provide a useful alternative with relatively simple tax considerations. However, it may be best from a business standpoint to actually establish operations abroad. In that case, different tax considerations come into play.

Operating within a Foreign Country

If a U.S. corporation or individual establishes a foreign corporation to carry on activities abroad, its income generally is not subject to U.S. tax until the corporation pays a dividend to the U.S. shareholder. Therefore, U.S. tax on such foreign income may be deferred, although the foreign corporation is wholly owned by a U.S. corporation or individual.

When a dividend is paid, the United States will allow a credit for any withholding tax imposed by the foreign country on the dividend. In the case of a U.S. corporate shareholder owning at least 10 percent of the foreign corporation, a credit is also allowed for all or a portion of any foreign corporate income tax imposed on the foreign corporation.

USCO

Assume USCO establishes a wholly owned foreign subsidiary, FORCO. FORCO has $100 of income in 1981,
pays a foreign corporate income tax of $40, and pays the
remaining $60 as a dividend to USCO. However, since
this dividend of $60 is also subject to a 10 percent (i.e.,
$6) foreign withholding tax, only $54 reaches USCO.
USCO increases the $54 not only by the $6 foreign tax
withheld, but also by the $40 corporate income tax paid
by FORCO, and includes $100 in its corporate income
tax return. The U.S. tax of $46 (46 percent of $100) is
reduced by a foreign tax credit for the $6 withheld and
the $40 corporate tax paid by FORCO. Thus no net U.S.
tax is payable on this dividend.

Operating Abroad Through a Branch of a U.S. Corporation or a Partnership or Joint Venture

A U.S. corporation that has foreign source income through the operation of a branch incurs U.S. corporate taxes on that income as it is
earned. If there are foreign losses, those losses may be used to reduce
its taxable U.S. source income. If foreign income taxes are paid on the
foreign source income, the foreign taxes may be credited against its U.S.
taxes. U.S. partners or joint venturers, in either a U.S. or foreign-based
partnership or joint venture, must include a share of foreign source
income in their U.S. tax returns. U.S. tax is payable on this income, but
a credit is allowed for a share of foreign income taxes incurred. Alternatively, the U.S. partner or joint venturer is allowed to reduce U.S.
taxable income by a share of foreign losses experienced by the partnership or joint venture.

"Subchapter S" Corporations

Certain provisions of the Internal Revenue Code allow a U.S. corporation that is owned by a small group of shareholders and that operates

abroad to elect to pay no U.S. corporate taxes. However, each shareholder is taxed on a share of the corporation's income as it is earned and may deduct a share of any losses. There are limits on how much of such a corporation's income may be from foreign sources, but any foreign corporate income taxes paid by the corporation are allowed as credits on the shareholder's U.S. individual tax return. Since the corporation is not taxed, the usual double tax burden of operating in the corporate form (i.e., the corporation taxed and the shareholders taxed when dividends are remitted to them) is avoided.

Possessions Corporations

Some U.S. possessions, like Puerto Rico, will exempt a U.S. corporation that organizes a business there from paying any income tax on profits earned there for periods up to ten years. If the corporation also elects to be taxed as a possessions corporation, the corporation will receive a special tax credit against its U.S. corporate income tax. The credit will equal the U.S. income tax that would have been levied on profits earned by that corporation in the possession. Thus the corporation will also pay no U.S. income tax on those profits. Also, if more than 80 percent of that corporation is owned by a U.S. parent company, any dividends received by that parent company from the possessions corporation will be exempt from U.S. income tax. A U.S. corporation can elect to be taxed as a possessions corporation if at least 80 percent of its gross income is from sources in a possession and 65 percent of that gross income is from the active conduct of business in the possession.

Exemption from Gross Income for Employees Based Abroad

Self-employed individuals or employees of a U.S. company residing in a foreign country can exempt from U.S. income tax up to $80,000 of foreign earned income (income from the performance of personal services in the foreign country) during 1983. To qualify for this exemption, the employee or self-employed individual must be resident abroad for an entire tax year or be physically present abroad for at least 330 days during a 12-month period. An employee may also be exempt from U.S.

income tax amounts received from his or her employer to cover certain excess housing costs incurred in the foreign country.

Many employers take advantage of these exemptions by reducing the compensation of their overseas employees by an amount equal to the U.S. income tax that the employees would have paid had they remained in the United States.

TAXES: TIM JONES

To illustrate the exemption from gross income for U.S. employees based abroad, assume that for all of 1983, Tim Jones is employed abroad by USCO and is in the 30 percent tax bracket. His salary of $50,000 is entirely excluded from his U.S. income tax return for 1983 because Jones meets either the "residence abroad" or "presence abroad" test. Jones is required to pay $5000 of income taxes to the foreign country in which he resides. Pursuant to USCO's policy, USCO reduces Jones' wages by an amount equal to the $15,000 of U.S. income tax ($50,000 × 30 percent) that Jones would have paid if he had been based in the United States, but it reimburses Jones for the $5000 of foreign income tax he pays to the foreign country.

Foreign Tax Credit Limitation

All U.S. taxpayers are permitted to credit against their U.S. income tax liability foreign income taxes paid or accrued during the taxable year on foreign-source income. In addition, U.S. corporate taxpayers that receive dividends from a foreign subsidiary in which they own at least 10 percent of the voting stock are allowed to credit the corporate income taxes paid by that subsidiary. However, there are limitations on the credit designed to ensure that the foreign tax credit claimed will not exceed the U.S. income tax payable by the U.S. taxpayers on the foreign-source income. To the extent the limitation prevents a U.S. taxpayer from crediting all of the foreign income tax paid or accrued, double taxation (U.S. plus foreign) or excessive taxation of the same income may result. Because of a variety of factors, including differences in U.S. and foreign concepts of income, it is not unusual for the amount of creditable foreign tax to be limited in a taxable year. However, businesses may be able to "spread" their foreign tax credits over a number of years and take advantage of a foreign tax credit that cannot be fully used in a single year.

Transfers of Property to a Foreign Corporation

When a U.S. business organizes a foreign corporation to do business abroad, it often transfers to that foreign corporation property that has appreciated in value, such as patents or technical know-how, necessary to the conduct of that business. The gain realized on this transfer would ordinarily not be taxed by the U.S. at this time. However, since the foreign corporation's income may not be currently subject to U.S. income tax, it is possible for that corporation to subsequently sell that property at a gain and avoid any U.S. income tax. To prevent such avoidance, the law requires the IRS to rule that transfers of property to foreign corporations are not done principally for tax avoidance. If no ruling is obtained, the U.S. business will be taxable on the gain realized when the appreciated property is initially transferred to the foreign corporation.

The Closely Held Foreign Corporation— Passive Income

As discussed previously, if a U.S. individual organizes a foreign corporation to conduct activities abroad, the income earned by that corporation will normally not be subject to U.S. income tax until the U.S. corporation pays dividends to that individual. However, if more than 50 percent of the corporation's gross income is securities, and more than 50 percent in value of the corporation's stock is owned by U.S. citizens or residents, the corporation will be a "Foreign Personal Holding Company." As such, the corporation's net income will be taxed directly to its U.S. shareholders although not actually distributed to those shareholders as dividends.

Tax Haven Corporations

Because the income of a foreign corporation is generally not taxed by the United States until distributed as dividends to its U.S. shareholders, some taxpayers sought to shift income currently taxable by the U.S. to a foreign subsidiary to defer U.S. income tax. The Internal Revenue Code attempts to prevent this by requiring that shareholders of so-called controlled foreign corporations (CFC) pay tax currently on the following types of income earned by the CFC even though such income has not been distributed to the shareholders:

Foreign Personal Holding Company. Passive income realized by the CFC such as dividends, interest, rentals, royalties, and gain from the sale of securities.

Foreign Base Company Sales Income. Income realized by the CFC from buying products manufactured by its U.S. parent at a non-arm's-length price and selling them at a profit for use in another foreign country.

Foreign Base Company Services Income. Income realized by the CFC from performing services outside its country of incorporation "on behalf of" its U.S. parent or for a related corporation.

Income from Insurance of United States Risks. Income realized by the CFC from insuring property, people, or products situated in the U.S.

Investment of Earnings in U.S. Property. To avoid paying taxable dividends to its U.S. parent, the CFC invests its earnings in bonds, stock, or other property of its U.S. parent.

Non-Arm's-Length Dealing with a Foreign Corporation

If a U.S. corporation deals with its foreign subsidiary in other than an "arm's-length" fashion, the IRS may adjust the U.S. taxpayer's income as if the parties were unrelated. Thus the arm's-length standard requires a related taxpayer to report its income and expenses from transactions with its parent as if it were not related to its parent.

Gain on Sale of Foreign Subsidiary by U.S. Parent Taxed as Ordinary Income

If a U.S. corporation sells stock of a foreign subsidiary that is a controlled foreign corporation (CFC), any gain recognized by the U.S. corporation on the stock sale will be taxable as ordinary income to the extent the gain does not exceed the foreign corporation's earnings and profits attributable to the stock which were not previously taxed by the U.S.

USCO 2

Suppose USCO, the U.S. parent, sells its 100 percent Controlled Foreign Corporation, FORCO, at a gain of $90. FORCO has accumulated earnings and profits of $80 not previously taxed by the United States while USCO held its stock. Up to $80 of USCO's gain will be taxable to USCO as ordinary income, and the remaining $10 is taxable as a capital gain.

Bribe- and Boycott-Related Income

U.S. taxpayers who use foreign corporations to make illegal bribes or other payments to foreign officials or to participate in economic boycotts against Israel may be denied credits for foreign income taxes, deferral from U.S. tax on the foreign subsidiary's income, and DISC benefits.

Miscellaneous U.S. Tax Disincentives to Operating Abroad

Special accelerated cost recovery tables are applicable to property used primarily outside the United States, so that the depreciation deductions are smaller on this property than on comparable property used in the United States. Generally, property used predominantly outside the United States does not qualify for the investment credit. With limited exceptions, a foreign corporation cannot file a consolidated U.S. income tax return with its U.S. parent. Also, there are extensive and complicated tax reporting requirements for foreign operations.

HOST-COUNTRY INCENTIVES

The following is a checklist, provided by Deloitte Haskins & Sells, of some incentives offered by countries to attract investment. Of course, the "package" of incentives given varies with the country and may vary significantly within a country, depending on how attractive a particular investment is to the country's economy. The most attractive investment would have some of the following attributes:

Be a large employer of local labor.

Earn hard currencies from exports.

Use local raw materials.

Train local managers and technicians.

Help develop locally owned suppliers.

Make a maximum reinvestment of profits in the local company.

Provide goods that are a substitute for imports.

1. Tax and Tariff Incentives

Income Tax Incentives

Corporate income tax holidays (exemptions from income tax) that may be limited or unlimited in time and amount.

Accelerated depreciation.

Investment tax credit in addition to depreciation.

Tax exemption or rebate of taxes to the extent funds are used to acquire public bonds.

Increased deduction allowed for business entertainment in connection with export sales.

"Double deduction" of export promotion expenses.

Royalty or fee income of a foreign transferor of technology may be free of withholding of income tax.

Foreign contractor's taxable income may be determined by a favorable formula.

Reduced personal taxation of foreign managers and technicians.

Reduced withholding of income tax on dividends to foreign share-holders from approved investment.

Other Tax Incentives

Exemption from excise taxes on imported machinery and equipment.
Exemption from registration duties, stamp taxes, or capital taxes upon incorporation.
Exemption from property taxes.
Exemption from sales, value added, and excise taxes with respect to export sales.

Tariff Incentives

Waivers on import of machinery, equipment, and raw materials.
Access to regional common markets.
Tariff-free foreign trade zones.

2. **Non-Tax Incentives**

Financial Assistance

Grants for purchase of land, buildings, and machinery.
Grants for expenditure of export market development.
Grants to aid research and feasibility studies.
Government land provided for factory sites.
Low-cost rentals in government-owned industrial parks.
Low-cost financing.

Other

Assistance in locating plant sites, employees, suppliers, and markets.
Preference in purchases by government agencies.
Protection of market from competition.

Purchase of government-owned raw materials (e.g., oil and gas) at less than market price.

Guarantee of availability of foreign exchange to purchase equipment and raw materials and to pay interest, fees for technology, and dividends.

Work permits granted to imported technicians and managers.

Employee training provided.

The foregoing checklist is intended only to make you aware of a variety of incentives that are offered by host countries, many of which are negotiable during the preinvestment stage. A prospective investor's market and investment feasibility study should include a very thorough investigation of the tax and non-tax incentives, as well as the disincentives to doing business in a particular country. Further information can be obtained from major accounting firms, foreign ministries, U.S. embassies, and financial institutions abroad, as well as government agencies in the United States.

CHAPTER SEVEN

FINANCING THE DEAL

The final decision to invest or do business in a country may depend on the availability of financing for the project. This chapter describes the sources of financing available within the U.S. government for three types of overseas operations:

Capital Investment. Programs for establishing and funding a fixed-asset investment overseas.

Transactional Investment. Government programs for funding operations that may not require initial capital investment, such as leasing companies, distributorships, and other service-related groups.

Export Sale. Funding assistance for the export of goods and services associated with investment projects. In addition, these financial programs may be used to create and develop overseas markets for products and services apart from investments.

CAPITAL INVESTMENT

Project Financing

The Overseas Private Investment Corporation (OPIC) provides medium- to long-term financing for U.S. business ventures in some 100 developing countries. Two types of loan program are available.

Direct Loans

These loans from OPIC funds generally range in amount from $100,000 to $4,000,000 and are reserved exclusively for projects sponsored by or significantly involving U.S. "small businesses" or cooperatives. A "small business" is defined as a firm having revenues or net worth less than that of the smallest firm listed on the "Fortune 1000."

Guaranteed Loans

OPIC also issues loan guarantees, under which funding can be obtained through U.S. financial institutions. These loan guarantees, which cover both commercial and political risks, are available for projects having significant U.S. involvement. Typical OPIC loan guarantees range from $1 to $25 million, but they can be as large as $50 million. This program is available for projects sponsored by any U.S. company, regardless of size.

Eligibility
OPIC's criteria are the same whether it makes a direct loan in dollars or issues a loan guarantee. The project must be commercially and financially sound, and it must be sponsored by an investor having a proven record of success in a closely related business. Eligible enterprises include, but are not limited to, manufacturing, agricultural production, fishing, forestry, mining, energy development, processing, storage, and certain service industries involving significant capital investment.

OPIC financing is available for new ventures or expansion of existing enterprises in those developing countries where the agency operates. The project must contribute to the economic and social development of the host country, be consistent with the economic interests of the

United States, and not have a significant adverse effect on the U.S. economy or employment.

Terms

Repayment of both direct loans and loan guarantees is usually made in equal, semiannual principal payments following a suitable grace period, with a final maturity of five to twelve years. The length of the grace period is usually based on the time needed by the project to generate a positive cash flow. Direct loan interest rates generally parallel the commercial equivalent. Interest rates on guaranteed loans are comparable to those of other U.S. government–guaranteed issues of similar maturity. In addition, OPIC charges the borrower a guarantee fee ranging from 1.5 to 3 percent. OPIC's financing commitment to a new venture may range up to 50 percent of total project costs. Greater OPIC participation may be considered in the case of an expansion of a successful existing enterprise.

Application Procedure

The sponsor of a potential project should provide OPIC with the following preliminary information:

Name, location, and business of the proposed project.

Identity, background, and financial statements of the principal sponsors.

Planned sources of supply, anticipated output and markets, distribution channels, and the basis for projecting market share.

Summary of costs and sources of procurement of capital goods and services.

Proposed financing plan, including the amount of OPIC participation anticipated, and financial projections.

Brief statement of the contribution the business is expected to make to local economic and social development.

Contact

Overseas Private Investment Corporation
1129 20th Street, N.W.
Washington, DC 20527

Officer	Program	Telephone
Brooks Browne	Direct loan	(202) 653-2883
Robert Draggon	Loan guarantee	(202) 653-2872

JAMAICA BROILERS, LTD.

Small business companies can turn to the Overseas Private Investment Corporation's direct loan program to consolidate and expand ongoing operations. In 1981 Jamaica Broilers, Ltd. took out a $1 million loan from OPIC to build and equip a fully integrated poultry breeder farm at White Marl, Jamaica. The following year the company obtained an additional $750,000 to expand its blast freeze and cold room capacity and to purchase new incubators for its hatchery. Today its facilities are among the largest and most efficient in the Caribbean. At the same time, to increase production, the company has contracted with 250 farmers within 40 miles of its Kingston processing plant to raise poultry. Jamaica Broilers now produces about 60 percent of the poultry consumed in the country—or about 40 million pounds of dressed broilers annually. As a result, chicken, an important source of protein for Jamaicans, is available at a reasonable cost. Jamaica Broilers, as it has from the start, continues to buy equipment, breeder eggs, and feed grain from the United States.

Direct Loans and Financial Guarantees

The Export-Import Bank provides financing assistance for U.S. exports of heavy capital equipment and large-scale installations that are normally financed for a term of more than five years. Eximbank's long-term financing takes the form of either a direct credit to a public or private overseas buyer, or a financial guarantee assuring repayment of a private credit to an overseas buyer. It often blends these two forms of support in a single financing package. Reviews of requests for financing include appraisal of the financial, economic, and technical aspects of the transaction as well as analysis of the degree of foreign, publicly supported export credit competition for the sale. Reviews also consider the effect the transaction will have on the U.S. economy.

Eligibility

Eximbank will not provide credit support for sales likely to go forward without its support. Major projects or large product purchases (projects involving $5 million or more and repayment terms generally more than five years) are eligible.

Terms

Eximbank will provide credit for up to 65 percent of the U.S. export value of each transaction when necessary. It requires a cash payment to the U.S. seller from the foreign buyer of at least 15 percent of the export value of the U.S. purchases. The balance of the financing is usually provided from private lenders, with financing arranged by the borrower. At times, to meet officially supported foreign competition, Eximbank may consider a credit of up to 75 percent if the U.S. exporter is prepared to provide 10 percent of export value at the same rate of interest. The financing from private lenders may be denominated in an acceptable foreign currency. Repayment of principal and interest is scheduled in equal semiannual installments, normally beginning six months from the date of product delivery or project completion. Eximbank usually agrees to be repaid from the later installments to encourage financing by private banks, which are repaid from the earlier maturities. Repayment terms normally range between five and ten years. However, Eximbank may lengthen repayment terms to enable U.S. exporters to counter foreign export credit competition, on a case-by-case basis.

Rates and Fees

Interest rates are fixed for the life of the loan at the time of authorization. Effective January 18, 1983, the interest rate is 10 percent for loans to relatively poor countries, 11.35 percent for loans to intermediate countries, and 12.4 percent for loans to relatively rich countries. These rates match those offered by foreign competitors under an arrangement with the Organization for Economic Cooperation and Development (OECD).

Eximbank charges a one-time credit application fee of 2 percent of the loan value, plus a commitment fee of 0.05 percent per year on the undisbursed amount of each direct loan. There is a guarantee fee, generally 0.05 percent, on the outstanding balance of a guaranteed loan, and a guarantee commitment fee of 0.0125 percent for the undisbursed amount of each guaranteed loan.

Repayment Assurance

To assure repayment, Eximbank may require a repayment guarantee by a financial organization in the buyer's country. Frequently a central bank, finance ministry, or government development bank will provide this guarantee. In some cases, larger commercial banks or parent firms are acceptable.

Application Procedure

Eximbank does not use a standard application form for its direct loan and financial guarantee programs. Applications should be submitted on the letterhead of the organization making the application and should outline the nature of the financing request. Requests for assistance can take two forms, depending on the state of development of the transaction being financed.

Preliminary Commitments. These are used primarily when the project is in an early stage, but U.S. exporters need to include a financing package as part of their marketing efforts. Eximbank's Preliminary Commitment (PC) outlines the amount, terms, and conditions of financial assistance it is prepared to offer to purchasers of U.S. equipment and services. The duration of a PC is normally 180 days. Once the foreign buyer decides to purchase U.S. goods, and before the PC expires, the buyer must apply to Eximbank to convert the PC to a loan and/or financial guarantee. Applications for PCs may be submitted by the overseas buyer, a U.S. exporter, or a U.S. or foreign bank involved in the transaction. The letter of application must include sufficient information to permit Eximbank to appraise the financial, economic, and technical aspects of the transaction.

Final Loan/Guarantee Applications. These must be submitted by the prospective borrower or obligor. The letter must include or be supplemented by information that is sufficient for Eximbank to appraise the financial, economic, and technical aspects of the transaction. The following basic information is normally required:

Name and address of borrower, ownership of borrower, and brief history of its operation.

Purpose of the proposed U.S. financing and its relationship to total project cost. If known, the letter should also describe the overall financing plan for the project or product transaction, including the amount of equity investment, any local or other foreign borrowings, the terms and security conditions of such borrowings, and contemplated provisions for coverage of cost overruns.

Description of the equipment and/or services to be purchased with the proposed financing, the name and address of U.S. supplier if any, estimated date of U.S. equipment delivery, project completion and start-up of commercial operations dates.

Copy of bid document if responding to bid invitation.

Latest audited financial statements of the borrower and explanatory notes (in English) and, if readily available, the borrower's audited financial statements for the two preceding years.

Whether the proposed financing will be guaranteed by the government of the host country, a foreign financial institution, or other guarantor. If a bank or corporate guarantor is offered, the latest audited financial statements of the guarantor should be supplied.

The borrower's financial projections for the next five years, or length of the construction period, whichever is longer. This should normally include the borrower's projected profit and loss statements, balance sheets and sources and applications of funds statement, and appropriate supporting documents. All borrowings should be indicated separately and statements should show repayment terms, interest rates, currency of repayment, and any guarantees or security conditions.

Appropriate engineering and marketing data demonstrating the economic and technical feasibility of the transaction. Marketing data should indicate whether the production will be exported and to what markets. As a minimum, the application should include a summary of the engineering and marketing data. Detailed back-up data should be supplied with the application for a final commitment. Whatever information is known about foreign competition for this sale, including the availability of similar items from other countries and the financing terms offered. To the extent possible, the source and accuracy of this information should be noted.

If the request is from a U.S. company, it is helpful for the applicant to describe the effect of the sale upon employment in the particular plant or facility from which the goods and services are to be provided. Applicant should also include any impact on major subcontractors and small and minority-owned enterprises, if known. Information on man-hours or man-years of direct and indirect labor to be provided by the sale would be desirable, as would unemployment statistics in the seller's community, county, and state. Applicant should also specify whether the equipment or services to be sold are known to be in short supply in the United States.

Efforts made to obtain the requested financing from private sources, and the extent of any preliminary or firm commitment from such sources to provide part of the total financing required.

Such additional information as may be required to evaluate the reasonable assurance of repayment factor.

Contact
Office of the Senior Vice President for Direct Credits and Financial Guarantees
Export-Import Bank of the United States
811 Vermont Avenue, N.W.
Washington, DC 20571
(202) 566-8187

Private Export Funding Corporation

The Private Export Funding Corporation (PEFCO) works with Eximbank in using private capital to finance U.S. exports. PEFCO makes loans to public and private borrowers located outside the United States who require medium- and long-term financing for the purchase of U.S. goods and services. All PEFCO loans must be covered by an unconditional guarantee of Eximbank for principal and interest. PEFCO is a private corporation owned by 54 commercial banks, seven industrial corporations, and one investment banking firm. It was established in 1970 and began operation in 1971.

YUGOSLAVIAN TEXTILE PLANT

Many American companies are repeat customers of U.S.-assisted investment programs. A New York City textile company, for example, had been involved in six overseas ventures financed by the Export-Import Bank when, in 1979, it and two Yugoslavian partners requested a $6.3 million loan from Eximbank to expand a polyester fiber plant at Skopje.

Four years earlier, the Skopje plant, which was equipped with American-made textile machinery, had been built as a joint venture by the New York company and the two Yugoslavian textile firms. Eximbank at that time made a direct loan of $8.3 million and guaranteed another loan of $8.3 million to the venture. The Overseas Private Investment Corporation insured the Skopje investment against currency inconvertibility and expropriation.

Eximbank judged that the fiber plant was operating satisfactorily when the request for the expansion loan was received. Consequently, in the fall of 1979 Eximbank approved the $6.3 million loan to more than double the output of fiber and filament at the Yugoslavian factory.

Eligibility
To date, most of PEFCO's loans have been made to the foreign users of U.S. goods and services. However, they also have been made to commercial or special-purpose lessors when a leasing transaction has been employed in the financing.

Terms
PEFCO generally does not make loans of less than $1 million. Individual PEFCO loans have ranged from approximately $1 to $225 million,

with an average of about $23 million. There is no maximum loan amount.

PEFCO may offer, at its discretion, one or more of the following alternatives in determining fixed interest rates for its loan commitments.

Immediate Pricing

Under this alternative, PEFCO offers an interest rate determined at the time the offer is requested. Generally, this is a fixed rate applicable to the total amount of the loan for the life of the loan.

Alternatively, PEFCO may offer a fixed interest rate which, although determined in a similar manner, would apply for a predetermined period of time (for example, the first five or six years of the PEFCO loan). At the end of this period, PEFCO would recompute the fixed rate of interest on the basis of the current market conditions applicable to the remaining life of the loan. At that time, the borrower has the option of accepting the new PEFCO rate or repaying the loan without penalty.

Under either of these alternatives, a commitment fee of 0.05 percent per annum on the unused and uncanceled amount of the commitment accrues from the date the borrower accepts the PEFCO offer.

Deferred Pricing

This alternative has been designed to assure borrowers of the availability of funds on fixed interest rate terms. It permits them to delay the actual interest rate determination until a later date if they believe that rates will decline. It also offers borrowers the opportunity to use their own funds temporarily or to obtain bridge financing from traditional lenders on a floating rate basis. It gives private-sector lenders an opportunity to provide bridge loans to their traditional customers.

A variation of deferred pricing would result from an agreement with the borrower that when the general level of PEFCO's lending rate declines to a predetermined level (the "drop-lock" rate) the borrower and PEFCO are then committed to a loan transaction at that rate.

PEFCO's lending rates for fixed rate loans are based on the estimated cost of funds to PEFCO at the time the rate is determined. PEFCO's estimated cost of funds reflects market-oriented spreads over the current yields on marketable U.S. Treasury securities with maturities similar to those of the PEFCO loan. To this estimated cost of funds, PEFCO adds a spread for administrative expenses, risk, and return to shareowners. PEFCO interest rates are subject to approval by Eximbank.

Application Procedure
The initial contact with PEFCO generally occurs after the potential borrower or the supplier obtains an indication from Eximbank that its Board will issue a Financial Guarantee for a part of the required financing. The approach to PEFCO should be made in conjunction with a traditional lender, such as a commercial bank, or with the U.S. supplier. The bank or supplier will determine whether a PEFCO loan would be a reasonable supplement to the funds provided by other sources. When contacted, PEFCO will give a prompt indication of its willingness to become a member of the lending group. Before PEFCO will indicate a specific interest rate for a proposed loan, the following minimum information is necessary: amount of loan required, approximate schedule of disbursements and final availability date, and repayment schedule.

Contact
Private Export Funding Corporation
280 Park Avenue
New York, NY 10017
(212) 557-3100

Foreign Bank Loans

The Agency for International Development (AID) has funded a number of foreign development and commercial banks that can provide project financing for joint ventures between U.S. and host-country investors. For 1984, AID has allocated funds to banks in Costa Rica, Haiti, Jamaica, the Eastern Caribbean, Kenya, and Peru.

Eligibility
U.S. businesses that enter into joint-venture arrangements with indigenous firms may be eligible for this financing.

Terms
Established by each bank.

Contact

U.S. companies seeking project financing should consult the appropriate AID country officer in Washington (see appendix) to determine whether a development bank in a particular country has received AID funds.

Capitalization of Financial Institutions

The Bureau for Private Enterprise within AID provides funds to capitalize private intermediate credit institutions, including leasing companies and venture capital firms, that serve the private sector (particularly small businesses) in Costa Rica, Egypt, Haiti, Indonesia, Ivory Coast, Jamaica, Kenya, Pakistan, Peru, Sri Lanka, Sudan, Thailand, Zimbabwe, and the Caribbean.

Eligibility

Joint ventures between U.S. companies and host-country firms may be eligible to receive loans from these institutions.

Terms

Determined by the local financial institution.

Contact

Bruce Bouchard
Bureau for Private Enterprise
Agency for International Development
State Annex 14, Room 633
Washington, DC 20523
(703) 235-2274

Agribusiness Financing

The Bureau for Private Enterprise within AID will consider financing for projects located in Egypt, Costa Rica, Kenya, Pakistan, Ivory Coast, Thailand, Zimbabwe, Indonesia, Sri Lanka, Sudan, Peru, and Jamaica, Haiti, and other Caribbean countries. Proposals for projects in other countries may be considered where there is a viable private sector enjoying support by the government and where there is a bilateral AID program.

Eligibility
Although projects in many industries are eligible, agricultural projects
are given high priority. The Bureau will consider only ventures with
substantial local ownership. Sponsors must be either host-country na-
tionals, U.S. firms, or U.S. citizens. Minority participation by host-government entities may be allowed. Projects must have a substantial developmental impact by generating net employment opportunities;
earning net foreign exchange; developing managerial, technical, or
other skills; or transferring technologies. The intended sources of goods
and services to be used in proposed projects will be a consideration in
determining eligibility for loans. Loans may be used to capitalize a new
enterprise and/or expand an existing enterprise.

Terms
The Bureau has flexibility in negotiating terms and conditions, depending on the nature, risk, and developmental impact of the project. Financing is available up to $2.5 million with emphasis in the range of
$250,000 to $1,000,000, but not for more than 25 percent of total
project cost. Maximum term of the loan is 15 years with a negotiable
grace period for principal. There are no fixed or minimum requirements for collateral. Repayment is on a quarterly or semiannual basis.

Application Procedure
If sponsors can demonstrate that they meet these criteria, a business
plan should be submitted to the Bureau for Private Enterprise. The
plan should include:

A. Project Description

    1. Brief background, description, and present status of the pro-
        ject.

        a. If an established firm: company name, ownership, manage-
            ment, joint venture agreement, articles of incorporation,
            and other legal arrangements; brief history and back-
            ground of firm and owners.
        b. If a proposed venture: proposed legal arrangement; name,
            ownership, management; source of funds; and experience
            with indigenous or foreign enterprises.

B. **Financing Requirements (from all sources)**

1. Total costs, itemized by project requirement.
2. Proposed financial structure, including source of funds and anticipated terms, and critical factors affecting investment opportunity.

C. **Technical Plan**

1. Technology to be used—its appropriateness, feasibility, and source.
2. Ease of incorporating the technology given existing levels of management and technical skills.
3. Advisory assistance and training requirements and how they will be provided.
4. Sources of raw materials, equipment, and labor.
5. Location in relation to markets and suppliers.
6. Relationship between activity and production.

D. **Marketing Plan**

1. Market and customer profile.
2. Transportation and distribution.
3. Pricing.
4. Competition.

E. **Financial Plan**

1. Source and application of funds statement (five years).
2. Projected pro forma income statement and balance sheet (five years).
3. Projected cash flow analysis and/or rate of return.

F. **Legal Requirements**

1. Legal impediments and requirements that will affect project success.
2. Import and export duties.

3. Tax implications (e.g., dividends and profits, interest payments).
4. Foreign exchange restrictions and regulations on repatriation of dividends, profits, interest, and principal repayments.
5. Ownership and management requirements.
6. Barriers to free market private enterprise activities.

G. Management Plan

1. Structure.
2. Skills (existing and needed).
3. Training requirements.

H. Implementation Plan

As much detail as possible should be given under each of the major topic areas described above. Any other factors or commitments critical to project success should also be described.

Contact

Bruce Bouchard
Office of Investment
Bureau for Private Enterprise
Agency for International Development
State Annex 14, Room 633
Washington, DC 20523
(703) 235-2274

Loans in Egypt

In 1984 the Agency for International Development will make $50 million available to Egypt through a production credit project. Medium- and long-term loans are available to U.S. companies that invest in Egypt.

Eligibility

U.S. companies must have an Egyptian joint-venture partner to be eligible.

Terms
Loans will range from $5 to $15 million.

Contact
Keith Brown
Near East Project Development Office
Agency for International Development
Room 4440
Washington, DC 20523
(202) 632-9734

TRANSACTIONAL INVESTMENT

Financing for Financial and/or Leasing Companies

The Bureau for Private Enterprise within AID will consider financing projects located in Egypt, Costa Rica, Kenya, Pakistan, Ivory Coast, Thailand, Zimbabwe, Indonesia, Sri Lanka, Sudan, Peru, Jamaica, Haiti, and other Caribbean nations. (For description of program eligibility, terms, and application procedures, see description under Agribusiness Financing, pages 168 and 169).

Contact
Bruce Bouchard
Office of Investment
Bureau for Private Enterprise
Agency for International Development
State Annex 14, Room 633
Washington, DC 20523
(703) 235-2274

BCN LEASING

The high cost of credit and capital equipment is stimulating strong interest abroad in equipment leasing. In Brazil, BCN Leasing-Arrendamento Mercentil, S.A. of São Paulo recently received a U.S. government-guaranteed loan for $10 million to expand its leasing enterprise. BCN, a joint venture in which Walter E. Heller, Intl. of Chicago has a 20 percent ownership, purchases Brazilian-made equipment which it then leases to small- and medium-sized manufacturing and construction companies. While Brazilian laws restrict local leasing companies to purchases of Brazilian equipment, much of this equipment is made there by U.S. subsidiaries. Heller's partner in BCN Leasing is a private banking company, Banco de Credito Nacional, S.A. Besides helping the expansion of the Brazilian economy, BCN promotes the sales of U.S. subsidiaries' equipment there.

Lease Financing

The Overseas Private Investment Corporation (OPIC) offers financial assistance to foreign leasing companies in which there is a significant U.S. private business interest. The funds are used to encourage U.S. exports of productive equipment for projects that contribute to host-country development.

Eligibility

The borrowing company or U.S. sponsor must be an established leasing company with a history of successful leasing operations. Companies must demonstrate the capability to proceed with the proposed leasing plan. Leases should be made to private companies on a medium- to long-term basis.

Terms

OPIC will guarantee loans to leasing firms in the range of $5 to $30 million. Terms of the guarantees are typically from four to seven years, with appropriate grace periods before principal repayment begins. U.S. dollar loans are provided by a U.S. lender under an OPIC guarantee, which covers 100 percent of all lender risks. The loans can carry fixed rates or floating rates priced at a small premium over the London Interbank Offering Rate (LIBOR), U.S. bank prime rate, or U.S. Treasury obligations. The borrower also pays an annual guarantee fee to OPIC in the range of 1.5 to 3 percent.

In addition to guaranteed loans, direct loans from OPIC are available to foreign companies or projects in which a U.S. small business has a significant interest. Small business is defined as a firm with revenues or a net worth less than that of the smallest firm listed on the "Fortune 1000." OPIC lends up to $4 million per project at a fixed rate priced at prevailing U.S. government agency rates of comparable maturity.

Security for the loans may include first liens on the assets financed and/or other collateral or pledges as required to adequately secure OPIC's financing.

Contact

Finance Applications Officer
Overseas Private Investment Corporation
1129 20th Street, N.W.
Washington, DC 20527
(202) 653-2870

Distributorship Financing

The Overseas Private Investment Corporation's distributorship program provides ongoing financing for the sale and service of U.S. equipment in eligible developing countries. The program helps to increase U.S. exports and fosters local skills in the distribution of goods and service/maintenance capabilities. It also provides an important transitional step between exports to overseas markets and actual investment. The program enables companies to test the market and their ability to service the product before committing to an overseas manufacturing operation.

Eligibility
The criteria for eligibility are generally the same as for other OPIC financing programs discussed earlier in this chapter. Where the foreign distributor is wholly owned by local interests, OPIC requires that the U.S. manufacturer and/or exporter be at risk in the financing of the project. The exporter must provide a loan to the distributor, subordinate to OPIC's loan, at a ratio of one to three.

Terms
The distributorship program provides medium-term commercial financing for up to 50 percent of the cost of a new dealer facility or 75 percent of the cost for expanding an existing operation. For additional information on terms, refer to the OPIC Finance Program described earlier in this chapter.

Contact
Finance Applications Officer
Overseas Private Investment Corporation
1129 20th Street, N.W.
Washington, DC 20527
(202) 653-2870

Small Contractors' Guaranty Program

The Overseas Private Investment Corporation (OPIC) has recently developed a Small Contractors' Guaranty Program to assist small business construction and service contractors.

Eligibility

The program is limited to small business contractors having revenues or net worth less than the smallest company on the "Fortune 1000."

Terms

OPIC will guarantee an eligible financial institution for up to 75 percent of an on-demand standby letter of credit or other form of performance or advance payment guarantee issued on behalf of a contractor. The contractor may also apply for OPIC's political risk insurance for up to 90 percent of that portion of the letter of credit not guaranteed by OPIC. (See discussion of OPIC insurance programs in Chapter 8.)

Contact

Brian Treadwell, Senior Investment Officer
Overseas Private Investment Corporation
1129 20th Street, N.W.
Washington, DC 20527
(202) 653-2884

BELIZE CEMCOL LTD.

The Overseas Private Investment Corporation in 1980 guaranteed a $420,000 loan to Belize Cemcol Ltd. to help it establish a dealership for Caterpillar Tractor equipment in Belize. The sales agency, owned by Caterpillar's Honduran dealer, sells equipment and spare parts; its repair center, the only one of its kind in the country, trains skilled mechanics to repair and maintain Caterpillar machinery used primarily in construction and farming.

EXPORT SALE

Small Manufacturer Discount Loan Program

This Eximbank program enables U.S. commercial banks to extend fixed-rate, medium-term export loans to small manufacturers. It provides standby assurance that the bank can borrow from Eximbank against the principal outstanding value of a medium-term foreign debt obligation.

Eligibility

"Small manufacturers" are defined as companies which—together with all affiliates, subsidiaries, and parent companies—had total gross annual sales of $25 million or less in the previous fiscal year. (Evidence of sales volume and company affiliations must be submitted with the applications.) If a bank (as exporter of record) or supplier, agent, export management company, or export trading company is selling products of a "small manufacturer," and if the eligibility of the manufacturer of the products is established, the transaction is eligible.

Eximbank will issue advance commitments to make fixed-rate loans to eligible U.S. commercial banks when the applicant bank is not prepared to offer fixed-rate financing unless Eximbank provides a discount commitment. Eximbank's lending rate on a discount commitment allows for up to 1 percent mark-up on Eximbank's lending rate in effect at time of approval. The current rate is 9 percent for exports to poor countries, 9.85 percent to intermediate countries, and 11.15 percent to rich countries. These interest rates match OECD guidelines.

Terms

The Eximbank's loan commitment covers up to 85 percent of the contract price of an export sale financed by the U.S. bank on terms ranging from 366 days to 5 years. Eximbank will either commit to make a discount loan to the commercial bank secured by a promissory note, or it will commit to purchase the foreign debt obligation from the U.S. bank. In either case, Eximbank will have full recourse to the U.S. bank for the amount of the loan.

Eximbank's loan commitment provides the applicant bank with the assurance that it can fund its own fixed-rate loan with Eximbank should interest rates and its cost of money rise. The loan may be prepaid at any time without penalty. This program is a standby mechanism. A bank will usually request disbursement from Eximbank when its alternative cost of funds is greater than Eximbank's committed discount loan rate. A commercial bank may draw on the discount loan only once for each commitment, and only after shipment has gone forward. Multiple disbursements may be made to accommodate multiple shipments.

Application Procedure

Applications must be accompanied by a commitment fee in the form of a check, which will not be refunded unless Eximbank denies the application. Eximbank's commitment fee is a one-time, front-end fee based on the amount of the discount loan commitment, the total term, and the full shipping period. On a five-year obligation with a one-year shipping period, the fee would be 65 cents per $100 of the loan amount. If there is a bid situation, Eximbank will allow the applicant bank to pay the fee up to 30 days after the contract is awarded, but not later than 120 days from the date of Eximbank's commitment letter. A copy of the bid invitation must be submitted with the application. Eximbank limits aggregate discount commitments per buyer to $10 million per year. Maximum contract value is $2.5 million per transaction.

Contact

James Crist
Office of Exporter Credits and Guarantees
Export-Import Bank of the United States
811 Vermont Avenue, N.W.
Washington, DC 20571
(202) 566-8819

Medium-Term Credit Program

Eximbank's medium-term loan program provides fixed interest rate support for those medium-term export sales that are facing officially supported export credit competition from abroad. It will make a fixed interest rate loan commitment to a U.S. bank that is financing the export sale and will lend its funds to the U.S. bank. The guidelines, fee rates, and internal administration of this program are nearly identical to the Small Manufacturers' Discount Loan Program, with the following exceptions.

Evidence of Competition

Unlike the Small Manufacturers' Discount Loan Program, there must be evidence of foreign, officially supported export credit competition for the sale. The U.S. suppliers and the applicant banks must submit the best information available regarding the existence of the foreign, officially supported export credit competition, preferably including the name of the foreign suppliers, the terms, and interest rates they are offering. When the specific identity of the foreign competitor or its financing offer is not known, other means of indirectly establishing the reasonable assurance of subsidized official export credit competition will be pursued by Eximbank. If the sale involves an invitation to bid, a copy of the bid document must accompany the application for financing.

Eligibility

Supplier credit transactions (products, not projects), which are normally financed on one- to five-year terms. The contract value of such transactions usually will not exceed $5 million. However, larger sales of products and/or longer terms may be eligible.

Advance Commitment Fees

The commitment fee is a one-time fee based on the amount and total term of the medium-term loan offered by Eximbank. The total term of the commitment includes the shipping period and term of repayment. The calculation of the fee and the fee rates are identical to the fee rate calculation for the Small Manufacturers' Discount Loan Program. All fees will be payable within 30 days after the U.S. exporter has won the contract but not later than 120 days from the date of Eximbank's commitment. Extensions of the fee payment date will be considered on a case-by-case basis.

Terms

The buyer must make a cash payment of 15 percent of the contract value. Eximbank normally will lend up to 85 percent of the contract value.

Contact
Office of Exporter Credits and Guarantees
Export-Import Bank of the United States
811 Vermont Avenue, N.W.
Washington, DC 20571
(202) 566-8819

Export Trading Company and Other Exporters' Loan Guarantee Program

Eximbank's Export Trading Company Loan Guarantee Program provides export trading companies and other exporters access to working capital loans. The loans are available only if they would not have been provided without Eximbank's assistance and if the trading company or exporter would not be able to support these exports sales through other means. Most of the working capital loans guaranteed by Eximbank are expected to support exports from small- to medium-sized minority or agricultural producers, especially new-to-export or new-to-market producers.

Eligibility
Eligible exporters are Export Trading Companies as defined in Section 4(c)(14)(F)(I) of the Bank Holding Company Act of 1956 and other exporters. Eximbank will issue its guarantee to the lender if, in its judgment, the eligible exporter is to be creditworthy for the loan or line of credit to be guaranteed. Generally, any financial institution or other public or private creditor will be eligible to apply for Eximbank's Loan Guarantee. If Eximbank has no working experience with the creditor, two years of full financial data, including balance sheets, income statements, corporate ownership, and a brief corporate history, are required. An eligible lender must be able to demonstrate the ability to perform and service loans to trading companies and exporters. Eligible loans for this program are specific loans or revolving lines of credit advanced by an eligible lender to an eligible exporter for export-related activities. The purpose of the loan must be clearly stated and it must be for a specific export-related activity. The guarantee applicant must also state why the subject loan cannot be guaranteed by the Small Business Administration under its Export Revolving Line of Credit Program (discussed later in this chapter). It is Eximbank's intention not to compete with the SBA program but to supplement it. The applicant must

demonstrate to Eximbank's satisfaction that the loan would not be made without its guarantee.

Terms

The terms of the guaranteed loan generally will range from 1 to 12 months but may be longer if required. The guarantee will be for 90 percent of the principal amount of the loan. It will cover interest up to the lesser of the stated rate of the loan or 1 percent above the U.S. Treasury borrowing rate for comparable maturities up to the date of default. The lender will be at risk for 10 percent of the principal amount of the loan, interest in excess of the guaranteed rate, and late interest, if any. Eximbank requires that the eligible lender be secured with inventory of exportable goods, or accounts receivable on goods or services already exported, or any combination of the first two mentioned. Such security must have a value, as determined by the lender and Eximbank, of not less than 110 percent of the outstanding loan balance. Eximbank will not impose any interest rate or fee rate ceiling on the lender for guaranteed loans. However, it will monitor rates and fees being charged. The guarantee fee will be calculated against the lender's loan amount as follows:

Maturity of Loan	Fee (%)
Up to 180 days	1.0
181 days to 1 year	1.5
Over 1 year	1.5 plus .5% for each additional 6 months

Application Procedure

Eximbank requires the following information from each exporter for the requested loan guarantee:

A summary of the exporter's business plan and history of activities.*

Two years of financial statements with cash flow projections.*

At least two credit or bank reports.*

*For newly formed trading companies or other exporters, an opening balance sheet in addition to other pertinent financial data may be submitted in lieu of this information.

A summary of management's experience in related and nonrelated fields.

Contact

Special Assistant for Small Business
Export-Import Bank of the United States
811 Vermont Avenue, N.W.
Washington, DC 20571
(202) 566-8944

Small Business Advisory Service

Eximbank maintains a special office to provide information and materials on the availability and use of export financing to encourage small businesses to sell overseas.

Contact

Office of Export Counseling
Export-Import Bank of the United States
811 Vermont Avenue, N.W.
Washington, DC 20571
(800) 424-5201 (in Washington, DC, (202) 566-8860)

Small Business Export Loan Guarantees

The Small Business Administration (SBA) may guarantee up to $500,000 of commercial financing to firms wishing to establish or expand their export operations.

Eligibility

For loan programs, SBA defines a "small business" as a concern (including its affiliates) that is independently owned and operated, not dominant in its field, and falls within employment or sales standards developed by the agency. For most industries, the standards are as follows:

Manufacturing. Maximum number of employees ranges from 250 to 1500, depending on the industry in which the applicant is primarily engaged.

Wholesaling. Annual sales not exceeding $9.5–22 million, depending on the industry.

Services. Annual receipts not exceeding $2–8 million, depending on the industry.

Construction. For *general construction* firms, annual receipts not exceeding $9.5 million for the three most recent completed fiscal years. For *special trade* construction firms, average annual receipts not exceeding $1 to $2 million for the three most recent completed fiscal years, depending on the industry.

Retailing. Annual sales or receipts not exceeding $2–7.5 million, depending on the industry.

Agriculture. Annual receipts not exceeding $1 million.

A new standard definition of a small business has been proposed, generally increasing the sales volume and/or employees permitted in each industry category. If this proposal is formally adopted, SBA district offices can advise firms which standard applies.

Terms
If the loan is $100,000 or less, the guarantee is not less than 90 percent. If the loan is more than $100,000, the guarantee may not be less than 70 percent, unless such a guarantee would be necessary to insure that the guaranteed portion of the loan would not exceed $500,000. The maximum guarantee percentage for loans or portions of loans that refinance prior indebtedness may not exceed 80 percent. Interest rates are negotiated between the borrower and lender with the maximum set by the SBA. At present, the maximum allowable rate for loans with maturities of up to 18 months is 2.25 percent above the prime rate. For maturities longer than 18 months, the maximum allowable rate is 2.75 percent above prime. Certain additional one-time fees may also be charged by the lender in accordance with allowable SBA limits.

Contact
Nearest SBA district office (see appendix).

Small Business Export Revolving Line of Credit Loan Program

The SBA's Export Revolving Line of Credit (ERLC), available only under the loan guaranty program, helps small businesses export their products and services. The request for the SBA to participate in the ERLC financing must come from the applicant's bank or lending institution. Any number of withdrawals and repayments can be made, as long as the dollar limit of the credit line is not exceeded and the disbursements are made within the stated maturity period. Proceeds can be used only to finance labor and materials needed for manufacturing or wholesaling for export and to develop foreign markets. Professional export marketing advice or services, foreign business travel, and participation in trade shows are examples of eligible expenses to develop foreign markets. Funds may not be used to pay existing obligations or to purchase fixed assets, nor can the SBA provide funds to establish overseas joint ventures. A cash flow projection depicting monthly activity and cash balances, covering expected activity during the term of the line of credit, must be submitted with the application.

Eligibility

Applicants must qualify under the SBA's size standards and meet the other eligibility criteria applicable to all SBA loans. In addition, an applicant must have been in business (not necessarily in exporting) for at least 12 full months prior to filing an application. The business must be current on all payroll taxes and have a depository plan for the payment of future withholding taxes.

Terms

The SBA can guarantee up to 90 percent of a bank line of credit to a small business exporter. An applicant may have other SBA loans in addition to loans under this program, as long as the SBA's share of the total outstanding balance of all loans does not exceed $500,000. The maturity of an Export Revolving Line of Credit is based on an applicant's business cycle but cannot exceed 18 months, including all extensions. No provisions exist for renewals, but borrowers can reapply for a new credit line when their existing line of credit expires. A new credit line may not be used to pay off an existing line of credit. The rate of interest that may be charged by the lender will be the same as for other SBA-guaranteed loans. Interest may be up to 2.25 percent greater than the prime rate.

Lenders must also pay a guarantee fee to the SBA, based on the length of maturity for the loan. For maturities of 12 months or less, the fee is .25 percent of the guaranteed portion of the loan. For maturities exceeding 12 months, the fee is 1 percent of the guaranteed portion of the loan.

The lender may also charge the borrower a commitment fee equal to .25 percent of the loan amount, or a $200 minimum. This fee cannot be charged until the SBA approves the line of credit. Collateral may include accounts receivable, inventories, assignments of contract proceeds, and bank letters of credit. Only collateral that is located in the United States and its territories and possessions—or other assets under the jurisdiction of U.S. courts—is acceptable. SBA may not guarantee a letter of credit, nor may loan proceeds be used to secure a letter of credit.

Contact
Nearest SBA district office (see appendix).

Small Business Investment Company

Small Business Investment Companies (SBICs) are limited partnerships or corporations certified under state law that are licensed and regulated by the Small Business Administration. The primary purpose of an SBIC is to provide equity capital and long-term financing to small business concerns for growth, expansion, and modernization.

Eligibility
Generally an SBIC finances small businesses located in the United States. However, funds may be provided to small business concerns for use outside the United States if the funds are used *(a)* to acquire materials abroad for its domestic operations; *(b)* for its foreign branch operations and foreign joint ventures; or *(c)* for transfer to a foreign subsidiary it controls. If used for a foreign branch or subsidiary operation, or for foreign joint ventures, the major portion of the assets and activities of the concern must remain in the United States. This means that the SBIC cannot finance a foreign corporation directly even if there is some U.S. small business ownership. The entity receiving the financing must be a domestic company with a majority of its assets and activities in the United States. However, that entity may use SBIC funds for its foreign branch operations or for relending to its foreign subsidiaries and foreign joint ventures.

Terms
An SBIC finances small firms in two ways:

Direct Loans. Although most SBICs want an opportunity to share in the growth and potential profits of the small companies they finance, some make loans that involve no equity participation. The interest rate on a loan is determined by negotiation between the SBIC and the small business but is subject to the state's legal limit. Collateral requirements, terms of repayment, and other parts of the loan agreement are also determined by negotiation, within the boundaries of the regulations.

Equity Investments

Loans with Warrants.

In return for a loan, the small business issues warrants enabling the SBIC to purchase common stock in the company, usually at a favorable price, during a specified period of time.

Convertible Debenture.

The SBIC loans money to a company and in return receives a debenture. The SBIC then either can accept repayment of the loan or can convert the debenture into an equivalent amount of common stock of the small business.

Common Stock.

The SBIC purchases common stock from the small business.

An SBIC may invest up to 20 percent of its private capital in a single business. Several SBICs may participate in financing the same business and thereby increase the maximum investment.

Contact

John L. Werner, Director
Office of SBIC Operations
Investment Division
U.S. Small Business Administration
Washington, DC 20416
(202) 653-6584

Agricultural Export Credit Guarantee Program

The Export Credit Guarantee Program (GSM-102) of the Commodity Credit Corporation (CCC) is designed to expand U.S. agricultural exports by stimulating U.S. bank financing of foreign purchases. The Program operates in cases where credit is necessary to increase or maintain U.S. exports to a foreign market and where private financial institutions would be unwilling to provide financing without a guarantee. This Program guarantees letters of credit from foreign financial institutions against default.

Eligibility

Eligible countries are those where the guarantees are necessary to secure financing of the exports and where the destination country has the foreign exchange to make the scheduled payments. Commodities are reviewed on a case-by-case basis to determine eligibility.

Terms

Guarantees are provided for up to three years.

Contact

Melvin E. Sims, General Sales Manager and Associate Administrator
Foreign Agricultural Service
U.S. Department of Agriculture
14th and Independence Avenue
Room 4071
Washington, DC 20250
(202) 447-5173

Agricultural Export Credit Sales Program

The Commodity Credit Corporation's (CCC) Export Credit Sales Program (GSM-5) is a commercial export financing program for U.S. agricultural commodities. A basic objective is to use credit to maintain, expand, or establish new commercial markets for eligible U.S. agricultural commodities. The Program is designed to meet competition from other suppliers and is currently exercised only in cases of "blended credits" (described in the Blended Credit Program on pages 187 and 188).

Eligibility

U.S. agricultural commodities eligible for financing are announced monthly. The export financing is provided through the CCC's purchase of the private U.S. exporter's accounts receivable.

Criteria for CCC Credit Financing

Permits U.S. exporters to meet competition.

Prevents a decline in U.S. commercial export sales.

Substitutes commercial dollar sales for sales made pursuant to concessional aid programs.

Results in a new use of the imported agricultural commodities in the importing country.

Permits expanded consumption of agricultural commodities in the importing country and increases total commercial sales of agricultural commodities to that country.

Terms

Interest rate is zero when the program is used in blended credit.

Contact

Melvin E. Sims, General Sales Manager and Associate Administrator
Foreign Agricultural Service
U.S. Department of Agriculture
14th and Independence Avenue
Room 4071
Washington, DC 20250
(202) 447-5173

Agricultural Blended Credit Program

The Blended Credit Program provides for up to three-year credit terms on a combination of interest-free direct credit under the Export Credit Sales Program (GSM-5) and credit guarantees under the Export Credit Guarantee Program (GSM-102). The blended credit program is available on exports to specific countries announced periodically by the Commodity Credit Corporation (CCC).

Eligibility

To qualify, the exporter must have an office and a representative in the United States upon whom judicial processes may be served. For sales to be eligible for export credit guarantees (GSM-102), U.S. exporters must submit an application along with the appropriate guarantee fee to the CCC before the goods are exported.

Contact

Kerry Reynolds
U.S. Department of Agriculture
South Building, Room 4526
Washington, DC 20250
(202) 447-6211

CHAPTER
EIGHT

PROTECTING
THE
DEAL

Any overseas venture involves a certain amount of risk. The programs discussed in this chapter are designed to protect your interests by providing insurance to cover the common commercial and political risks of doing business overseas. Included are discussions on insurance for three types of overseas enterprises:

Capital Investments. Government insurance programs to protect U.S. businesses with fixed-asset overseas investments against losses due to expropriation, currency inconvertibility, and political hostilities.

Transactional Investments. Government insurance programs similar in coverage to those above, but designed for U.S. firms whose overseas operations are of a transactional investment nature, such as leasing, contracting, and servicing.

Export Sales. Government insurance programs to protect U.S. exporters against the risk of nonpayment by foreign buyers because of commercial or political reasons.

AMF CORPORATION

In 1982 OPIC insured AMF Corporation's investment of $950,000 in a Chinese venture for the production of sports equipment. AMF is providing machinery, equipment, and technical assistance for the project, which will produce volleyballs, soccer balls, and basketballs. The agreement is for 10 years.

AMF's associates in the venture include Shanghai Light Industrial Products, Shanghai Rubber Industrial Corporation, and Shanghai Leather and Leather Products Corporation.

AMF will purchase all of the balls manufactured on its machinery, with the price based on a formula involving labor, material costs, and market conditions. Under the terms of the agreement, AMF will export the products to markets in the Far East, Southeast Asia, Europe, and South America.

The project will employ approximately 70 persons and is expected to earn significant foreign exchange for the People's Republic of China.

The new China facility will make AMF more competitive, enabling it to open new world markets. The project is expected to generate initial U.S. exports of machinery, equipment, and materials estimated at $1 million. Annual remittances to the United States are projected at $100,000.

CAPITAL INVESTMENT

The Overseas Private Investment Corporation (OPIC) offers a number of insurance programs designed to encourage U.S. private investment in the developing countries of the world.

Insurance Program

OPIC insures investments in qualified projects in friendly less developed countries against loss caused by certain political risks. Insurance is provided against three major types of political risk:

Inability to convert into dollars local currency received by the investor as profits or earnings or return on the original investment.

Losses due to expropriation, nationalization, or confiscation by action of a foreign government.

Loss due to war, revolution, insurrection, or civil strife.

Eligible Investors

OPIC's charter requires that its insurance be issued only to "eligible investors." OPIC may thus insure an investment by an eligible investor in a project controlled by foreign interests, but it is only the eligible investor's investment that is insured, not the entire project.

Eligible investors are:

Citizens of the United States.

Corporations, partnerships, or other associations created under the laws of the United States, or of any state or territory of the United States, which are substantially beneficially owned by U.S. citizens.

A foreign business at least 95 percent owned by investors eligible under the preceding criteria.

OPIC recognizes a corporation organized under the laws of the United States or of any state or territory of the United States to be substantially beneficially owned by U.S. citizens if more than 50 percent of each class of its issued and outstanding stock is owned by U.S. citizens either directly or beneficially.

Eligible Countries

OPIC programs are available to cover U.S. private investments in over 100 countries defined as "less developed friendly countries and areas," with which the United States has agreements for the operation of the OPIC programs. A list of eligible countries is available from OPIC. The availability of OPIC insurance is generally restricted to investments in countries with per capita GNPs lower than $2950 (in 1979 dollars). In countries with higher GNP levels, insurance is available for investments sponsored by U.S. small businesses or cooperatives, projects involving minerals or energy (except oil and gas exploration in OPEC countries), construction projects, projects using OPIC's letter of credit or contractors coverage, and other projects that OPIC's Board of Directors determines to merit insurance, such as those offering exceptionally significant developmental or trade benefits. Small businesses are defined as firms having revenue or net worth less than the smallest firm listed on the "Fortune 1000."

Eligible Investment

OPIC insures not only new investments but also those used for the enlargement or modernization of existing plant and equipment as well as additional working capital in an expanded business. It may, in some cases, include the cost of acquiring an existing business. The investor should apply for insurance sufficient to cover possible project cost overruns. Coverage is available not only for conventional equity investments and loans but also for investment or exposure of funds and goods or services under various contractual arrangements. To be eligible for insurance, an investor must apply for and receive an OPIC Registration Letter before the investment is made or irrevocably committed.

Other Criteria

Investors are asked to supply data on a project's developmental effect on the host country, including information relating to job creation, skill development, balance of payments effects, taxes and host-government revenues, and contribution to basic human needs.

OPIC will deny coverage for investments that are likely to have a negative effect on U.S. domestic employment. It may also refuse coverage for investments in projects that are likely to have adverse effects on the U.S. balance of payments and those used primarily to finance the procurement of goods or services for a particular project in other industrialized countries.

OPIC's agreements with the governments of countries in which OPIC programs are offered require that the foreign government specifically approve of OPIC's insurance of each individual project. Insurance coverage cannot begin until OPIC receives an acceptable Foreign Government Approval (FGA) covering the investment. (See Chapter 6.)

Coverage

Inconvertibility. Inconvertibility coverage assures that earnings, capital, principal and interest, and other eligible remittances, such as payments under service agreements, can continue to be transferred into U.S. dollars. The insured will be compensated for currency blockage whether it is active (when host-country authorities deny access to foreign exchange on the basis of new, more restrictive regulations) or whether it is passive (when the monetary authorities fail to act within a specified period on an application for foreign exchange—usually 60 days). In either case, OPIC makes dollar payments upon receipt of the local currency.

Expropriation. OPIC insurance contracts define the insurable event of "expropriatory action" to include not only a direct taking of property but also a variety of situations that might be described as "creeping expropriation." An action taken by the host-country government which has a specified impact on either the properties or operations of the foreign enterprise or on the rights or financial interests of the insured investor may be considered expropriatory. For an action to be considered expropriatory, it must continue for at least one year for most investments, six months for contracts covering oil and gas projects, and three months or less for contracts covering institutional loans.

OPIC compensation for expropriatory actions is based on the amount of the original insured investment adjusted for retained earnings or losses and accrued and unpaid interest as of the date of expropriation, and for return of capital.

War, Revolution, and Insurrection (WRI)/Civil Strife. Coverage extends to losses from actions taken to hinder, combat, or defend against hostile action during war, revolution, or insurrection. As part of the WRI coverage, an investor may also elect coverage against civil strife of a lesser degree than that contemplated under the standard WRI policy. Civil strife coverage includes damage due to politically motivated violent acts by a group or individual, including acts of terrorism and sabotage. A loss caused by an individual or group acting primarily to achieve demands of labor or students, however, would be excluded from the coverage. Civil strife coverage is available only in conjunction with WRI coverage (although WRI coverage may still be purchased separately).

Terms

OPIC insurance contracts generally require the insurance premium to be paid annually in advance. Premiums are computed for each type of coverage on the basis of a contractually stipulated maximum insured amount and a current insured amount chosen by the investor on a yearly basis. The current insured amount represents the insurance actually in force during any contract year. The difference between the current insured amount and maximum insured amount for each coverage is called the *standby amount.* The major portion of the premium is based on the current insured amount, with a reduced premium rate being applicable to the standby amount. For expropriation and war coverages, the insured must maintain current coverage at a level equal to the amount of investment at risk.

Premiums

Annual base rates for manufacturing, agribusiness, and services projects are given in the following list. Note that these rates vary for different industries and are discussed in greater detail in this chapter.

Coverage	Current (%)	Standby (%)
Inconvertibility	0.30	0.25
Expropriation	0.60	0.25
War, Revolution, Insurrection (WRI)	0.60	0.25
WRI and civil strife	0.75	0.30

Rates applied to individual investments may vary by as much as one-third from these base rates, depending on the risk profile of a specific project. Rates for natural resource and hydrocarbon projects or very large projects may vary by more than one-third of the base rates. OPIC insurance contracts (except for those covering institutional loans and certain service contracts) contain provisions that allow for an increase in the initial current coverage rate by up to 50 percent during the first 10 years of the contract period and another 50 percent during the second 10 years of the contract period.

SMITH KLINE & FRENCH
INTERNATIONAL COMPANY

In 1982 OPIC issued $2.8 million in insurance to Smith Kline & French International to cover its investment in a Bangladesh project for manufacturing a number of its pharmaceutical products. Twenty-five percent of the project is owned by Bangladesh nationals.

The project establishes a ready source of critically needed pharmaceutical products in one of the world's poorest countries. It is expected to supply hospitals and consumers with reasonably priced products in place of costly imports, thus contributing to improved health standards.

The project will employ 122 local workers. Anticipated returns to the host country are estimated at $100,000 annually during the first five years of operation, and $400,000 annually thereafter.

Contact
Applications Officer
Overseas Private Investment Corporation
1129 20th Street, N.W.
Washington, DC 20527
(202) 653-2972

Special Insurance Programs

Minerals Insurance

OPIC offers specialized coverage for investments in mineral exploration and development (including processing where it is an integral part
of a development project). OPIC will cover 50–90 percent of the initial
investment plus an equal amount of retained earnings. The percentage
of investment and retained earnings insured will depend on OPIC's
assessment of risk factors in the project, including the extent of multinational equity and/or debt participation.

Coverage

Exploration.   Insurance will be provided against all three covered
risks (see page 191) during the exploration phase for intangible costs as
well as tangible assets.

Breach of Specified Government Contractual Obligations.   Special
additional coverage may be provided against losses resulting from the
breach of certain host-government undertakings identified by the project sponsor at the outset as vital to the successful operation of the
project. Such special coverages will be individually rated.

War, Revolution, Insurrection (WRI), and Civil Strife.   In addition to
standard WRI (or WRI and civil strife) coverage, insurance may be
offered to cover consequential loss due to closing of operations for a
period of at least six months. This loss may be directly caused by WRI
(or WRI and civil strife) events in the project country or by certain
specified WRI (or WRI and civil strife) events in another country.

Premiums
Annual base rates for natural resource projects other than oil and gas
are as follows:

Coverage	Current (%)	Standby (%)
Inconvertibility	0.30	0.25
Expropriation	0.90	0.25
WRI	0.60	0.25
WRI and civil strife	0.75	0.30

Contact

Thomas Mansbach (202) 653-2958
Douglas Greco (202) 653-2956
Overseas Private Investment Corporation
1129 20th Street, N.W.
Washington, DC 20527

Energy Insurance

OPIC provides insurance for most types of investment in energy exploration, development, and production. This includes investments made pursuant to traditional concession agreements, production-sharing agreements, service contracts, risk contracts, and other agreements with host-country governments.

Coverage

Coverage is available for up to 90 percent of the investment and generally does not exceed $100 million per project. OPIC's insurance for energy investments includes coverage against inconvertibility, expropriation, war, revolution, insurrection, and civil strife, and interference with operations due to bellicose hostilities.

Coverage for oil and gas projects is issued for a maximum term of 12 years with an optional extension of 8 years after the original insured period. Insurance covering the construction period plus 10 years may be issued for coal mining projects, while projects involving the development of alternative energy sources may be insured for up to 20 years.

OPIC insurance is not available for investments in oil and gas exploration, development, and production projects in OPEC member countries. However, projects in OPEC countries involving investments in other petroleum service operations and downstream petrochemical projects, as well as investments in other energy and mineral sources, may be eligible.

Premiums

Premium rates are determined by the risk profile for a particular project. The annual base rates for oil and gas projects are as follows:

Coverage	Exploration Period (%)	Development/Production Period (%)
Inconvertibility	0.10	0.30
Expropriation	0.40	1.50
War, Revolution, and Insurrection (WRI)	0.60	0.60
WRI and civil strife	0.75	0.75
Interference with operations	0.40	0.40
Interference with operations and civil strife	0.55	0.55

The rates are applied to sums actually invested, beginning with the quarter in which each incremental investment is made. Coverage can be assured for future investments in the project by the payment of modest standby premiums.

The base rates for other types of energy project vary in accordance with the type of project and the method of investment.

Contact

Thomas Mansbach (202) 653-2958
Douglas Greco (202) 653-2956
Overseas Private Investment Corporation
1129 20th Street, N.W.
Washington, DC 20527

UNION OIL COMPANY OF CALIFORNIA

The Union Oil Company of California took out a $100 million political risk insurance policy with the Overseas Private Investment Corporation in 1981 on its investment in a natural gas venture in Thailand. The project involved developing and producing from an offshore natural gas field. The gas produced by the insured project is transported by an underwater pipeline, built and owned by the Petroleum Authority of Thailand and partially funded by the World Bank, to supply natural gas to two Bangkok power plants. The project will help Thailand begin to attain energy self-sufficiency and will produce significant foreign exchange savings.

Branch Banking Insurance

OPIC offers U.S. banks a number of services particularly designed to meet their needs.

Coverage

OPIC can cover a bank's capital investment in foreign branches and subsidiaries. It will provide coverage for up to 270 percent of an initial branch capital infusion and earnings thereon, with coverage tailored to each bank's definition of branch capital. OPIC is also able to provide coverage for a bank's foreign private loans. This coverage is available for up to 100 percent of a bank's loan (principal plus interest) to a foreign private enterprise. The annual premium base rate is 0.9 percent compared to 1.5 percent for intercompany investments.

Coverage for a bank's equity participation in a cross-border lease transaction is also available through OPIC. In addition to these possibilities, OPIC is also prepared to cover against arbitrary drawings of letters of credit posted as bid, performance, or advance payments guarantees.

This type of coverage is particularly well-suited to the needs of a bank's trade financing group.

Premiums

Annual base rate for institutional loans is as follows:

Coverage	Current (%)	Unused Commitment (%)
Inconvertibility	0.25	0.20
Expropriation	0.30	0.20
War, Revolution, and Insurrection (WRI)	0.60	0.20
WRI and civil strife	0.70	0.22
Inconvertibility and expropriation (combined)	0.50	0.30
Inconvertibility, expropriation, and WRI (combined)	0.90	0.50
Inconvertibility, expropriation, WRI, and civil strife (combined)	1.00	0.52

Contact

Cassandra Pulley
Overseas Private Investment Corporation
1129 20th Street, N.W.
Washington, DC 20527
(202) 653-2977

TRANSACTIONAL INVESTMENT

Leasing Program

OPIC offers political risk insurance coverage for cross-border operating and capital lease transactions with terms of at least 36 months. OPIC's insurance for assets leased under an operating lease provides coverage for the original costs (including duties, freight, and installation) incurred by the lessor. Insurance for capital leases covers the stream of payments due under the lease agreement. OPIC's insurance provides coverage against the following:

The inability to convert into dollars local currency received as lease payments.

Loss due to expropriation, nationalization, or confiscation by action of the host government.

Loss due to war, revolution, insurrection, and civil strife.

Coverage is also available for equity investments in, and loans to, off-shore leasing companies, for management and maintenance agreements involving leasing companies, and for consigned inventory.

Eligibility
See the description of OPIC's insurance program discussed earlier in this chapter.

Premiums
Premium rates are determined by the risk profile of a particular project. Annual base rates for leasing insurance are as follows:

Coverage	Current (%)
Inconvertibility	0.30
Expropriation	0.60
War, Revolution, Insurrection (WRI)	0.60
WRI and civil strife	0.75

Contact
Cassandra Pulley
Overseas Private Investment Corporation
1129 20th Street, N.W.
Washington, DC 20527
(202) 653-2977

Contractors and Exporters Program

OPIC insures letters of credit or on-demand bonds required as bid, performance, or advance payment guarantees against arbitrary drawings. OPIC also provides contractors or exporters with political risk protection against losses resulting from currency inconvertibility, confiscation, war/revolution/insurrection/civil strife, and unresolved disputes with the owner. Financial guarantees for the repayment of letters of credit are available to ensure that an issuing financial institution will be repaid by OPIC, if not by the contractor, if there is a drawing.

Eligibility
The project must benefit host-country development, and there must be reasonable assurance of adequate project funding. Military projects and projects harmful to U.S. economic interests are not eligible. Imported goods and services associated with the contract should be primarily either of U.S. origin or from developing countries.

Coverage

Bid, Performance, and Advance Payment Guarantees.   Through its insurance program, OPIC indemnifies the contractor or exporter for losses resulting from a foreign government owner's "arbitrary" drawing of a letter of credit or on-demand bond issued as a bid, performance, or advance payment guarantee. This insurance is also available to subcontractors and others who are not the prime contractor but who must post a guarantee for a particular project. The insurance policy provides coverage for up to 90 percent of the guarantee; the balance of the political risk must be borne by the contractor. OPIC does not indemnify if the guarantee is drawn because of the contractor's failure to perform its contractual obligations or if the contractor provokes or agrees to the drawing.

OPIC may issue bid guarantee coverage before a contract is in force but without obligating itself to insure against the arbitrary drawing of the performance or advance payment guarantee. This guarantee may be required if the contractor is the successful bidder.

Coverage also is available to contractors who post guarantees in favor of private parties. In these cases, an arbitrary drawing is defined as a drawing that is not justified by the terms of the contract and is directly caused by the host government or is followed by host government action that thwarts the proper functioning of the decisional procedure.

OPIC also offers the following coverages for certain additional risks incurred by U.S. contractors and exporters in the underlying contract.

Currency Inconvertibility.   Inconvertibility coverage provides contractors with protection against the inability to convert local currency contract payments or payments from the sale or other disposition of the insured party's property into U.S. dollars.

Confiscation.   Coverage is available against the loss of the contractor's tangible assets and bank accounts maintained in the project country in connection with the underlying contract. This loss may result from confiscation by the host government that continues uninterrupted for a period of six months.

War, Revolution, Insurrection (WRI), and Civil Strife.   Under WRI coverage, the contractor is compensated for loss or damage to assets that results directly from hostile actions occurring within the project country. Coverage against losses caused by civil strife of a lesser degree than revolution or insurrection is available at a surcharge to the WRI base rate; it may not, however, be elected separately from WRI coverage.

Disputes.   Disputes coverage compensates the contractor for losses sustained when a government owner fails to honor an arbitration award in favor of the contractor for a period of at least six months. Compensation is calculated at 90 percent of the portion of the award the government owner has failed to pay, less any valid obligations owed to the government owner by the contractor.

The coverage also provides for compensation when a government owner refuses, for a period of at least six months, to submit a dispute for resolution as outlined in the contract. In addition, if the government owner fails or refuses to pay valid invoices and the dispute resolution procedure has been exhausted, OPIC will compensate the contractor for up to 90 percent of such invoices. In either case, OPIC's indemnity is limited to 90 percent of the difference between the invoiced amounts for work performed and compensation received by the contractor for those amounts. In the event the insured party's contract is with a private entity, OPIC will compensate the contractor only if nonpayment is directly caused by the host government or if the host government thwarts the proper functioning of the decisional procedure.

Judicial Requirements

Insurance against arbitrary drawings of letters of credit provided as performance and advance payment guarantees, and disputes coverage, are available only where the underlying construction, sales, or services contract provides a decisional procedure to settle disputes between the owner and the contractor; local law and practice indicate that the procedure would be followed in the event of a dispute; and experience suggests that the procedure is likely to be fair and impartial.

Terms

The term of the insurance policy generally coincides with the term of the guarantee or the duration of the contract, but the minimum premium payment is for six months.

Binders.   OPIC offers binders committing it to issue, at a later date, policies of insurance covering specified risks. The binder fee is either 1/25 of 1 percent per year times the maximum amount of insurance or $1000, whichever is greater. Binders normally are offered for six-month periods. OPIC will refund half of the binder fee either upon the issuance of the insurance policy or upon the award of the contract to another party. OPIC will refund the full amount of the binder fee if it does not issue insurance because of the occurrence of an event that has been specified in the binder as an exception to the commitment to insure. No refund is made if the contractor receives the contract award but does not promptly seek OPIC insurance.

Premiums

The annual base rate for contractors' and exporters' guarantee coverage is as follows:

Coverage	Current (%)	Standby (%)
Inconvertibility	0.30	0.25
Expropriation	0.60	0.25
WRI	0.60	0.25
WRI and civil strife	0.75	0.30
Disputes	0.80	0.25
Bid, performance, and advance payment guarantees	0.60	0.25

Contact

Cassandra Pulley
Overseas Private Investment Corporation
1129 20th Street, N.W.
Washington, DC 20527
(202) 653-2977

BLOUNT, INC.

In 1981 the Overseas Private Investment Corporation issued insurance totalling $110 million against losses that might result from an arbitrary call on letters of credit issued on behalf of Blount, Inc., a Montgomery, Alabama construction firm working in Saudi Arabia. The letters of credit had been issued to the Alabama company by a consortium of eight banks, led by Chase Manhattan and American Express International Banking Corporation. The letters were to be used as performance and advance payment guarantees covering Blount's portion of a $2 billion project at King Saud University. The project includes construction of 17 major buildings, a 2-million volume library, and seven colleges in Riyadh. Blount's partner in the venture is a French firm, Bouygues.

EXPORT SALE

Commercial Bank Guarantee Program

Under the Commercial Bank Guarantee Program, the Export-Import Bank of the United States (Eximbank) guarantees the repayment of medium-term (181 days to 5 years) export obligations acquired by U.S. financial institutions from U.S. exporters. The purpose of this program is to increase U.S. exports of capital and quasi-capital goods by assuming commercial and political risks associated with international trade. Eximbank works closely with participating financial institutions such as U.S. commercial banks, Edge Act Corporations, Agreement corporations operating under Sections 25 and 25(a) of the Federal Reserve Act, and U.S. branches and agencies of foreign banks.

Terms

Eximbank requires a 15 percent cash payment from the buyer. For the financed portion, Eximbank's guarantee covers 100 percent of the political risks and up to 85 percent of the commercial risk. Repayment terms do not exceed those which are customary in international trade, and usually follow the schedule below:

Eximbank's General Guidelines

Contract Value	Maximum Repayment Terms
Up to $50,000	181 days to 2 years
$50,001 to $100,000	Up to 3 years
$100,001 to $200,000	Up to 4 years
Over $200,000	Up to 5 years

Interest guaranteed is limited to the lower of either *(a)* interest rate of the note, or *(b)* 1 percent above the effective rate of interest at the date of default for Treasury borrowings having the same maturity as the remaining term of the note. In the event of a claim, Eximbank will pay interest accrued to the date of default.

A number of special coverages are available to exporters:

206

Floor-Plan Coverage.   When Eximbank guarantees a revolving line of credit involving repeat sales to dealers/distributors, a floor-plan period of up to 270 days is also eligible. Products not resold to an end user during the floor-plan period are then financed under a medium-term debt obligation.

Switch-Cover Option.   This feature permits U.S. equipment that has been exported to a dealer/distributor to be guaranteed in the name of the end user.

Bank-to-Bank Lines.   In nonindustrial countries, Eximbank offers its guarantee to cover revolving medium-term lines of credit established by a U.S. bank with a foreign bank.

Preshipment Coverage.   When the export product is specially fabricated or requires a lengthy manufacturing period, Eximbank may issue its guarantee to the exporter.

Foreign Currency Guarantees.   Transactions may also be denominated in selected foreign currencies.

Contact
Office of Exporter Credits and Guarantees
Export-Import Bank of the United States
811 Vermont Avenue, N.W.
Washington, DC 20571
(202) 566-8819

Foreign Credit Insurance Association

The Foreign Credit Insurance Association (FCIA) is a group of U.S. marine, property, and casualty insurance companies. FCIA helps U.S. exporters compete on favorable terms with exporters from other countries. FCIA also helps expand U.S. exports. FCIA, as agent for Eximbank, insures U.S. exporters against the risk of nonpayment by foreign buyers for commercial and political reasons. Commercial risks include losses from a buyer's bankruptcy or failure, due to insolvency, to pay within six months after the due date of an insured obligation. Political risks are losses from dollar transfer delays, war, revolution, license revocation, diversion of goods, and similar politically related incidents occurring in the buyer's country that cause a loss to the U.S. company. This credit insurance generally covers 100 percent of the financed portion for political risks and up to 90 percent for commercial risks.

FCIA works in cooperation with the Export-Import Bank and markets and issues the credit insurance on behalf of Eximbank.

Eligibility

Any company, corporation, partnership, or similar entity registered to do business in the United States and engaged in the export or export financing of U.S. products is eligible to participate in FCIA programs. A qualified U.S. exporter may obtain FCIA coverage by becoming a policyholder directly or by working through an FCIA policy held by a commercial bank. Short-term coverage is available when at least 50 percent of the value of a product consists of labor and materials exclusively of U.S. origin. A medium-term product normally must be 100 percent of U.S. origin, but FCIA will consider contracts with a minor foreign-content percentage.

Virtually any product can be insured, though there are some exceptions:

Military or defense-related equipment generally is not eligible for coverage (exceptions require advance approval).

Cattle or livestock and used equipment require the completion of a special questionnaire with each application for coverage.

Insured products usually are shipped from the United States. However, coverage is available for sales made either from an exporter's consigned stock in a foreign country or from the insured's wholly owned subsidiary overseas, provided the U.S. content requirement is met.

Terms

FCIA covers transactions using credit terms that generally do not exceed those recognized internationally as customary for the products in question. Short-term products (such as consumer goods and spare parts) carry maximum repayment terms of 180 days. Repayment terms for

---

SOLAREX CORPORATION

The Export-Import Bank approved both guarantee protection and discount loan support for a $300,000 export sale to a Colombian utility of American-made solar power generating equipment. The sale was made in 1982 against competition from suppliers in France, Germany, and Japan.

The Solarex Corporation of Rockville, Maryland, which manufactures solar power equipment, worked with Eximbank to arrange the financing of the sale.

The purchaser, Empresas Departamentales de Antioquia, will use the solar generators to power a telecommunication system for 99 small villages.

---

medium-term products (capital and quasi-capital goods) can range from 181 days to five years.

The following programs are available to the U.S. exporter.

Single-Buyer Programs

The three separate policies written on an individual buyer basis are the Medium-Term Single Sale (MTS), Medium-Term Repetitive (MTR), and Combined Short Term–Medium Term (MSC). Each policy covers transactions of capital or quasi-capital goods with one buyer only, on terms of credit ranging from one to five years. Transaction endorsements to the policies outline in detail the specific terms of coverage authorized.

1. Appropriate Repayment Terms. The policies cover transactions typically with terms of payment ranging from 181 days to five years. Goods eligible for medium-term cover generally are capital or quasi-capital goods of relatively high unit value. The size of the order is important in determining the appropriate repayment terms for such product transactions, as shown in the following tabulation.

Contract Price	Maximum Repayment Term
Up to $50,000	2 years
$50,001–100,000	3 years
$100,001–200,000	4 years
$200,001 and over	5 years

The buyer must make a minimum down payment of at least 15 percent of the contract price on or before delivery. The balance of the transaction is payable in equal installments usually made monthly, quarterly, or semiannually.

2. **Medium-Term Single Sale (MTS).** The MTS policy is designed for the exporter making one-time sales of capital goods to end users. It offers regular coverage on the sale, without requiring the exporter to submit future sales for coverage. Separate shipments can be made during a policy period (usually six months), and FCIA can extend this period if a delay in shipment is expected. Terms can range from 181 days to five years. The down payment must be made prior to delivery of goods to the buyer. The policy requires promissory notes to be executed within 30 days of shipment. Upon application, FCIA can consider cover on multiple shipments evidenced by a single note.

3. **Medium-Term Repetitive (MTR).** The MTR policy covers capital goods shipments to a particular buyer on an ongoing and repeated basis. Although the coverage is the same as the MTS, the buyer generally is a dealer or distributor. The policy carries a final shipment date of one year from the date of issue but is renewable at the end of that period, based on the exporter's experience.

4. **Combined Short Term–Medium Term (MSC).** The MSC policy covers sales of capital and quasi-capital goods, including related spare parts and accessories to overseas dealers and distributors. Regular short-term coverage (up to 180 days) is provided on the parts and accessories. In addition to the traditional short-term coverage for normal shelf items, the MSC policy provides inventory and receivable financing for the capital and quasi-capital goods portion of the sale. Inventory financing is provided under a floor-plan arrangement, during which time no payment is required (up to 270 days). At the end of the floor-planning period, the short-term obligation may be rolled over into medium-term

coverage. When the obligation is rolled over, the policyholder must make a down payment of 15 percent of the cost of the policy.

Premiums

When setting premiums, FCIA will consider a number of factors, including repayment terms, markets for the exporter's products, and the amount of the sale.

Multibuyer Programs

The FCIA's Multibuyer Program is designed for the exporter doing business with numerous overseas buyers on a continuous basis. The program permits the exporter to react quickly to market changes and opportunities and also acknowledges the need of the exporter to decide how and when to do business. Features of the Multibuyer Program include authority to make credit decisions independently, ability to cover a wide range of products, and terms to fit the marketplace.

Five policies are available to exporters in the Multibuyer Program.

1. **Short-Term Master (SD).** The Short-Term Master Policy is available to a company making shipments of U.S. products to foreign buyers on repayment terms not in excess of 180 days. The policy features a discretionary credit limit, allowing the exporter to exercise credit judgment, and a commercial first-loss deductible. Exporters of consumer and industrial items are the main users of this policy. Typical products shipped under the policy include auto parts, clothing, electronics, agricultural commodities, and metals.

2. **Short Term–Medium Term Master (CMR).** The Short Term–Medium Term Master Policy offers the same coverage and credit judgment flexibility as the Short-Term Master Policy plus the ability to insure export transactions of capital and quasi-capital goods on medium-term credit. The policy is designed for the large-volume exporter with multiple credit lines. This policy is used by exporters in every sector of American business, especially those in the construction, machinery, transportation, air conditioning, and chemical industries.

3. **Medium-Term Master (MD).** This version of the master policy is suited to the needs of the capital equipment manufacturer who maintains repetitive sales arrangements with overseas dealers or distributors

or who seeks an aggressive sales approach with end users. The exporter receives continuous coverage on medium-term sales at more advantageous premium rates.

Note.

Medium-term transactions insured under a CMR or MD policy must comply with the same repayment terms as those applicable to single-buyer policies.

4. **Comprehensive Services Policy (CV).**   The Comprehensive Services Policy is for the company providing U.S. expertise and technology to foreign customers. It insures the service company against failure of its clients to make agreed-upon progress payments caused by defined commercial and political risks. Services must be performed by U.S. personnel. This policy can be tailored to the needs of any company performing services overseas and receiving progress payments at regular intervals. These intervals range from payment on receipt of invoice to payment at 180 days after the invoice date.

5. **Small Business Policy (SB).**   The Small Business Policy offers the same basic protection as the SD but with an increase in the commercial coverage to 95 percent. There is no first-loss commercial deductible applied to this policy.

All companies must meet the following requirements when applying for a Small Business Policy:

Net worth not exceeding $2 million.

Average annual export sales during the preceding two fiscal years not exceeding $750,000.

No prior coverage under any FCIA insurance program, either through the company's own policy or through a commercial bank or merchant exporter policy.

Special Coverages

Exporters also can obtain a number of special coverages from FCIA. Preshipment coverage, for example, insures against specified risks from the date of execution of the sales contract rather than from the date of shipment. Exporters find this coverage desirable when their products are specially fabricated or require a long factory lead time (up to a maximum of 18 months). In addition, FCIA will insure against political risks for goods on consignment, where the exporter retains title until the products are sold. If an exporter consummates a sale requiring payment in foreign currency rather than U.S. dollars, FCIA will cover such transactions under all policies. No exchange or transfer risk is insurable under this endorsement. In addition, FCIA also offers special support for the sale of bulk agricultural commodities sold on irrevocable letter-of-credit terms. The bulk agricultural programs provide for terms of up to 360 days and coverage up to 98 percent.

Contact
Your insurance broker or:

Atlanta
Foreign Credit Insurance Association
520 South Omni International
Atlanta, GA 30303
(404) 522-2780

Chicago
Foreign Credit Insurance Association
20 North Clark Street, Suite 910
Chicago, IL 60602
(312) 641-1915

Houston
Foreign Credit Insurance Association
Texas Commerce Tower
Houston, TX 77002
(713) 227-0987

Los Angeles
Foreign Credit Insurance Association
707 Wilshire Boulevard
Los Angeles, CA 90017
(213) 624-8412

New York
Foreign Credit Insurance Association
40 Rector Street, 11th Floor
New York, NY 10006
(212) 306-5000

Washington, DC
Foreign Credit Insurance Association
1425 H Street, N.W.
Washington, DC 20005
(202) 638-5028

San Francisco
Foreign Credit Insurance Association
1990 North California Boulevard
Walnut Creek, CA 94596
(415) 930-9652

CHAPTER NINE

TRAINING, ADVICE, AND ASSISTANCE

Once the decision has been made to begin operations abroad, several U.S. government programs are available to assist in the start-up phase. Government programs also can provide assistance when a business is expanded at a later date. Additional programs are available for handling the typical needs faced by a U.S. enterprise overseas. This chapter discusses three types of federal programs:

Training for Employees. Assistance for training and educating employees in skills required for overseas business.

Advice. How to benefit from the large pool of experienced business executives, government officials, and industry specialists willing to help.

Special Assistance. Information and assistance with problems or questions that might arise with an overseas venture as well as promotional assistance for the export of agricultural products.

TRAINING FOR EMPLOYEES

Vocational Management Training

The Bureau for Private Enterprise within the Agency for International Development provides grants for vocational management training to projects it finances. These projects must have significant foreign ownership. Decisions to fund training are based on specific needs of individual projects. Grants usually are limited to 10 percent of the amount of financing that has been provided.

Contact
Bruce Bouchard
Bureau for Private Enterprise
Agency for International Development
State Annex 14, Room 633
Washington, DC 20523
(703) 235-2274

FUND FOR MULTINATIONAL MANAGEMENT EDUCATION

A New York City educational firm is establishing, with the help of a grant from OPIC, a three-year program to train management executives in five Southeast Asian countries in the use of American technology. Each year the Fund for Multinational Management Education (FMME) plans to train approximately 50 management executives in each of the five countries on how to plan, purchase, install, and manage U.S. technology in their companies. The program grew out of the desire of these nations to learn about alternatives to Japanese and European technology. OPIC is insisting that the FMME obtain a substantial contribution toward the cost of the program from private-sector sources.

Technical and Managerial Skills Training

OPIC provides funding for training projects related to OPIC-financed or insured investments in a developing country. These training projects improve the technical and managerial skills of developing country personnel. Funding, which is provided on a concessional loan or grant basis, is typically not more than $50,000. Funds cover travel or living expenses related to the training project. Project sponsors must contribute at least 25 percent of the cost of the training project.

Contact
  Michael Stack
  Overseas Private Investment Corporation
  1129 20th Street, N.W.
  Washington, DC 20527
  (202) 653-2907

Agricultural Education and Training

USDA International Training Division

The Agriculture Department's International Training Division offers a variety of courses to develop the skills of foreign agriculturalists. These courses include Animal Science and Natural Resources; Economics and Policy; Management, Education, and Human Resource Development; and Production and Technology.

The courses are open to agricultural and rural development technicians, scientists, trainers, administrators, and policymakers from developing nations. Courses are held in the Washington area, at universities in over 20 states, and in foreign countries. Applications for course enrollment must be submitted no later than two months before a course begins. For most courses, enrollment is on a space-available basis. Organizations sponsoring participants include the Agency for International Development, the Food and Agriculture Organization of the United Nations, international development banks, developing country governments, foundations, and private organizations. In addition, there are opportunities for foreign agriculturalists to participate in research in over 200 subject areas. This research is conducted in laboratories operated by the Science and Education Administration and other research laboratories. This allows foreign scientists to update, increase, and refine their research skills while working together with U.S. scientists in ongoing research programs.

Contact

David P. Winkelmann, Deputy Administrator for International Training
Office of International Cooperation and Development
U.S. Department of Agriculture
Auditors Building, Room 4118
Washington, DC 20250
(202) 447-4711

USDA Graduate School

The Graduate School of the U.S. Department of Agriculture is a nonprofit, self-supporting educational institution established by the U.S. government in 1921. The Graduate School has trained over 400,000 people at the international, national, state, and local levels. The International Programs Division provides training and technical assistance for participants from other countries. Training areas include financial and industrial management, economics, business administration, energy, human resource development, computer sciences, statistics, marketing, employment, forestry, agricultural and rural development, transportation, telecommunications, appropriate technology, and health and nutrition. Courses are taught in English, French, Spanish, Arabic, and Portuguese, and they are offered both in the United States and overseas.

The Graduate School also offers cross-cultural education, English-language training, custom-designed programs to meet specific needs of an organization, a masters degree program in management, and an International Management Development program.

Contact

Arthur F. Byrnes or Michael J. Marquardt
International Programs
The Graduate School
U.S. Department of Agriculture
600 Maryland Avenue, S.W., Suite 134
Washington, DC 20024
(202) 447-7476

ADVICE

In-Country Management Advice

The Agency for International Development provides funds to support the International Executive Service Corps, a not-for-profit corporation run by U.S. business executives dedicated to serving developing countries. The Corps' experienced volunteers take on short-term assignments to advise overseas groups, including locally owned and operated private enterprises, government entities, and educational and health care institutions on how to upgrade management skills, increase productivity and employment, and improve basic technologies.

Contact

Charles Neiswender, Vice President, Projects
International Executive Service Corps
622 Third Avenue
New York, NY 10017
(212) 490-6800

Specialized Management Counseling

The Active Corps of Executives, with the support of the Small Business Administration, offers free management counseling by its more than 2600 members. The members are active executives from major industries, professional and trade associations, educational institutions, and other professions. Executives volunteer their specialized expertise upon request by a U.S. business.

Contact

Nearest Small Business Administration district office (see appendix).

Advice on Technical and Managerial Problems

The Bureau for Private Enterprise within the Agency for International Development provides advice and technical assistance to joint ventures between U.S. companies and developing country enterprises to help resolve specific technical and/or managerial problems. The Bureau will advise on laws and regulations related to private investment, mobilizing resources, nontraditional exports and marketing, and new business planning.

INTERNATIONAL EXECUTIVE SERVICE CORPS

In the late 1970s a group of Philippine businessmen provided the necessary funding for establishment of a small project involving the design and production of ceramics. Their goal was to establish an enterprise that would create local employment and whose profits would be used to provide an ongoing source of revenue to the families of patients at a leprosarium located not far from the plant.

Recognizing that the ultimate success of the project would depend to a great extent on management expertise and knowledge of the ceramics industry, the investors sought help from the International Executive Service Corps (IESC). In response, the corporation sent John Lux, retired vice-president of a Buffalo, New York porcelain-ceramics company, to Manila, where he spent two months working shoulder-to-shoulder with the plant manager and employees.

The teamwork paid off. Just one year later, the project had doubled its sales and added 100 new employees to the original staff of 60. By the end of the second year, annual enrollment in its training school had risen to 45, and more recently a major building program for the construction of production line and electric kiln housing was completed.

Contact

Bruce Bouchard
Bureau for Private Enterprise
Agency for International Development
State Annex 14, Room 633
Washington, DC 20523
(703) 235-2274

SPECIAL ASSISTANCE

Expropriation Information

The State Department's Office of Investment Affairs is a point of contact in the U.S. government for multinational corporations. In addition to its role in expropriation matters, it formulates State Department policy on bilateral investment treaties. The Office assesses the investment climate for U.S. businesses in developing nations by monitoring host-country investment policies and regulations. In the event a country's legislation or other government actions threaten the integrity of its commitments to investors, the Office formulates an appropriate U.S. government response. The Office also develops and coordinates U.S. policy concerning investment and multinational corporation issues, consults with Congress on investment issues, and maintains formal liaison with the U.S. business community on developments in international investment policy.

Contact
Philip T. Lincoln, Jr., Acting Director
Office of Investment Affairs
U.S. Department of State
Room 2533A
Washington, DC 20520
(202) 632-2728

Patents, Trademarks, and Copyrights

The State Department's Office of Business Practices is responsible for policies relating to the foreign protection of U.S. patents, trademarks, and copyrights. It closely follows developments that might lead to the erosion of this protection, especially in developing nations. It also works with the U.S. Patent and Trademark Office and the Copyright Office. The Office provides consultation and assistance to U.S. companies faced with possible patent, trademark, or copyright violations.

Contact
Harvey J. Winter, Director
Office of Business Practices
U.S. Department of State
Room 3531A
Washington, DC 20520
(202) 632-1486

International Telecommunications Information

The Federal Communications Commission provides information on communications systems worldwide, including the availability of particular communications services and regulations governing communications in foreign countries.

Contact

Kalmann Schaefer, International Telecommunications Advisor
Federal Communications Commission
1919 M Street, N.W., Room 846
Washington, DC 20554
(202) 632-4161

Labor Information

The Department of Labor provides a number of services to Americans interested in doing business abroad, including information on the labor climate in certain countries and on foreign projects for which technical assistance is sought. The Department has made the Caribbean Basin a high-priority area and offers current information on labor conditions in countries in this region.

Contact

Robert W. Searby, Deputy Undersecretary for International Affairs
Bureau of International Labor Affairs
Department of Labor
200 Constitution Avenue, N.W.
Washington, DC 20210
(202) 523-6243/6043

Agricultural Export Promotion

The Department of Agriculture's Export Incentive Program assists private U.S. firms in promoting agricultural consumer products overseas. Under this program, the Foreign Agricultural Service reimburses firms for up to 50 percent of their export promotion expenditures. The amount of reimbursement is determined by the level of gross export sales (generally 1 percent, but not exceeding 3 percent of the growth in sales) and the extent of the company's promotional activities. The criteria for program approval include probable success in maintaining or increasing consumption of U.S. products, long-range contributions to U.S. agricultural exports and balance of payments, and competition in the export markets. The following products are eligible for promotion assistance: wine, green peppers and other fresh vegetables, almonds, walnuts, canned corn, processed vegetables, cranberries, frozen peas, celery, citrus, and prunes.

This program is available only when at least one-half to two-thirds of the members of an industry seek assistance together. However, at the suggestion of a single firm, the Foreign Agricultural Service will contact others who might be willing to join. This program is not available when the industry's Cooperator group is active in the same market.

Contact
Jimmy D. Minyard, Assistant Administrator for Commodity and Marketing Programs
Foreign Agricultural Service
U.S. Department of Agriculture
Washington, DC 20250
(202) 447-4761

CHAPTER
TEN

A
FINAL
NOTE

When operating abroad, not all problems or opportunities can be anticipated. Special situations requiring special remedies may arise. The U.S. government, as your partner, stands ready to support American investors overseas not only through management advice and training programs, but also through all the programs described in this book.

AGRO-TECH INTERNATIONAL, INC.

To initiate its poultry operations in the Dominican Republic, the Miami-based Agro-Tech International, Inc. turned to OPIC in 1979 for an $800,000 loan. The company, founded by Francisco Hernandez, used the OPIC loan to begin enlarging its poultry breeding and broiler farm capacity. But Hurricane David severely damaged the incomplete project, causing Agro-Tech to return to OPIC in 1980 for an additional $400,000 loan and an extension of its first loan OPIC granted. Agro-Tech and its subsidiaries, which supply farm equipment, feed grains, and technical services abroad in addition to its feed and poultry operations, has prospered: since 1979 its sales have increased by 50 percent. Over the next five years, its Dominican operation is expected to import some $6 million worth of U.S. feed grains.

APPENDIX

U.S. DEPARTMENT OF COMMERCE DISTRICT OFFICES

ALABAMA

908 South 20th Street, Suite 200–201
Birmingham, AL 35205
(205) 254-1331

ALASKA

Federal Building
701 C Street
P.O. Box 32
Anchorage, AK 99513
(907) 271-5041

ARIZONA

2950 Valley Bank Center
201 North Central Avenue
Phoenix, AZ 85073
(602) 261-3285

ARKANSAS

320 West Capitol Avenue, Room 635
Little Rock, AR 72201
(501) 378-5794

CALIFORNIA

11777 San Vicente Boulevard,
Room 800
Los Angeles, CA 90049
(213) 209-6707

Federal Building
Box 36013
450 Golden Gate Avenue
San Francisco, CA 94102
(415) 556-5860

COLORADO

U.S. Customhouse
721 19th Street, Room 119
Denver, CO 80202
(303) 837-3246

CONNECTICUT

Federal Building
450 Main Street, Room 610-D
Hartford, CT 06103
(203) 244-3530

FLORIDA

Federal Building
51 Southwest First Avenue, Suite 224
Miami, FL 33130
(305) 350-5267

GEORGIA

1365 Peachtree Street, N.E., Suite 600
Atlanta, GA 30309
(404) 881-7000

222 U.S. Courthouse
27 East Bay Street
P.O. Box 9746
Savannah, GA 31412
(912) 944-4204

HAWAII

Federal Building
300 Ala Moana Boulevard
P.O. Box 50026
Honolulu, HI 96850
(808) 546-8694

ILLINOIS

Mid-Continental Plaza Building
55 East Monroe Street,
Room 1406
Chicago, IL 60603
(312) 353-4450

INDIANA

357 U.S. Courthouse and
Federal Office Building
46 East Ohio Street
Indianapolis, IN 46204
(317) 269-6214

IOWA

817 Federal Building
210 Walnut Street
Des Moines, IA 50309
(515) 284-4222

KENTUCKY

U.S. Post Office and Courthouse Building,
Room 636B
Louisville, KY 40202
(502) 582-5066

LOUISIANA

432 International Trade Mart
2 Canal Street
New Orleans, LA 70130
(504) 589-6546

MARYLAND

415 U.S. Customhouse
Gay and Lombard Streets
Baltimore, MD 21202
(301) 962-3560

MASSACHUSETTS

441 Stuart Street, 10th Floor
Boston, MA 02116
(617) 223-2312

MICHIGAN

445 Federal Building
231 West Lafayette
Detroit, MI 48226
(313) 226-3650

MINNESOTA

218 Federal Building
110 South 4th Street
Minneapolis, MN 55401
(612) 725-2133

MISSISSIPPI

300 Woodrow Wilson Boulevard
Suite 3230
Jackson, MS 39213
(601) 960-4388

MISSOURI

601 East 12th Street, Room 1840
Kansas City, MO 64106
(816) 374-3142

120 South Central Avenue
St. Louis, MO 63105
(314) 425-3302

NEBRASKA

Empire State Building, 1st Floor
300 South 19th Street
Omaha, NE 68102
(402) 221-3664

NEVADA

1755 East Plum Lane, Room 152
Reno, NV 89502
(702) 784-5203

NEW JERSEY

240 West State Street, 8th Floor
Trenton, NJ 08608
(609) 989-2100

NEW MEXICO

505 Marquette Avenue, N.W., Room 1015
Albuquerque, NM 87102
(505) 766-2386

NEW YORK

1312 Federal Building
111 West Huron Street
Buffalo, NY 14202
(716) 846-4191

Federal Office Building
26 Federal Plaza, 37th Floor
Foley Square
New York, NY 10278
(212) 264-0634

NORTH CAROLINA

203 Federal Building
West Market Street
P.O. Box 1950
Greensboro, NC 27402
(919) 378-5345

OHIO

9504 Federal Building
550 Main Street
Cincinnati, OH 45202
(513) 684-2944

666 Euclid Avenue, Room 600
Cleveland, OH 44114
(216) 522-4750

OKLAHOMA

4024 Lincoln Boulevard
Oklahoma City, OK 73105
(405) 231-5302

OREGON

1220 Southwest 3rd Avenue, Room 618
Portland, OR 97204
(503) 221-3001

PENNSYLVANIA

9448 Federal Building
600 Arch Street
Philadelphia, PA 19106
(215) 597-2866

2002 Federal Building
1000 Liberty Avenue
Pittsburgh, PA 15222
(412) 644-2850

PUERTO RICO

Federal Building, Room 659
Chardon Avenue
San Juan, PR 00918
(809) 753-4555, Ext. 555

SOUTH CAROLINA

Strom Thurmond Federal Building
1835 Assembly Street
Columbia, SC 29201
(803) 765-5345

TENNESSEE

1 Commerce Place, Suite 1427
Nashville, TN 37239
(615) 251-5161

TEXAS

1100 Commerce Street, Room 7A5
Dallas, TX 75242
(214) 767-0542

2625 Federal Building
515 Rusk Street
Houston, TX 77002
(713) 229-2578

UTAH

U.S. Post Office and Courthouse Building
350 South Main Street, Room 340
Salt Lake City, UT 84101
(801) 524-5116

VIRGINIA

Federal Building
400 North 8th Street, Room 8010
Richmond, VA 23240
(804) 771-2246

WASHINGTON

706 Lake Union Building
1700 Westlake Avenue North
Seattle, WA 98109
(206) 442-5616

WEST VIRGINIA

3000 New Federal Office Building
500 Quarrier Street
Charleston, WV 25301
(304) 343-6181, Ext. 375

WISCONSIN

605 Federal Building
517 East Wisconsin Avenue
Milwaukee, WI 53202
(414) 291-3473

WYOMING

8007 O'Mahoney Federal Center
2120 Capitol Avenue
Cheyenne, WY 82001
(307) 772-2151

U.S. SMALL BUSINESS ADMINISTRATION DISTRICT OFFICES

ALABAMA

908 South 20th Street, Room 202
Birmingham, AL 35256
(205) 254-1338

ALASKA

Room 1068, Module G
8th and C Street
Anchorage, AK 99501
(907) 271-4022

ARIZONA

3030 North Central Avenue, Suite 1201
Phoenix, AZ 85012
(602) 241-2203

ARKANSAS

320 West Capital Avenue, Room 601
Little Rock, AR 72201
(501) 378-5871

CALIFORNIA

2202 Monterey Street
Fresno, CA 93721
(209) 487-5657

350 South Figueroa Street, 6th Floor
Los Angeles, CA 90071
(213) 688-4375

880 Front Street, Room 4-S-29
San Diego, CA 92188
(714) 293-6515

211 Main Street, 4th Floor
San Francisco, CA 94105
(415) 974-0596

COLORADO

U.S. Customhouse
721 19th Street, Room 407
Denver, CO 80202
(303) 837-2607

CONNECTICUT

1 Hartford Square West
Hartford, CT 06106
(203) 244-2544

DISTRICT OF COLUMBIA

1111 18th Street, N.W., 6th Floor
Washington, DC 20417
(202) 634-6185

FLORIDA

400 West Bay Street, Room 261
P.O. Box 35067
Jacksonville, FL 32202
(904) 791-3107

2222 Ponce de Leon Boulevard, 5th Floor
Coral Gables, FL 33134
(305) 350-5833

GEORGIA

1720 Peachtree Road, N.W., 6th Floor
Atlanta, GA 30309
(404) 881-2441

HAWAII

P.O. Box 50207
300 Ala Moana Boulevard, Room 2213
Honolulu, HI 96850
(808) 546-3119

IDAHO

1005 Main Street, 2nd Floor
Boise, ID 83702
(208) 334-1780

ILLINOIS

219 South Dearborn Street, Room 838
Chicago, IL 60604
(312) 353-4578

INDIANA

New Federal Building
575 North Pennsylvania Street, 5th Floor
Indianapolis, IN 46209
(317) 331-7280

IOWA

373 Collins Road, N.E.
Cedar Rapids, IA 52402
(319) 399-2571

210 Walnut Street, Room 749
Des Moines, IA 50309
(515) 284-4026

KANSAS

110 East Waterman Street, Room 141
Wichita, KS 67202
(316) 269-6273

KENTUCKY

P.O. Box 3517
600 Federal Place, Room 188
Louisville, KY 40202
(502) 582-5976

LOUISIANA

1661 Canal Street, 2nd Floor
New Orleans, LA 70112
(504) 589-2354

MAINE

40 Western Avenue, Room 512
Augusta, ME 04330
(207) 622-6265

MARYLAND

8600 LaSalle Road, Room 630
Towson, MD 21204
(301) 962-2233

MASSACHUSETTS

150 Causeway Street, 10th Floor
Boston, MA 02114
(617) 223-3293

MICHIGAN

McNamara Building
477 Michigan Avenue, Room 515
Detroit, MI 48226
(313) 226-4276

MINNESOTA

100 North 6th Street
Minneapolis, MN 55403
(612) 349-3541

MISSISSIPPI

New Federal Building
100 West Capitol Street
Suite 322
Jackson, MS 39269
(601) 969-4384

MISSOURI

Scarritt Building
818 Grand Avenue
Kansas City, MO 64106
(816) 374-5868

815 Olive Street, Room 242
St. Louis, MO 63101
(314) 425-6600

MONTANA

301 South Park Avenue, Room 528
Helena, MT 59601
(406) 449-5381

NEBRASKA

Empire State Building
19th and Farnum Streets
Omaha, NE 68102
(402) 221-3604

NEW JERSEY

970 Broad Street, Room 1635
Newark, NJ 07102
(201) 645-3830

NEW MEXICO

Patio Plaza Building
5000 Marble Avenue, N.E.
Albuquerque, NM 87110
(505) 766-1162

NEW YORK

Federal Office Building
26 Federal Plaza, Room 3100
New York, NY 10278
(212) 264-5272

100 South Clinton Street, Room 1071
Syracuse, NY 13260
(315) 423-5381

NORTH CAROLINA

230 South Tryon Street, Room 700
Charlotte, NC 28202
(704) 371-6578

NORTH DAKOTA

653 2nd Avenue North, Room 218
P.O. Box 3068
Fargo, ND 58102
(701) 237-3984

OHIO

AJA Federal Building
1240 East 9th Street, Room 317
Cleveland, OH 44199
(216) 522-4195

85 Marconi Boulevard
Columbus, OH 43215
(614) 469-5548

OKLAHOMA

200 Northwest 5th Street, Suite 670
Oklahoma City, OK 73102
(405) 231-4491

OREGON

Federal Building
1220 Southwest 3rd Avenue, Room 676
Portland, OR 97202
(503) 294-3441

PENNSYLVANIA

231 St. Asaphs Road
East Lobby, Suite 400
Bala Cynwyd, PA 19004
(215) 597-5822

960 Pennsylvania Avenue, 5th Floor
Pittsburgh, PA 15222
(412) 644-5438

PUERTO RICO

Carlos Chardon Avenue, Room 691
Hato Rey, PR 00919
(809) 753-4422

RHODE ISLAND

40 Fountain Street
Providence, RI 02903
(401) 528-4583

SOUTH CAROLINA

Strom Thurmond Federal Building
1835 Assembly Street, 3rd Floor
Columbia, SC 29201
(803) 765-5131

SOUTH DAKOTA

101 South Main Avenue, Suite 101
Sioux Falls, SD 57102
(605) 336-5131

TENNESSEE

404 James Robertson Parkway, Suite 1012
Nashville, TN 37219
(615) 251-7176

TEXAS

1100 Commerce Street
Dallas, TX 75242
(214) 767-0495

222 East Van Buren Street, Suite 500
Harlingen, TX 78550
(512) 423-4534

2525 Murworth, Room 112
Houston, TX 77054
(713) 660-2407

1611 10th Street, Suite 200
Lubbock, TX 79401
(915) 543-7560

Federal Building
727 East Durango Street, Room A-513
San Antonio, TX 78206
(512) 229-6287

UTAH

125 South State Street, Room 2237
Salt Lake City, UT 84138
(801) 524-5805

VERMONT

P.O. Box 605
Federal Building
Montpelier, VT 05602
(802) 229-4422

VIRGINIA

Federal Building
400 North 8th Street, Room 3015
Richmond, VA 23240
(804) 771-2765

VIRGIN ISLANDS

Veterans Drive, Room 283
St. Thomas, VI 00801
(809) 774-8530

WASHINGTON

915 2nd Avenue, Room 1744
Seattle, WA 98174
(206) 442-4518
U.S. Court House
920 West Riverside Avenue, Room 651
P.O. Box 2167
Spokane, WA 99210
(509) 456-3786

WEST VIRGINIA

109 North 3rd Street, Room 302
Clarksburg, WV 26301
(304) 343-6181

WISCONSIN

212 East Washington Avenue, Room 213
Madison, WI 53703
(608) 264-5518

WYOMING

100 East "B" Street, Room 4001
Casper, WY 82602
(307) 265-5761

WASHINGTON, D.C. COUNTRY OFFICERS

Country	U.S. Dept. of State Washington, DC 20520 State Officer/Phone*	U.S. Dept. of Commerce Washington, DC 20230 Commerce Officer/Phone*	Agency for Intl. Development† Washington, DC 20523 AID Officer/Phone*
Afghanistan	Ernestine Heck/632-9552	David Coale/377-2954	Christopher Crowley/632-9142
Albania	Ronald Neitzke/632-1457	Karen Jurew/377-2645	☐
Algeria	Ann Korky/632-0304	Cynthia McDonald/377-5737	George Lewis/632-9228
Andorra	Donald Planty/632-1633	Randy Miller/377-4508	☐
Angola	Michael Ranneberger/632-9429	Simon Bensimon/377-0357	Dominic D'Antonio/632-4287
Anguilla	Sandra Marsden/632-8451	Desmond Foynes/377-5563	Theodor Bratrud/632-2116
Antigua and Barbuda	Sandra Marsden/632-8451	Desmond Foynes/377-5563	Theodor Bratrud/632-2116
Argentina	Sheila-Kaye O'Connell/632-9166	Walter Bastian/377-5427	Robert Lindsay/632-2676
Australia	Bryan Baas/632-9690	Stephen Hall/377-3646	☐
Austria	Douglas Jones/632-2005	Philip Combs/377-2897	☐
Bahamas, The	Mary Kosheleff/632-7385	Libby Roper/377-2912	Theodor Bratrud/632-2116
Bahrain	Robert Campbell/632-1794	Claude Clement/377-5545	Richard Burns/632-8532
Bangladesh	Jackson McDonald/632-0466	Naomi Bradshaw/377-2954	Vovikka Mulldrem/632-9064
Barbados	Sandra Marsden/632-8451	Desmond Foynes/377-5563	Theodor Bratrud/632-2116
Belgium	Michael Lemmon/632-0498	Boyce Fitzpatrick/377-4104	☐
Belize	Robert Blohm/632-0467	Desmond Foynes/377-5563	Edward Campbell/632-3448
Benin	Nancy Morgan/632-0842	John Crown/377-4564	Warren Wolff/632-9808
Bermuda	Keith Smith/632-2622	Libby Roper/377-2912	Theodor Bratrud/632-2116
Bhutan	Nancy Powell/632-0653	Jeff Johnson/377-2954	George Carner/632-2076
Bolivia	Robert Millspaugh/632-3076	Richard Muenzer/377-4302	Penelope Farley/632-2196
Botswana	Cynthia Hanson/632-0916	David Savastuk/377-5148	Leonard Pompa/632-4287
Brazil	Thomas Coony/632-1245	Wilbur Garges/377-5427	Jerome Hulehan/632-2718
British Virgin Islands	Sandra Marsden/632-8451	Desmond Foynes/377-5563	Theodor Bratrud/632-2116

*Area code 202.
†AID does not operate in countries indicated by black square.

Country	State Officer/Phone	Commerce Officer/Phone	AID Officer/Phone
Brunei	Sylvia G. Stanfield/632-3276	Kent Stauffer/377-3875	☐
Bulgaria	Joseph McGhee/632-3747	Karen Jurew/377-2645	☐
Burma	Charles Smith/632-3276	Kyaw Win/377-3875	Carl Penndorf/632-8526
Burundi	Sally Gober/632-3138	David Savastuk/377-5148	Beatrice Beyer/632-9808
Cameroon	Frances Wurlitzer/632-0996	Philip Michelini/377-5148	William Faulkner/632-9810
Canada	James Nelson/632-2170	Nick Burakow/377-5327	☐
Cape Verde	Raymond Pardon/632-8436	John Crown/377-4564	Yvonne John/632-3034
Caroline Islands	D. Stephen May/632-3546	Gary Bouck/377-3647	☐
Caymans	Mary Kosheleff/632-7385	Libby Roper/377-2912	Theodor Bratrud/632-2116
Central African Republic	Sally Gober/632-3138	Philip Michelini/377-0357	William Faulkner/632-9810
Chad	Marie Huhtala/632-0725	Fred Stokelin/377-4564	Yvonne John/632-3034
Chile	David Kemp/632-2575	Herbert Lindow/377-4302	Robert Lindsay/632-2676
China	Barbara Schrage/632-1004	Christine Lucyk/377-3583	☐
Colombia	James Bell/632-3023	Richard Muenzer/377-4302	Penelope Farley/632-2196
Comoros	David H. Kaeuper/632-3040	Fred Stokelin/377-4564	Richard Eney/632-9762
Congo	Robert Boggs/632-1637	Philip Michelini/377-0357	Gary Nelson/632-1761
Cook Islands	D. Stephen May/632-3546	Gary Bouck/337-3647	☐
Costa Rica	Donna Hrinak/632-3385	Robert Bateman/377-2527	Penelope Farley/632-2196
Cuba	Timothy Brown/632-1476	Scott Wylie/377-3637	☐
Cyprus	Vacant/632-1429	Norman McLennan/377-2434	Christopher Crowley/632-9142
Czechoslovakia	Ronald Neitzke/632-1457	Karen Jurew/377-2645	☐
Denmark	C. Michael Konner/632-1774	L. Reid Thomas/377-2920	☐
Diego Garcia	David Kaeuper/632-3040	Fred Stokelin/377-4564	☐
Djibouti	Frank Day/632-3355	Fred Stokelin/377-4564	Thomas Cornell/632-2978
Dominica	Sandra Marsden/632-8451	Desmond Foynes/377-5563	Theodor Bratrud/632-2116
Dominican Republic	William Craft/632-2130	George Fitch/377-3637	Theodor Bratrud/632-2116
Ecuador	Stevan Ordal/632-5864	Fred Kayser/377-4302	Robert Lindsay/632-2676
Egypt	Kenneth Bril/632-1169	Cheryl McQueen/377-4652	Gerald Gower/632-9048
El Salvador	Peter Romero/632-8148	Scott Wylie/377-3637	John Clary/632-4795
Equatorial Guinea	Frances Wurlitzer/632-0996	Philip Michelini/377-5148	William Faulkner/632-9810

Country	State Officer/Phone	Commerce Officer/Phone	AID Officer/Phone
Estonia	Mildred Patterson/632-4138	Hertha Heiss/377-3647	☐
Ethiopia	Frank Day/632-3355	Fred Stokelin/377-4564	Thomas Cornell/632-2978
Fiji	D. Stephen May/632-3546	Gary Bouck/377-3647	Louis Kuhn/632-9844
Finland	Dennis Finnerty/632-0624	Maryanne Lyons/377-3254	☐
France	Jacklyn Cahill/632-1726	James Fitzgerald/377-4941	☐
French Antilles (or French Guyana)	William Craft/632-2130	Robert Dormitzer/377-2218	☐
French Polynesia	D. Stephen May/632-3546	Gary Bouck/377-3647	☐
Gabon	Frances Wurlitzer/632-0996	Philip Michelini/377-0357	William Faulkner/632-9810
Gambia, The	Melinda L. Kimble/632-2865	John Crown/377-4564	Herbert I. Woods/632-8393
Germany, East	Edward O'Donnell/632-2721	Suzanne Porter/377-2645	☐
Germany, West	William Gussman/632-2155	Velizer Stanoyevitch/377-2841	☐
Ghana	Raymond Pardon/632-8436	John Crown/377-4564	David Walsh/632-3305
Gibraltar	Keith Smith/632-2622	Marv Belden/377-3337	☐
Gilbert and Elise Islands	D. Stephen May/632-3546	Gary Bouck/377-3647	☐
Greece	Morton Dworken, Jr./632-1563	Yolanda Corro/377-3945	Christopher Crowley/632-9142
Greenland	C. Michael Konner/632-1774	L. Reid Thomas/377-2920	☐
Grenada	Sandra Marsden/632-8451	Desmond Foynes/377-5563	Theodor Bratrud/632-2116
Guadeloupe	William Craft/632-2130	Libby Roper/377-2912	Theodor Bratrud/632-2116
Guatemala	Robert Blohm/632-0467	Robert Bateman/377-5563	Gary Adams/632-5221
Guinea	Nancy Morgan/632-0842	John Crown/377-4564	Warren Wolff/632-9808
Guinea-Bissau	Raymond Pardon/632-8436	John Crown/377-4564	Yvonne John/632-3034
Guyana	Christopher Webster/632-6386	Robert Dormitzer/377-2218	Edward Campbell/632-3448
Haiti	Susan Lysyshyn/632-3449	George Fitch/377-2912	Elias Padilla/632-2129
Honduras	V. Manuel Rocha/632-0815	Scott Wylie/377-2527	Neil Billig/632-9158
Hong Kong	Keith Powell/632-1436	Nancy Chen/377-4681	☐
Hungary	Mildred Patterson/632-4138	John Fogarasi/377-2645	☐
Iceland	Dennis Finnerty/632-1774	Maryanne Lyons/377-3254	☐
India	Stephen Eisenbraun/632-1289	Dick Harding/377-2954	George Carner/632-2076

Country	State Officer/Phone	Commerce Officer/Phone	AID Officer/Phone
Indonesia	Alphonse LaPorta/632-3276	Don Ryan/377-3875	Steven Singer/632-9842
Iran	Ralph Lindstrom/632-0313	Kathleen Keim/377-4652	Christopher Crowley/632-9142
Iraq	Frank Ricciardone/632-0695	Mark Roth/377-5767	Thomas Miller/632-8408
Ireland	Michael Barry/632-1194	Marv Belden/377-3337	□
Israel	Edward Abington, Jr./632-3672	Kathleen Keim/377-4652	Ann Gooch/632-3585
Italy	Gilbert Kulick/632-2453	Noel Negretti/377-3462	Marx Sterne/632-8152
Ivory Coast	Nancy Morgan/632-0842	Peter Ryan/377-4388	Bernard Lane/632-0593
Jamaica	Christopher Webster/632-6386	Scott Wylie/377-3637	Richard Delaney/632-3447
Japan	A. Jack Croddy, Jr./632-3152	Maureen Smith/377-4527	□
Jordan	Marc Grossman/632-0791	Mark Roth/377-5767	Richard Brown/632-8237
Kampuchea	Robert Porter/632-3132	JeNelle Matheson/377-3583	□
Kenya	Jay Baker/632-0857	Fred Stokelin/377-4564	Sidney Chernekoff/632-9762
Korea, North	Barbara Harvey/632-7717	Jeffrey Lee/377-4681	Louis Kuhn/632-9844
Korea, South	Barbara Harvey/632-7717	Debbie Lamb/377-4390	Richard Burns/632-8532
Kuwait	Ralph Bresler/632-1334	Claude Clement/377-5545	□
Laos	Robert Porter/632-3132	Jeffrey Lee/377-4681	□
Latvia	Mildred Patterson/632-4138	Hertha Heiss/377-4655	Henry D. Merrill/632-8301
Lebanon	A. Elizabeth Jones/632-1018	Mark Roth/377-5767	Dominic D'Antonio/632-4287
Lesotho	Cynthia Hanson/632-0916	David Savastuk/377-5148	David Walsh/632-3305
Liberia	Peter Eicher/632-8354	John Crown/377-4564	□
Libya	William Pope/632-9373	Gwen Brown/377-5737	□
Liechtenstein	Douglas Jones/632-2005	Philip Combs/377-2897	□
Lithuania	Mildred Patterson/632-4138	Hertha Heiss/377-4655	□
Luxembourg	Michael Lemmon/632-0498	Boyce Fitzpatrick/377-5381	Carl Penndorf/632-3526
Macau	Keith Powell/632-1436	Nancy Chen/377-4681	Richard Eney/632-9762
Madagascar	David Kaeuper/632-3040	Simon Bensimon/377-0357	Robert Wrin/632-4326
Malawi	Philip King/632-8851	David Savastuk/377-5148	Louis Kuhn/632-9844
Malaysia	Sylvia G. Stanfield/632-3276	Kent Stauffer/377-3875	□
Maldives	Alan Eastham/632-2351	Naomi Bradshaw/377-2954	□
Mali	Joyce Leader/632-3066	Fred Stokelin/377-4564	Nicholas Mariani/632-3034

Country	State Officer/Phone	Commerce Officer/Phone	AID Officer/Phone
Malta	Robert Smolik/632-8210	Norman McLennan/377-2434	Christopher Crowley/632-9142
Marianas Islands	D. Stephen May/632-3546	Gary Bouck/377-3647	□
Marshall Islands	D. Stephen May/632-3546	Gary Bouck/377-3647	□
Martinique	William Craft/632-2130	Libby Roper/377-2912	Theodor Bratrud/632-2116
Mauritania	Melinda L. Kimble/632-2865	John Crown/377-4564	Nicholas Mariani/632-3034
Mauritius	David H. Kaeuper/632-3040	Simon Bensimon/377-0357	Richard Eney/632-9762
Mexico	T. Frank Crigler/632-9894	Dale Slaght/377-2332	Robert Queenar/632-0001
Monaco	Jacklyn Cahill/632-1726	James Fitzgerald/377-4941	
Mongolia	Keith Powell/632-1436	Lillian Monk/377-2462	
Montserrat	Sandra Marsden/632-8451	Desmond Foynes/377-5563	Theodor Bratrud/632-2116
Morocco	Edward Abington, Jr./632-0279	Gwen Brown/377-5737	George Lewis/632-9228
Mozambique	Emil Skodon/632-8433	David Savastuk/377-5148	Earl Yates/632-3229
Namibia	Peter Reams/632-8252	Urath Gibson/377-5148	Dominic D'Antonio/632-4287
Nauru	D. Stephen May/632-3546	Gary Bouck/377-3647	□
Nepal	Nancy Powell/632-0653	Jeff Johnson/377-2954	Howard Thomas/632-8226
Netherlands	Michael Lemmon/632-0498	Robert McLaughlin/377-5401	□
Netherlands Antilles	Mary Kosheleff/632-7385	Robert Dormitzer/377-2527	□
New Caledonia and Vanautu	D. Stephen May/632-3546	Gary Bouck/377-3647	□
New Zealand	Patricia Langford/632-9690	Gary Bouck/377-3647	□
Nicaragua	Lino Gutierrez/632-2205	Scott Wylie/377-3637	Gary Adams/632-5221
Niger	Joyce E. Leader/632-3066	Fred Stokelin/377-4564	Yvonne John/632-3034
Nigeria	Thomas E. Williams/632-3406	James Robb/377-4388	David Walsh/632-3305
Norway	C. Michael Konner/632-1774	James Devlin/377-4414	□
Oman	Ralph E. Bresler/632-1334	Mark Roth/377-5767	Richard P. Burns/632-8237
Pacific Islands	D. Stephen May/632-3546	Gary Bouck/377-3647	Louis Kuhn/632-9844
Pakistan	Gerald Feirstein/632-2441	Stan Bilinski/377-2954	David Mutchler/632-8226
Panama	Edward Woltman, Jr./632-4986	Robert Bateman/377-5563	Neil Billig/632-9158
Papua–New Guinea	D. Stephen May/632-3546	Gary Bouck/377-3647	Louis Kuhn/632-9844
Paraguay	Mirta Alvarez/632-1551	Mark Siegelman/377-5427	Jerome Hulchan/632-2718

Country	State Officer/Phone	Commerce Officer/Phone	AID Officer/Phone
Peru	Richard Watkins/632-3360	Herbert Lindow/377-4303	Jerome Hulchan/632-2718
Philippines	Charles W. Reynolds/632-1669	George Paine/377-3875	Carl Penndorf/632-8526
Poland	Dale R. Herspring/632-0575	Delores Harrod/377-2645	Ann Gooch/632-8940
Portugal	Lewis Girdler/632-0719	Randy Miller/377-4509	Marx Sterne/632-6517
Puerto Rico	John Upston/632-2621	Carlos Montoulieu/377-2623	☐
Qatar	Robert Campbell/632-1794	Claude Clement/377-5545	☐
Reunion Island	Jacklyn A. Cahill/632-1726	James Fitzgerald/377-4941	☐
Romania	Johnathon B. Rickert/632-3928	Jay Burgess/377-2645	☐
Rwanda	Sally M. Gober/632-3138	Simon Bensimon/377-0357	Beatrice Beyer/632-9808
Samoa (see Western Samoa)			
San Marino	Gilbert Kulick/632-2453	Noel Negretti/377-3462	☐
Sao Tome and Principe	Frances Wurlitzer/632-0996	Simon Bensimon/377-0357	Beatrice Beyer/632-9808
Saudi Arabia	Richard Dotson/632-3121	Karl Reiner/377-5767	☐
Senegal	Melinda L. Kimble/632-2865	John Crown/377-4564	Nicholas Mariani/632-3034
Seychelles	Jay Baker/632-0857	Fred Stokelin/377-4564	Nicholas Mariani/632-3034
Sierra Leone	Gregory Fergin/632-3395	John Crown/377-4564	David Walsh/632-3305
Singapore	Sylvia G. Stanfield/632-3276	George Paine/377-3875	Louis Kuhn/632-9844
Solomon Islands	D. Stephen May/632-3546	Gary Bouck/377-3647	☐
Somalia	Earle Scarlett/632-0849	Fred Stokelin/377-4564	Brian Kline/632-4030
South Africa	David Dlouhy/632-3274	Urath Gibson/377-5148	☐
Soviet Union	Raymond F. Smith/632-8671	Hertha Heiss/377-4655	☐
Spain	Donald J. Planty/632-2633	Randy Miller/377-4508	☐
Sri Lanka	Alan Eastham/632-2351	Naomi Bradshaw/377-2954	John Gunning/632-8226
St. Christopher and Nevis,			
St. Lucia,			
St. Vincent, and the Grenadines	Sandra Marsden/632-8451	Desmond Foynes/377-5563	Theodor Bratrud/632-2116
Sudan	Donald E. Booth/632-0668	Fred Stokelin/377-4564	Thomas Cornell/632-2978
Suriname	Susan Lysyshyn/632-3449	Robert Dormitzer/377-2218	Edward Campbell/632-3448
Swaziland	Cynthia G. Hanson/632-0916	David Savastuk/377-5148	Robert Wrin/632-4326

Country	State Officer/Phone	Commerce Officer/Phone	AID Officer/Phone
Sweden	Michael T. Barry/632-1194	James Devlin/377-4414	☐
Switzerland	Douglas H. Jones/632-2005	Philip Combs/377-2897	☐
Syria	Molly Williamson/632-4714	Mark Roth/377-5767	Richard Brown/632-8237
Taiwan	Donald C. Ferguson/632-7710	Betty Patrick/377-4957	☐
Tanzania	David H. Kaeuper/632-3040	Fred Stokelin/377-4564	Brian Kline/632-4030
Thailand	Jim Henderson/632-0978	Linda Droker/377-3875	Louis Kuhn/632-9844
Togo	V. Manuel Rocha/632-0815	John Crown/377-2527	Warren Wolff/632-9808
Tonga	D. Stephen May/632-3546	Gary Bouck/377-3647	
Trinidad and Tobago	Mary Kosheleff/632-7385	Thomas Moore/377-5563	Theodor Bratrud/632-2116
Tunisia	John Hamilton/632-3614	Cynthia McDonald/377-5737	Marilyn Arnold/632-9228
Turkey	Michael W. Cotter/632-1562	Norman McLennan/377-2434	
Uganda	Donald E. Booth/632-0668	Fred Stokelin/377-4564	Alfred Ford/632-9762
United Arab Emirates	Robert Campbell/632-1794	Claude Clement/377-5545	☐
United Kingdom	Keith C. Smith/632-2622	Marv Belden/377-3337	☐
Upper Volta	Joyce E. Leader/632-3066	Fred Stokelin/377-4564	Yvonne John/632-3034
Uruguay	Mirta Alvarez/632-1551	Mark Siegelman/377-5427	Robert Lindsay/632-2676
Vatican City	Robert J. Smolik/632-8210	Noel Negretti/377-3462	
Venezuela	Eleanor W. Savage/632-3338	Walter Earle/377-4302	
Vietnam	Brian Kirkpatrick/632-3132	JeNelle Matheson/377-3583	
Western Sahara	Melinda L. Kimble/632-2865	Gwen Brown/377-5737	
Western Samoa	D. Stephen May/632-3546	Gary Bouck/377-3647	Louis Kuhn/632-9844
Yemen Arab Republic	Bruce Ehrnman/632-2329	Tom Sams/337-5767	Christopher Crowley/632-8984
Yemen, People's Democratic Republic of	Bruce Ehrnman/632-2329	Tom Sams/337-5767	Christopher Crowley/632-8984
Yugoslavia	George M. Humphrey/632-3655	Geoffrey Jackson/377-4508	
Zaire	Robert K. Boggs/632-1637	Simon Bensimon/377-0357	Beatrice Beyer/632-9808
Zambia	Philip A. King/632-8851	David Savastuk/377-5148	Leonard Pompa/632-4287
Zimbabwe	Joseph M. Segars/632-8434	Urath Gibson/377-5148	Robert Wrin/632-4326

KEY PERSONNEL AT U.S. EMBASSIES

Instructions for Addressing Mail to a U.S. Foreign Service Post

Correspondence to a foreign service post should be addressed to a section or position rather than to an officer by name. Normally, correspondence concerning commercial matters should be addressed "Commercial Section," followed by the name and correct mailing address of the post.

Below are the three accepted forms of addressing mail to a foreign service post using the Economic/Commercial Section of the American Embassy in Manama, Bahrain as an example:

Economic/Commercial Section   or   Economic/Commercial Section
American Embassy   Manama
FPO NY 09526   Department of State
     Washington, DC 20520

or

Economic/Commercial Section
American Embassy
P.O. Box 26431*
Manama, Bahrain

Key

The following abbreviations are used in this chart:

ACM	Assistant Chief of Mission
ADM	Administration
AGR	Agricultural Section
AID	Agency for International Development
AMB	Ambassador
BO	Branch Office of Embassy
C	Consulate
CG	Consul General, Consulate General
COM	Commercial Section
CON	Consul, Consular Section

*Use street address only when P.O. box is not supplied.

DCM	Deputy Chief of Mission
DPO	Deputy Principal Officer
E	Embassy
ECO	Economic Section
LAB	Labor Officer
M	Mission
MIL	Military Officer
PO	Principal Officer
POL	Political Section
VC	Vice Consul

Description of Embassy Officers' Responsibilities

At the head of each U.S. diplomatic mission are the *Chief of Mission* (with the title of *Ambassador, Minister, or Chargé d'Affaires*) and the *Deputy Chief of Mission.* These officers are responsible for all components of the U.S. mission within a country, including consular posts.

Economic/commercial officers represent the entire spectrum of U.S. economic and commercial interests within their countries of assignment. Their activities range from trade promotion to economic reporting. At larger posts, where trade volume, travel, and private investment interest are high, there are *commercial officers* who specialize in export promotion, arrange appointments with local business and government officials, and provide maximum assistance to American business.

Political officers analyze and report on political developments and their potential impact on U.S. interests.

Consular officers extend to U.S. citizens and their property abroad the protection of the U.S. government. They maintain lists of local attorneys, act as liaison with police and other officials, and have the authority to notarize documents. The State Department recommends that business representatives residing overseas register with the consular officer; in troubled areas, even travelers are advised to register.

Agricultural officers promote the export of U.S. agricultural products and report on agricultural production and market developments in their area.

The *AID mission director* is responsible for AID programs, including dollar and local currency loans, grants, and technical assistance.

AFGHANISTAN

Kabul (E), Wazir Akbar Khan Mina
Tel 24230-9
Workweek: Sunday–Thursday

AMB: (Vacancy)
DCM: Lee O. Coldren (Acting)
POL: Richard C. Vandiver
ECO/COM: Peter T. Graham

ALGERIA

Algiers (E), 4 Chemin Cheich Bachir
Brahimi, B.P. Box 549 (Alger-Gare)
Tel 601425/255/186   Telex 52064
Workweek: Saturday–Wednesday

AMB: Michael H. Newlin
DCM: Joseph P. Lorenz
POL: Charles E. Redman
ECO: Ross C. Parr
COM: Andrew Grossman
AGR: Forrest K. Geerken
       (resident in Rabat)

Oran (C), 14 Square de Bamako
Tel 390972; 399941   Telex   22310
AMCONRN
Workweek: Saturday–Wednesday

ANTIGUA AND BARBUDA

ST. JOHNS (E), FPO Miami 34054
Tel AC 809-462-3506

AMB: Milan D. Bish
       (resident in Bridgetown)

ARGENTINA

BUENOS AIRES (E), 4300 Colombia, 1425
APO Miami 34034
Tel 774-7611/8811/9911
Telex 18156 USICA

AMB: Harry W. Shlaudeman
DCM: John A. Bushnell
POL: John F. King
ECO: John P. Crawford
COM: Richard Rueda, Jr.
AGR: Lawrence Hall

AUSTRALIA

CANBERRA (E), Moonah Pl., Canberra,
A.C.T. 2600

APO San Fran 96404
Tel (062) 73-3711
Telex USAEMB62104

AMB: Robert D. Nesen
DCM: Stephen R. Lyne
POL: Richard N. Kilpatrick
ECO: Paul L. Laase
COM: John W. Avard
AGR: Dale B. Douglas

Melbourne (CG), 24 Albert Rd., South
Melbourne, Victoria 3205
APO San Fran 96405
Tel (03) 699-2244
Telex 30982 AMERCON

CG: James W. White
COM: Donald R. Cleveland

Sydney (CG), 36th Fl., T&G Tower, Hyde
Park Square, Park and Elizabeth Sts.,
Sydney 2000, N.S.W.
APO San Fran 96209
Tel 264-7044   Telex 74223 FCSSYD

CG: Herbert E. Horowitz
COM: Edward G. Simonsen, Jr.

Perth (C), 246 St. George's Ter., Perth, WA
6000
Tel (09) 322-4466
Telex 93848 AMCON

COM: B. Paul Scogna

AUSTRIA

Vienna (E), IX Boltzmanngasse 16 A-1091
Tel (222) 31-55-11   Telex 74634

AMB: Helene A. von Damm
POL: Carl J. Clement
ECO: Felix S. Bloch
COM: Raymond W. Eiselt
AGR: Nicholas M. Thuroczy

BAHAMAS

Nassau (E), Mosmar Bldg., Queen St., P.O.
Box N-8197
Tel (809) 322-4753/6   Telex 20-138

AMB: Lev E. Dobriansky
DCM: Andrew F. Antippas
POL/ECO/COM: Ismael Lara
AGR: Marvin L. Lehrer (resident in
       Santo Domingo)

BAHRAIN

Manama (E), Shalkh Isa Rd., P.O. Box 26431

FPO NY 09526

Tel 714151   Telex 9398 USATO BN

Workweek: Saturday–Wednesday

AMB: Peter A. Sutherland
DCM: Charles H. Brayshaw
ECO/COM: Laraine N. Carter

BANGLADESH

Dhaka (E), Adamjee Court Bldg. (5th Fl.), Motijheel Commercial Area

G.P.O. Box 323, Ramna

Tel 237161–63 and 235093–99

Telex 642319 AEDKA BJ

AMB: Jane A. Coon
DCM: Carl W. Schmidt
POL: Peter J. Lydon
ECO/COM: Robert B. McMullen
AGR: Robert E. Haresnape
AID: James A. Norris

BARBADOS

Bridgetown (E), P.O. Box 302

Box B, FPO Miami 34054

Tel 63574-7

Telex 259 USEMBBG1 WB

AMB: Milan D. Bish
DCM: Ludlow Flower III
POL/ECO: Kenneth A. Kurze
ECO/COM: John E. Hope
AGR: Harry C. Bryan (resident in Caracas)
AID: William B. Wheeler

BELGIUM

Brussels (E), 27 Boulevard du Regent, B-1000, Brussels

APO NY 09667

Tel (02) 513-3830   Telex 846-21336

AMB: Charles H. Price II
DCM: Charles H. Thomas
POL: John P. Heimann
ECO: Mary E. McDonnell
COM: Hendrik N. Smit
ADM: Lawrence D. Russell
AGR: Roger Lowen

Antwerp (CG), Rubens Center, Nationale-straats, B-2000 Antwerp

APO NY 09667

Tel (03) 2321800   Telex 31966

CG: Thomas H. Gewecke
ECO/COM: James A. Minyard

BELIZE

Belize City (E), Gabourel Lane and Hutson St.

Tel 02–7161, 62, 63   Telex BH 213

AMB: Malcolm R. Barneby
POL: Jeanne M. Pryor
ECO/COM: Jonathan D. Farrar
AID: Neboysha R. Brashich
AGR: Robert R. Anlauf (resident in Guatemala)

BENIN

Cotonou (E), Rue Caporal Anani Bernard, B.P. 2012

Tel 30-06-50, 3017-92

AMB: (Vacancy)
AID: John Lundgren (resident in Lome)

BERMUDA

Hamilton (CG), Vallis Bldg., Front St.

FPO NY 09560

Tel (809) 295-1342

CG: Max L. Friedersdorf

BOLIVIA

La Paz (E), Banco Popular Del Peru Bldg., Corner of Calles Mercado and Colon, P.O. Box 425

APO Miami 34032

Tel 350251, 350120   Telex BX5240

AMB: Edwin G. Corr
POL/ECO: Daniel A. Strasser
AGR: Norval Francis (resident in Lima)
AID: Henry H. Bassford

BOTSWANA

Gaborone (E), P.O. Box 90

Tel 53982/3/4

Telex 2554 AMEMB BD

AMB: Theodore C. Maino
DCM: William L. Jacobsen, Jr.

POL/ECO/COM: John L. Berntsen
AGR: Guy L. Haviland (resident in Pretoria)
AID: J. Paul Guedet

BRAZIL

Brasilia (E), Avenida das Nocoes, Lote 3
APO Miami 34030
Tel (061) 223-0120   Telex 061-1091

AMB: (Vacancy)
CHG: Harry Kopp
POL: T. Elkin Taylor
ECO: Thomas J. O'Donnell
COM: Emilio F. Iodice
AGR: G. Stanley Brown

Rio De Janeiro (CG), Avenida Presidente Wilson, 147
APO Miami 34030
Tel (021) 292-7117   Telex 021-21466

CG: Samuel Lupo
DPO/POL: Douglas G. Hartley
ECO: James R. Sartorius
COM: John P. Steinmetz
AGR: Joseph F. Somers

Sao Paulo (CG), Rua Padre Joao Manoel, 933, P.O. Box 8063
APO Miami 34030
Tel (011) 881-6511   Telex 011-22183

CG: John C. Leary
POL: Thomas G. Martin
ECO: Hilton L. Graham
COM: Louis V. Riggio (located in Trade Center)
AGR: John T. Hopkins (located in Trade Center)

Porto Alegre (C), Rua Coronel, Genuino, 421 (9th Fl.)
APO Miami 34030
Tel (0512) 26-4288/4697
Telex (0512) 148

CON: Douglas B. Neumann

Recife (C), Rua Goncalves Maia, 163
APO Miami 34030
Tel (081) 221-1412, 222-6612, 222-6577
Telex 081-1190

PO: Edward A. Torre
CON: Arthur H. Mills

Salvador Da Bahia (C), Avenida Presidente Vargas, 1892 (Ondina)
APO Miami 34030
Tel (071) 245-6691/92
Telex 071-2780

ECO/COM/VC: Ray C. Rajan

BULGARIA

Sofia (E), 1 Stamboliiski Blvd
Tel 88-48-01 to 05   Telex 22690 BG

AMB: Robert L. Barry
DCM: H. Kenneth Hill
POL/ECO: Joseph E. Lake
ECO/COM: Lawrence E. Butler
AGR: Roger Lowen (resident in Belgrade)

BURMA

Rangoon (E), 581 Merchant St.
Tel 82055, 82181

AMB: Patricia M. Byrne
DCM: Jerrold M. Dion
POL: Hugh C. MacDougall
ECO/COM: Edward H. Goff
AID: David N. Merrill

BURUNDI

Bujumbura (E), Chaussee Prince Louise Rwagasore
B.P. 1720
Tel 34-54

AMB: James R. Bullington
DCM: Joseph C. Wilson IV
POL/ECO: Ravic R. Huso
ECO/COM: Dorothy A. Painter
AID: George T. Bliss

CAMEROON

Yaounde (E), Rue Nachtigal, B.P. 817
Tel 234014, 220512   Telex 8223KN

AMB: Myles R. Frechette
POL: Janean L. Mann
ECO: Duane Sams
COM: (Vacancy)
AGR: Christopher E. Goldthwait (resident in Lagos)
AID: Ronald D. Levin

Douala (CG), 21 Avenue du General De Gaulle, B.P. 4006
Tel 425331, 426003 Telex 5233KN

CG: Lois J. Matteson
ECO: Linus F. Upson III
COM: (Vacancy)

CANADA

Ottawa (E), 100 Wellington St. K1P 5T1
Tel (613) 238-5335 Telex 0533582

AMB: Paul H. Robinson, Jr.
DCM: Richard J. Smith
POL: Dwight N. Mason
ECO: Sandra L. Vogelgesang
COM: John W. Bligh, Jr.
AGR: Alexander Bernitz

Calgary, Alberta (CG), Rm. 1050, 615 Macleod Trail, S.E. Calgary, Alberta, Canada T2G 4T8
Tel (403) 266-8962

CG: Richard L. Wilson
COM: Carl R. Jacobsen

Halifax, Nova Scotia (CG), Suite 910, Cogswell Tower, Scotia Sq., Halifax, NS, Canada B3J 3K1
Tel (902) 429-2480-1
Telex 019-23566

CG: Lawrence R. Raicht

Montreal, Quebec (CG), Suite 1122, South Tower, Place Desjardins, P.O. Box 65, Montreal H5B 1G1, Canada
Tel (514) 281-1886 Telex 05-268751

CG: William D. Morgan
ECO: Frederick S. Vaznaugh
COM: Jerry Mitchell

Quebec, Quebec (CG), 2 Place Terrasse Dufferin C.P. 939, G1R 4T9
Tel (418) 692-2095 Telex 051-2275

CG: George W. Jaeger

Toronto, Ontario (CG), 360 University Ave., M5G 1S4
Tel (416) 595-1700 Telex 065-24132

ECO: David C. Holton
COM: Toby T. Zettler

Vancouver, British Columbia (CG), 1199 West Hastings St., V6E 2Y4
Tel (604) 685-4311

CG: George W. Ogg
ECO: Walter B. Lockwood, Jr.
COM: Peter G. Frederick

Winnipeg, Manitoba (CG), 6 Donald St. R3L OK7
Tel (204) 475-3344 Telex 07-55875

CG: Lillian P. Mullin

REPUBLIC OF CAPE VERDE

Praia (E), Rua Hoji Ya Yenna 81, 1st and 3d Fls.
C.P. 201
Tel 553 and 761

AMB: John M. Yates
AID: James Maher (resident in Bissau)

CENTRAL AFRICAN REPUBLIC

Bangui (E), Avenue President Dacko, B.P. 924
Tel 61-02-00, 05, 10 Telex 5216 EC

AMB: (Vacant)
POL: Christopher N. Darlington
CHG: Douglas A. Hartwick

CHAD

N'Djamena (E), Ave. Felix Eboue B.P. 413
Tel 32-29, 32-69, 35-15
Telex 5203 KD

AMB: Peter Moffat
AID: (Vacancy)

CHILE

Santiago (E), Codina Bldg., 1343 Agustinas
APO Miami 34033
Tel 710133/90; 710326/75
Telex 40062-ICA-CL

AMB: James D. Theberge
POL: Michael L. Durkee
ECO: Peter D. Whitney
COM: Daniel Taher
AGR: Lawrence R. Fouchs

CHINA

Beijing (E), Guang Hua Lu 17
Dept. of State, Wash., D.C. 20520

Box 50, FPO San Fran 96659
Tel 52-2033
AMB: Arthur W. Hummel, Jr.
POL: Richard R. Hart
ECO: David G. Brown
COM: Melvin W. Searls, Jr.
ADM: James B. Moran
AGR: Norman R. Kallemeyn
Guangzhou (CG), Dong Fang Hotel, Box 100
FPO San Fran 96659
Tel 69900 (ext. 1000)
POL: Brian V. Evans
ECO: Brian Page
COM: Ying Price
Shanghai (CG), 1469 Huai Hai Middle Rd., Box 200
FPO San Fran 96659
Tel 379-880
CG: Donald M. Anderson
POL: Thomas V. Biddick
ECO: (Vacancy)
COM: Genevieve C. Dean

COLOMBIA
Bogota (E), Calle 37, 8-40
APO Miami 34038
Tel 285-1300   Telex 44843
AMB: Lewis A. Tambs
POL: Adolph H. Eisner
ECO: Ralph E. Winstanley II
COM: Ricardo Villalobos
AGR: Lloyd I. Holmes
Barranquilla (C), Calle 77 Carrera 68, Centro Commercial Mayorista
APO Miami 34038
Tel 245-7560; 245-7088
CON: Clyde I. Howard

PEOPLE'S REPUBLIC OF THE CONGO
Brazzaville (E), Avenue Amilcar Cabral, B.P. 1015
Box C, APO NY 09662
Tel 81-20-70; 81-26-24
AMB: Kenneth L. Brown
POL/CON: Gene H. Williams
ECO/COM: David R. Burnett

COSTA RICA
San Jose (E), Avenida 3 and Calle I
APO Miami 34020
Tel 33-11-55
AMB: Curtin Winsor Jr.
POL: Ronald Godard
ECO: John H. Curry
COM: (Vacancy)
AGR: Frank D. Lee
AID: Daniel A. Chaij

CUBA
Havana (USINT), Swiss Embassy, Calcado entre L & M, Vedado Seccion
Tel 320551; 329700
POL/ECO: James C. Todd

CYPRUS
Nicosia (E), Therissos St. and Dositheos St.
FPO NY 09530
Tel 65151/5
AMB: Raymond C. Ewing
DCM: James L. Tull
POL: Richard Hoover
ECO/COM: Herbert Yarvin
AGR: Gerald W. Sheldon (resident in Tel Aviv)

CZECHOSLOVAKIA
Prague (E), Trziste 15-12548 Praha, Amembassy Prague, c/o Amcongen
APO NY 09757
Tel 53 66 41/8
Telex 121196 AMEMBC
AMB: Jack F. Matlock, Jr.
DCM: Martin A. Wenick
POL: James K. Connell
ECO: Nicholas R. Lang
COM: Stephan Wasylko
AGR: Nicholas M. Thuroczy (resident in Vienna)

DENMARK
Copenhagen (E), Dag Hammarskjolds Alle 24
2100 Copenhagen O or APO NY 09170
Tel (01) 42 31 44   Telex 22216

AMB: John L. Loeb, Jr.
DCM: Arthur H. Hughes
POL: James C. Whitlock, Jr.
ECO: Matthew T. Lorimer
COM: Max Miles
AGR: Edmund L. Nichols

REPUBLIC OF DJIBOUTI
Djibouti (E), Villa Plateau du Serpent Blvd,
Marechal Joffre, B.P. 185
Tel 35-38-49; 35-39-95; 35-29-16/17
Workweek: Sunday–Thursday

AMB: Alvin P. Adams, Jr.
POL: Eugene D. Schmiel
ECO/COM: Malcom Gray
AID: Ellsworth M. Amundson

DOMINICAN REPUBLIC
Santo Domingo (E), Corner of Calle Cesar
Nicolas Penson & Calle Leopoldo
Navarro
APO Miami 34041
Tel 682-2171   Telex 3460013

AMB: Robert Anderson
DCM: John D. Blacken
POL: Richard Hines
ECO: Carl B. Cunningham
COM: Rafael Fermoselle
AGR: Marvin L. Lehrer
AID: Philip R. Schwab

ECUADOR
Quito (E), 120 Avenida Patria
APO Miami 34039
Tel 548-000
Telex 02-2329 USICAQ ED

AMB: Samuel F. Hart
DCM: John J. Youle
POL: Arnold A. Isaacs
ECO: Oscar J. Olson
COM: Robert C. Fraser
AGR: Leonidas P. Emerson
AID: Orlando Llenza

Guayaquil (CG), 9 de Octubre y Garcia
Moreno
APO Miami 34039
Tel 511-570
Telex 04-3452 USICAG ED

CG: Charles W. Grover
COM: Robert M. Shipley

EGYPT (ARAB REPUBLIC OF)
Cairo (E), 5 Sharia Latin America
Box 11, FPO NY 09527
Tel 28219, 774666
Telex 93773 AMEMB
Workweek: Sunday–Thursday

AMB: Alfred L. Atherton, Jr.
DCM: Henry Precht
POL: Thomas J. Carolan
ECO: David J. Dunford
COM: Theodore A. Rosen
AGR: Clarence Jean
AID: Michael P. Stone

Alexandria (CG), 110 Ave. Horreya
FPO NY 09527
Tel 801911; 25607; 22861; 28458
Workweek: Monday–Friday

CG: Frances D. Cook
ECO/CON: Gerald J. Loftus
COM: (Vacancy)

EL SALVADOR
San Salvador (E), 25 Avenida Norte No.
1230
APO Miami 34023
Tel 26-7100; 25-9984

AMB: Thomas R. Pickering
DCM: Kenneth W. Bleakley
POL: James F. Mack
ECO/COM: Bonnie M. Lincoln
AGR: Robert R. Anlauf (resident in
            Guatemala)
AID: Martin Dagata

EQUATORIAL GUINEA
Malabo (E), Tel 2607; 2467

AMB: Alan M. Hardy

ETHIOPIA
Addis Ababa (E), Entoto St., P.O. Box 1014
Tel 110666/117/129

AMB: (Vacancy)
POL/ECO: Joseph P. O'Neill

FIJI

Suva (E), 31 Loftus St., P.O. Box 218
Tel 23031
Telex 2255 AMEMBASSY FJ

AMB: Fred J. Eckert
DCM: Russell J. Surber
AID: Robert V. Craig

FINLAND

Helsinki (E), Itainen Puistotie 14A
APO NY 09664
Tel 171931
Telex 121644 USEMB SF

AMB: Keith F. Nyborg
DCM: C. Arthur Borg
POL: William R. Salisbury
ECO: Leo Cecchini, Jr.
COM: Max J. Ollendorff
AGR: William P. Huth (resident in Stockholm)

FRANCE

Paris (E), 2 Avenue Gabriel, 75382 Paris
Cedex 08
APO NY 09777
Tel 296-1202; 261-8075
Telex 650-221

AMB: Evan G. Galbraith
DCM: John J. Maresca
POL: Francis DeTarr
ECO: Michael E. Ely
COM: E. William Tatge
AGR: Frank Padovano

Bordeaux (CG), 22 Cours du Marechal
Foch, 33080 Bordeaux Cedex
Tel 56/52-65-95   Telex 540918F

CG: Charles T. Sylvester

Lyon (CG), 7 Quai General Sarrail,
69454 Lyon Cedex 3
Tel 824-68-49
Telex USCSUL 380597F

CG: Peter R. Chaveas

Marseille (CG), No. 9 Rue Armeny 13006
Tel 54-92-00   Telex 430597

CG: Edward M. Sacchet
ECO: Daniel P. Carbognin

Strasbourg (CG), 15 Ave. D'Alsace
67082 Strasbourg Cedex or APO NY
09777
Tel (88) 35-31-04/05/06
Telex 870907

CG: Robert O. Homme
ECO/COM: (Vacancy)

FRENCH CARIBBEAN DEPARTMENT

Martinique (CG), 14 Rue Blenac
B.P. 561, Fort-de-France 97206
Tel 71.93.01/03   Telex 912670 MR

AGR: Marvin L. Lehrer (resident in Santo Domingo)

GABON

Libreville (E), Blvd. de la Mer
B.P. 4000
Tel 762003/4; 761337; 721348
Telex 5250 GO

AMB: Francis Terry McNamara
POL: William P. Wagner III
ECO/COM: John R. Trowbridge

THE GAMBIA

Banjul (E), Fajara East, Pipeline Road,
P. O. Box 596
Tel 526; 527

AMB: (Vacancy)
AID: Bryon Bahl

GERMAN DEMOCRATIC REPUBLIC

Berlin (E), 108 Berlin, Neustaedtische
Kirchstrasse 4-5
USBER Box E, APO NY 09742
Tel 2202741
Telex 112479 USEMB DD

AMB: Rozanne L. Ridgway
DCM: M. James Wilkinson
POL: Bruce W. Clark
ECO/COM: W. Wyatt Martin
AGR: Steven D. Yoder

FEDERAL REPUBLIC OF GERMANY

Bonn (E), Delchmannsaue, 5300 Bonn
2
APO NY 09080
Tel (0228) 339-3390   Telex 885-452

AMB: Arthur F. Burns
DCM: William M. Woessner
POL: Richard C. Barkley
ECO: William H. Edgar
COM: Kenneth D. Blum
AGR: Richard L. Barnes

Berlin (M), Clayallee 170, D-1000 Berlin 33 (Dahlem)
APO NY 09742
Tel (030) 832 40 87
Com. Unit: Tel (030) 819-7561
Telex 183-701 USBER-D

ACM: Nelson C. Ledsky
POL: George M. Humphrey
ECO: John P. Jureky
COM: Edward B. O'Donnell, Jr.

Duesseldorf (CG), Cecillenallee 5, 4000 Duesseldorf 30
Box 515, APO NY 09712
Tel (0211) 49 00 81   Telex 8584246

CG: David K. Edminster
COM: Patrick T. O'Connor

Frankfurt am Main (CG), Siesmayerstrasse 21, 6000 Frankfurt
APO NY 09757
Tel (0611) 740071; after hours (0611) 745004   Telex 412589 USCON-D

CG: William Bodde, Jr.
COM: Walter Hage

Hamburg (CG), Alsterufer 27/28, 2000 Hamburg 36
APO NY 09215
Tel (040) 44 10 61   Telex 213777
US Agricultural Trade Office: Grosse Theaterstrasse 42
Tel (040) 341207
Telex 02163970 ATO D

CG: Grant E. Mouser III
COM: Suresh (Sam) Dhir

Munich (CG), Koeniginstrasse 5, 8000 Muenchen 22
APO NY 09108
Tel (089) 2 30 11
Telex 5-22697 ACGM D

CG: Carroll Brown
POL: Victor S. Gray, Jr.
COM: Kay R. Kuhlman
Stuttgart (CG), Urbanstrasse 7, 7000 Stuttgart;
APO NY 09154
Tel (0711) 21 02 21   Telex 07-22945
CG: Thomas T. Turqman
COM: Thomas L. Boam
ADM: Leroy Beal

GHANA
Accra (E), Liberia & Kinbu Rds.
P.O. Box 194
Tel 66811   Com Off: Tel 66125
AMB: Robert E. Fritts
DCM: John S. Brims
ECO/COM/POL: William C. Mithoefer, Jr.
AGR: Christopher E. Goldthwait (resident in Lagos)
AID: Leroy L. Wagner

GREECE
Athens (E), 91 Vasilissis Sophias Blvd. or
APO NY 09253
Tel 721-2951 or 721-8401 (area code from U.S.: 01130-1)   Telex 21-5548
AMB: Monteagle Stearns
DCM: Alan D. Berlind
POL: Charles W. McCaskil
ECO: William E. Rau
COM: Robert Kohn
AGR: Gerald W. Shelden
Thessaloniki (CG), 59 Vasileos Constantinou St.
APO NY 09693
Tel 266-121   Telex 041/2285
CG: Michael D. Sternberg
POL/ECO/COM: Alan W. Barr

GUATEMALA
Guatemala (E), 7-01 Avenida de la Reforma, Zone 10
APO Miami 34024
Tel 31-15-41
AMB: Frederic L. Chapin
DCM: Paul D. Taylor

POL: Richard C. Graham
ECO: David H. Stebbing
COM: Robert W. Miller
AGR: Robert R. Anlauf
AID: Charles E. Costello

GUINEA

Conakry (E), 2d Blvd. and 9th Ave.
B.P. 603
Tel 415-20 thru 24

AMB: James D. Rosenthal
DCM: Kathryn Clark-Bourne
POL: Victor P. Kohl, Jr.
ECO/COM: John Stepanchuk
AGR: Walter A. Stern (resident in Abidjan)
AID: Edward T. Costello

GUINEA-BISSAU

Bissau (E), Avenida Domingos Ramos
C.P. 297
Tel 212816/7

AMB: Wesley W. Eagan, Jr.
AID: Louis F. Macary (Acting)

GUYANA

Georgetown (E), 31 Main St.
Tel 02-54900
Telex GY-213 AMEMSY GY

AMB: Gerald E. Thomas
DCM: David R. Beall
POL: William H. Moore
ECO/COM: Karen S. Brown
AGR: Harry C. Bryan (resident in Caracas)
AID: Harry P. Johnson (Acting)

HAITI

Port-au-Prince (E), Harry Truman Blvd.
Tel 20200   Telex 0157 EMPAP

AMB: Ernest H. Preeg
DCM: Stephen P. Dawkins
POL: Lino Gutierrez
ECO/COM: John H. Lewis
AGR: Marvin L. Lehrer (resident in Santo Domingo)
AID: Harlan Hobgood

HONDURAS

Tegucigalpa (E), Avenido La Paz
APO Miami 34022
Tel 32-3120 to 29

AMB: John D. Negroponte
DCM: Shepard C. Lowman
POL: Raymond F. Burghardt
ECO: James W. Lamont
COM: (Vacancy)
AGR: Robert R. Anlauf (resident in Guatemala)
AID: Anthony J. Cauterucci

HONG KONG

Hong Kong (CG), 26 Garden Rd
Box 30, FPO San Fran 96659
Tel 239011

CG: Burton Levin
POL: Dennis G. Harter
ECO: Richard Mueller
COM: Paul Walters
AGR: Michael L. Humphrey

HUNGARY

Budapest (E), V. Szabadsag Ter 12
Am Embassy; APO NY 09757
Tel 329-375   Telex 224-222
Commercial Devel Ctr: Telex 227136
USCDC H

AMB: Harry E. Bergold, Jr.
DCM: Keith C. Smith
POL: G. Jonathan Greenwald
ECO: Thomas A. Schlenker
COM: Michael J. Hegedus
AGR: Nicholas M. Thuroczy (resident in Vienna)

ICELAND

Reykjavik (E), Laufasvegur 21
FPO NY 09571
Tel 29100

AMB: Marshall Brement
DCM: Paul F. Canney
POL: Elizabeth P. Spiro
ECO/COM: Algirdas Rimas

INDIA

New Delhi (E), Shanti Path, Chanakyapuri 21
Tel 690351   Telex USCS IN 031-4589
USICA Tel 46841

AMB: Harry G. Barnes, Jr.
DCM: Marion V. Creekmore, Jr.
POL: Rufus G. Smith
ECO: Martin G. Heflin
COM: Hallock R. Lucius
AGR: W. Garth Thorburn
AID: Priscilla Boughton

Bombay (CG), Lincoln House, 78 Bhulabhal Desai Rd.
Tel 823611/8
Telex 011-6525 ACON IN

CG: J. Bruce Amstutz
POL/ECO: Emily Perreault
COM: Monroe E. Aderhold

Calcutta (CG), 5/1 Ho Chi Minh Sarani, Calcutta 700071
Tel 44-3611/6   Telex 021-2483

CG: George Sherman
POL: James E. Burkart
ECO/COM: Michael E. McNaull

Madras (CG), Mount Rd.-6
Tel 83041

CG: Douglas M. Cochran
POL/ECO: Roy Whitaker
ECO/COM: Lloyd D. Davis

INDONESIA

Jakarta (E), Medan Merdeka Selatan 5
APO San Fran 96356
Tel 340001-9
Telex 44218AMEMB JKT

AMB: John H. Holdridge
DCM: Richard C. Howland
POL: W. Scott Butcher
ECO: Joseph A. Winder
COM: Franklin J. Kline
AID: William P. Fuller IV
AGR: George J. Pope

Medan (C), Jalan Imam Bonjol 13
APO San Fran 96356
Tel 322200   Telex 51764

PO: Susan M. Klingaman
ECO/COM: Kevin F. Herbert

Surabaya (C), Jalan Raya Dr. Sutomo 33
APO San Fran 96356
Tel 69287/8   Telex 031-334

PO: James H. McNaughton
ECO: Alfreda Meyers
COM: (Vacancy)

IRAQ

Baghdad (USINT) Opp. For. Ministry Club (Masbah Quarter), P.O. Box 2447 Alwiyah, Baghdad, Iraq
Tel 96138/9
Telex 212287 USINT IK
Workweek: Sunday–Thursday

The Embassy was closed on June 7, 1967. The Government of Belgium serves as protective power for the United States in Iraq. The United States Interests Section is staffed by the following American personnel:

PO: William L. Eagleton, Jr.
POL: Gene M. McGill
ECO: William T. Monroe
COM: Hampton E. Brown III
AGR: Clyde Gumbmann (resident in Damascus)

IRELAND

Dublin (E), 42 Elgin Rd., Ballsbridge
Tel Dublin 688777   Telex 25240

AMB: Peter H. Dailey
DCM: John A. Boyle
POL: W. Alan Roy
ECO/COM: E. Mark Linton
AGR: Pitamber Devgon

ISRAEL

Tel Aviv (E), 71 Hayarkon St.
APO NY 09672
Tel 03-654338   Telex 33376

AMB: Samuel W. Lewis
DCM: Robert A. Flaten
POL: Paul J. Hare
ECO: Richard D. Kauzlarich
COM: Thomas Roesch
AGR: Alfred R. Persi

ITALY

Rome (E), Via Veneto 119/A, 00187-Rome
APO NY 09794
Tel (06) 4674   Telex 610450 AMB-
RMA or 613425 AMBRMB
USIS: Via Boncompagni 2, 00187-Rome
Telex 614437 or 614431 USICAR

AMB: Maxwell M. Rabb
DCM: Peter Bridges
POL: Charles R. Stout
ECO: William B. Whitman, Jr.
COM: Raymond J. De Paulo
AGR: James P. Rudbeck

Genoa (CG), Banca d'America e d'Italia
Bldg., Piazza Portello 6
Box G, APO NY 09794
Tel (010) 282-741 thru 5
Telex 270324 AMCOGE I

CG: Peter K. Murphy
POL/COM: Claretta Scott

Milan (CG), Piazza Repubblica 32, 20124
Milano
c/o U.S. Embassy, Box M, APO NY
09794
Tel (02) 652-841 thru 5
Commercial Section: Via Gattamelata 5,
20149 Milano
Tel 498-2241/2/3

CG: Robert D. Collins
COM: David A. Ross
ECO: George M. White
AGR: Harold Rabinowitz

Naples (CG), Piazza della Repubblica
80122 Naples
Box 18, FPO NY 09521
Tel (081)660966
Telex ICA NAPLES 720442 ICANA

CG: Walter J. Silva
POL/ECO/COM: William H. Skok
AID: Richard M. Dangler

Palermo (CG), Via Baccarini 1, 90143
APO NY 09794 (c/o AmEmbassy Rome-
P)
Tel (091) 291532-35
Telex 910313 USACON I

CG: Ralph T. Jones
ECO/COM: David Bloch

Florence (CG), Lungarmo Amerigo Ves-
pucci 38
APO NY 09019
Tel (055) 298-276
Telex 570577 AMCOFI I

CG: Frederick H. Hassett
POL/ECO/COM: Thomas H. Gerth

Trieste (C), Via Roma 9 (4th Fl.)
APO NY 09293
Tel (040) 68728/29
Telex 460354 AMCOTS

PO: Frank R. Golino

IVORY COAST

Abidjan (E), 5 Rue Jesse Owens
01 B.P. 1712
Tel 32-09-79   Telex 3660

AMB: (Vacant)
DCM: Carl C. Cundiff
POL: John J. Hartley II
ECO: Bruce Duncombe
COM: Frederic J. Gaynor
AGR: James Benson
AID: Laurance Bond

JAMAICA

Kingston (E), Jamaica Mutual Life Center,
2 Oxford Rd., 3d Fl.
Tel 809-92-94850

AMB: William A. Hewitt
DCM: W. Robert Warne
POL: Alexander Sleght
ECO/COM: Alan P. Larson
AGR: Marvin L. Lehrer (resident in
Santo Domingo)
AID: Lewis Reade

JAPAN

Tokyo (E), 10-1, Akasaka 1-chome, Minato-
ku (107)
APO San Fran 96503
Tel 583-7141   Telex 2422118

AMB: Michael J. Mansfield
DCM: William Clark, Jr.
POL: Robert M. Immerman
ECO: William Piez
COM: William V. Rapp
AGR: William L. Davis, Jr.

Naha, Okinawa (CG), No. 2129, Gusukuma, Urasoe City, Okinawa (901-21)
APO San Fran 96248
Tel (0988) 77-8142/8627
PO: Edward M. Featherstone
POL: Lawrence M. Enomot

Osaka-Kobe (CG), APO San Fran 96503
Osaka Office: 9th Fl., Sankei Bldg., 4-9, Umeda 2-chome, Kita-ku, Osaka (530)
Tel (06) 341-2754/7
Telex 5623023 AMCON J
(Includes American Merchandise Display)
CG: W. Lawrence Dutton
ECO: Norman S. Hastings
COM: Herbert A. Cochran

Kobe Office: 3-1, Kano-cho 6-chome, Chuo-ku, Kobe (650)
Tel (078) 331-6868, 331-9677/8
Telex 5623023 AMCON J
CG: W. Lawrence Dutton

Fukuoka (C), 5-26 Ohori 2-chome, Chuo-ku, Fukuoka-810
Box 10, FPO Seattle 98766
Tel (092) 751-9331/4   Telex 725679
PO: Marilyn A. Meyers
ECO/COM: Thomas A. Steele

Sapporo (C), Kita 1-Jyo Nishi 28-chome, Chuoku, Sapporo 064
APO San Fran 96503
Tel (011) 641-1115/7
PO: Robert C. Reis

JERUSALEM

JERUSALEM (CG), 18 Agron Rd.
APO NY 09672
Tel 234271 (via Israel)
Consular & Cultural Sections: 27 Nablus Rd.
Tel 282231/272681 (both offices via Israel)
CG: Brandon Grove, Jr.
DPO: Jock Covey
POL: Thomas E. Dowing
ECO/COM: Wesley D. Johnson

JORDAN

Amman (E), Jebel Amman; P.O. Box 354
APO NY 09892
Tel 44371-6   Telex 21510 USEMB JO
Workweek: Sunday-Thursday
Com. Off.: 4th Fl., Zeyad Saleh Contracting Estab. Bldg. (Opp. Ambassador Hotel in Shmeisani District)
Tel 664874/664576
Workweek: Sunday-Thursday
AMB: Richard N. Viets
DCM: Edward P. Djerejian
POL: James F. Collins
ECO/COM: David S. Robins
AGR: Clyde E. Gumbmann (resident in Damascus)
AID: Walter G. Bollinger

KENYA

Nairobi (E), Moi/Haile Selassie Ave., P.O. Box 30137
APO NY 09675
Tel 334141   Telex 22964
AMB: William C. Harrop
DCM: Robert G. Houdek
POL: Louis F. Janowski
ECO: Duane C. Butcher
COM: Edward R. Stumpf
AGR: Harold L. Norton
AID: Allison Herrick

Mombasa (C), Palli House, Nyerere Avenue, P.O. Box 88079
Tel. 315101
PO: Robert Gribben III

KOREA

Seoul (E), 82 Sejong-Ro: Chongro-ku:
APO San Fran 96301
Tel 722-2601 thru 19
Telex AMEMB 23108
US Agricultural Trade Office: 63, 1-KA, Eulchi-Ro, Choong-Ku
AMB: Richard L. Walker
DCM: Paul M. Cleveland
POL: David L. Blakemore
ECO: Walter A. Lundy, Jr.
COM: Norman D. Glick
AGR: James A. Freckmann

KUWAIT
Kuwait (E), P.O. Box 77 SAFAT
Tel 424-151 thru 9
Workweek: Saturday-Wednesday

AMB: (Vacancy)
CHG: Philip J. Griffin
POL: Gordon D. Barnes
ECO: Norman T. Shaft
COM: Wanda L. Ale
AGR: Theodore Horoschak (resident in Manama)

LAOS
Vientiane (E), Rue Bartholonie; B.P. 114
Box V, APO San Fran 96346
Tel 3126, 3570

AMB: (Vacancy)
POL: Marion L. Gribble
ECO/COM/CON: Karla Reed

LEBANON
Beirut (E), Corniche at Rue Ain Mreisseh,
P.O. Box 110301
Tel 361-800; 361-964

AMB: Robert S. Dillon
DCM: Robert L. Pugh
POL: Ryan C. Crocker
ECO/COM: H. Huntington Janin
AGR: Clyde E. Gumbmann (resident in Damascus)
AID: William R. McIntyre

LESOTHO
Maseru (E), P.O. Box MS 333, Maseru 100
Tel 22666/7; 23892

AMB: Keith L. Brown
POL/ECO/COM: Edward J. Michal
AGR: Guy L. Haviland (resident in Pretoria)
AID: Edna A. Boorady

LIBERIA
Monrovia (E), APO N Y 09155
111 United Nations Dr.; P.O. Box 98
Tel 222991 thru 4

AMB: William L. Swing
DCM: Leonard G. Shurtleff
POL: Marshall McCallie

ECO: Dane F. Smith
AGR: Walter A. Stern (resident in Abidian)
AID: Lois Richards

LIBYA
Tripoli (E), Shari Mohammad Thabit, P.O.
Box 289
Tel 34021/6
Workweek: Sunday-Thursday

On May 2, 1980, all Embassy working activities were suspended and all American personnel were withdrawn from the Embassy.

LUXEMBOURG
Luxembourg (E), 22 Blvd. Emmanuel-Servais, 2535 Luxembourg
APO NY 09132
Tel 40123 thru 7

AMB: John E. Dolibois
DCM: James H. Madden
POL: James L. Pavitt
ECO/COM: Matthew Ward
AGR: James F. Lankford (resident in Brussels)

MADAGASCAR
Antananarivo (E), 14 and 16 Rue
Rainitovo, Antsohavola; B.P. 620
Tel 212-57, 209-56   Telex USA EMB
MG 22202 ANTANANARIVO

AMB: Robert B. Keating
POL/CON: John M. Wilcox
ECO/COM: Eugene P. Tuttle

MALAWI
Lilongwe (E), P.O. Box 30016
Tel 730-166

AMB: John A. Burroughs, Jr.
DCM: Robert J. Kott
ECO/COM: Jay T. Smith
AID: Sheldon W. Cole

Blantyre (BO), Unit House 4th Fl., Victoria
Ave.
P.O. Box 380
Tel 635721

MALAYSIA

Kuala Lumpur (E), A.I.A. Bldg. Jalan Ampang
P.O. Box No. 35
Tel 226322

AMB: Ronald D. Palmer
DCM: M. Lyall Breckon
POL: Murray Zinoman
ECO: Donald McConville
COM: Theodore J. Villinski
AGR: Daniel B. Conable

MALI

Bamako (E), Rue Testard and Rue
Mohamed V.
B.P. 34
Tel 225834, 225663   Telex 448

AMB: Parker W. Borg
DCM: Charles O. Cecil
POL: Rebecca A. Joyce
ECO/COM: Robert A. Benedetti
AID: David M. Wilson

MALTA

Valletta (E), 2d Fl., Development House,
St. Anne St., Floriana, Malta
P.O. Box 535, Valletta
Tel 623653, 620424, 623216

AMB: James M. Rentschler
DCM: Thomas L. Price
ECO/COM: Peter R. De Castro

MAURITANIA

Nouakchott (E), B.P. 222
Tel 52660/3
Telex AMEMB 558 MTN

AMB: Edward L. Peck
DCM: Edward Brynn
POL/ECO: Alfred Fonteneau
AID: Peter Benedict

MAURITIUS

Port Louis (E), Rogers Bldg. (4th Fl.), John
Kennedy St.
Tel 2-3218/9

AMB: Robert C.F. Gordon
DCM: Leo R. Wollemborg
ECO/COM: Michael D'Andrea

MEXICO

Mexico, D.F. (E), Paseo de la Reforma 305,
Mexico 5, D.F.
Tel (905) 553-3333
Telex 017-73-091; 017-75-685

AMB: John A. Gavin
DCM: George B. High
POL: Arthur P. Shankle, Jr.
ECO: Alton L. Jenkens
COM: Calvin C. Berlin
AGR: John E. Montel

Guadalajara (CG), Jal.; Progreso 175
Tel 25-29-98, 25-27-00
Telex 068-2-860

CG: Julio J. Arias
COM: (Vacancy)

Hermosillo (C), Son.; Isssteson Bldg. 3d Fl.,
Miguel Hidalgo y Costilla No. 15
Tel 3-89-22 thru 25   Telex 058-829

PO: Anthony Arredondo

Monterrey (CG), N.L., Avenida Constitu-
cion 411 Poniente
Tel 4306 50/59   Telex 0382853

CG: Frank M. Tucker, Jr.
COM: (Vacancy)

Tijuana (CG), B.C., Tapachula 96
Tel 86-1001/5   Telex 056-6836

CG: Robert E. Ezelle

Ciudad Juarez (CG), 924 Avenue Lopez
Mateos
Tel 34048   Telex 033-840

CG: William S. Tilney

Matamoros (C), Tamps.; Ave. Primera No.
232
Tel 2-52-50/1/2   Telex 035-827

PO: George B. Kettenhofen

Mazatlan (C), Sin.; 6 Circunvalacion No. 6
(at Venustiana Carranza)
Tel 1-29-05   Telex 066-883

PO: Elayne J. Urban

Merida (C), Yuc.; Paseo Montejo 453,
Apartado Postal 130
Tel 5-54-09, 5-50-11   Telex 0753885
AMCONME

PO: Virginia S. Carson

Nuevo Laredo (C), Tamps.; Avenida Allende 3330, Col. Jardin
Tel 4-05-12, 4-06-18   Telex 036-849
PO: Victor A. Abeyta

MOROCCO
Rabat (E), 2 Ave. de Marrakech
P.O. Box 120
APO N Y 09284
Tel 622-65   Telex 31005
AMB: Joseph V. Reed, Jr.
DCM: R. T. Curran
POL: Richard L. Jackson
ECO: Joel S. Spiro
AGR: Forrest K. Geerken
AID: Robert C. Chase
Casablanca (CG), 8 Blvd. Moulay Youssef
Tel 22-41-49
CG: Fred J. Galanto
POL/LAB: Richard V. Fisher
COM: Donald F. Meyers
Tangier (CG), Chemin des Amoureux
Tel 359-05   Telex 33025
CG: Kenneth N. Rogers
CON/COM: Lili Ming

MOZAMBIQUE
Maputo (E), 35 Rua Da Mesquita, 3d Fl.
P.O. Box 783
Tel 26051/2/3
AMB: (Vacancy)
POL: (Vacancy)
ECO/COM: Vicente Valle, Jr.

NEPAL
Kathmandu (E), Pani Pokhari
Tel 11199, 12718, 11603/4
AMB: Carleton S. Coon
DCM: James R. Cheek
POL/ECO: Eric D. Tunis
ECO/COM: Craig A. Arness
AGR: Dennis J. Brennan

NETHERLANDS
The Hague (E), Lange Voorhout 102
APO NY 09159
Tel (070) 62-49-11   Telex (044) 31016
AMB: L. Paul Bremer III
DCM: Arthur H. Hughes

POL: Michael J. Habib
ECO: Richard E. Hecklinger
COM: Stanley P. Harris
AGR: Roland Anderson
Amsterdam (CG), Museumplein 19
APO NY 09159
Tel (020) 790321
Telex 044-16176 CGUSA NL
CG: Hawthorne Q. Mills
COM: Mike R. Frisby
Rotterdam (CG), Vlasmarkt 1
APO NY 09159
Tel (010) 117560   Telex 044-22388
CG: Lewis D. Junior

NETHERLANDS ANTILLES
Curacao (CG), St. Anna Blvd. 19; P.O. Box 158, Willemstad, Curacao
Tel 613066, 613350, 613441
Telex 1062 AMCON NA
CG: Alta F. Fowler
AGR: Harry C. Bryan (resident in Caracas)

NEW ZEALAND
Wellington (E), 29 Fitzherbert Ter., Thorndon
Am. Emb., Private Bag, Wellington
FPO San Fran 96690
Tel 722-068   Telex NZ 3305
AMB: H. Monroe Browne
DCM: Richard W. Teare
POL: Linda C. Stillman
ECO: Charles S. Ahlgren
COM: Kenneth L. Norton
AGR: L. Ben Thompson
Auckland (CG), 4th Fl., Yorkshire General Bldg., Shortland and O'Connell Sts., Private Bag, Auckland 1
FPO San Fran 96690
Tel 32-724   Telex NZ 3305
CG: Peter T. Higgins

NICARAGUA
Managua (E), Km. 4½ Carretera Sur
APO Miami 34021
Tel 23061, 23881-7

AMB: Anthony C. Quainton
DCM: Roger R. Gamble
POL: John Joyce
ECO/COM: Wendell L. Belew
AGR: Robert R. Anlauf (resident in Guatemala)
AID: R. Carey Coulter

NIGER

Niamey (E) (No street address)
B.P. 11201
Tel 72-26-61 thru 4, 72-26-70

AMB: William R. Casey, Jr.
DCM: E. Michael Southwick
ECO/CON: James F. Entwhistle
AID: Irving Rosenthal
COM: Michael B. Doyle

NIGERIA

Lagos (E), 2 Eleke Crescent; P.O. Box 554
Tel 610097   Telex 21670 USEMLA NG

AMB: Thomas R. Pickering
DCM: Herbert D. Gelber
POL: Walter S. Clarke
ECO: Chester E. Norris
COM: George G. Griffin
AGR: Christopher E. Goldthwait

Kaduna (C), 5 Ahmadu Bellow Way, P.O. Box 170
Tel (062) 213276

PO: Donald D. Haught
ECO: Robert W. Merrigan
COM: Harry Ryder

NORWAY

Oslo (E), Drammensveien 18, Oslo 2, or APO NY 09085
Tel 44-85-50   Telex 18470

AMB: Mark E. Austad
DCM: Ronald Woods
POL: James H. Holmes
ECO: William H. Dameron
COM: Clifton Stanley
AGR: Edmund L. Nichols (resident in Copenhagen)

OMAN

Muscat (E). P.O. Box 966
Tel 745-006 or 745-231
Workweek: Saturday-Wednesday

AMB: John R. Countryman
DCM: Charles O. Cecil
POL: Frederic Lundahl
ECO/COM: Robert W. Dry

PAKISTAN

Islamabad (E), Temporarily located in AID/UN Bldg.; P.O. Box 1048
Tel 24071   Telex 82-5-864
Workweek: Sunday-Thursday

AMB: Ronald I. Spiers
DCM: Barrington King, Jr.
POL: John L. Hirsch
ECO: Andrew D. Sens
AGR: John J. Reddington
AID: Donor M. Lion

Karachi (CG), 8 Abdullah Haroon Rd.
Tel 515081   Telex 82-2-611
Workweek: Sunday-Thursday

CG: Alexander L. Rattray
POL/ECO: Albert A. Thibault, Jr.
COM: David E. Brantley
AID: William T. White

Lahore (CG), 50 Zafar Ali Rd., Gulberg 5
Tel 870221 thru 5
Workweek: Sunday-Thursday

CG: Arnold P. Schifferdecker
POL/ECO: Eugene D. Price, Jr.

Peshawar (C), 11 Hospital Rd
Tel 73361, 73405   Telex 82-5-264
Workweek: Sunday-Thursday

AID: Richard Scott
PO: Ronald D. Lorton

PANAMA

Panama (E), Avenida Balboa y Calle 38, Apartado 6959, R.P. 5; Box E
APO Miami 34002
Tel Panama 27-1777

AMB: Everett E. Briggs
DCM: William T. Pryce
POL: Ashley C. Hewitt
ECO: J. Peter Becker
COM: F. Miguel Pardo de Zela

AGR: Franklin D. Lee (resident in San Jose)
AID: Robin Gomez

PAPUA NEW GUINEA
Port Moresby (E), Armit St.; P.O. Box 3492
Tel 211455/594/654
Telex 70322189

AMB: M. Virginia Schafer
DCM: Morton R. Dworkey, Jr.
POL/ECO/COM: Alan Krause
AID: William Paupe (resident in Suva)

PARAGUAY
Asuncion (E), 1776 Mariscal Lopez Ave.
APO Miami 34036
Tel 201-041

AMB: Arthur H. Davis
DCM: J. Ford Cooper
POL: John P. Leonard
ECO/COM: Paul F. Hurley
AGR: Lawrence Hall (resident in Buenos Aires)
AID: Abe M. Pena

PERU
Lima (E), Corner Avenidas Inca Garcilaso de la Vega & Espana
APO Miami 34031
P.O. Box 1995, Lima 100
Tel 286000

AMB: Frank V. Ortiz, Jr.
DCM: Gerald P. Lamberty
POL: Daniel H. Clare
ECO: M. Gordon Jones
COM: T. Porter Clary
AGR: Norval Francis
AID: Malcolm H. Butler

PHILIPPINES
Manila (E), 1201 Roxas Blvd.
APO San Fran 96528
Tel 598-011   Telex 722-7366
Com. Off.: 395 Buendia Ave. Extension Makati
Tel 818-6674
Telex 66887 COSEC PN

AMB: Michael H. Armacost
DCM: Robert G. Rich
POL: Scott S. Hallford

ECO: John H. Penfold
COM: Thomas C. Moore
AGR: Verle E. Lanier
AID: Anthony Schwarzwalder
Cebu (C), 3d Fl., Philippine American Life Insurance Bldg., Jones Ave.
APO San Fran 96528
Tel 7-96-10/24

PO: Stanley R. Ifshin

POLAND
Warsaw (E), Aleje Ujazdowskie 29/31
AmEmbassy Warsaw, c/o AmConGen
APO NY 09213
Tel 283041-9
Telex 813304 AMEMB PL

AMB: (Vacancy)
POL: Mark S. Ramee
ECO: Hugh G. Hamilton Jr.
COM: August Maffrey, Jr.
AGR: Frank A. Coolidge
Krakow (C), Ulica Stolarska 9, 31043 Krakow
AmConsul Krakow, c/o AmConGen
APO NY 09213
Tel 29764, 21400   Telex 0325350

PO: Michael J. Metrinko
POL/ECO: Charles B. Smith
Poznan (C), Ulica Chopina 4
c/o AmConGen, APO NY 09213
Tel 595-86/87, 598-74
Telex 041-34-74 USA PL

PO: John A. Purnell

PORTUGAL
Lisbon (E), Avenida das Forcas Armadas, 1600 Lisboa
APO NY 09678
Tel 72–5600   Telex 12528 AMEMB

AMB: H. Allen Holmes
DCM: Alan H. Flanigan
POL: James F. Creagan
ECO: Mark Lore
COM: Ralph Griffin
AGR: Mollie J. Iler
AID: Michael Lukomski
Oporto (C), Apartado No. 88, Rua Julio Dinis 826-30
Tel 6-3094/5/6

PO: Robert F. Illing

Ponta Delgada, Sao Miguel, Azores (C), Avenida D. Henrique
APO NY 09406
Tel 22216/7   Telex 82126 AMCNPD P

PO: Terry D. Hansen

QATAR

Doha (E), Fariq Bin Omran (opp. TV station): P.O. Box 2399
Tel 870701/2/3
Workweek: Saturday-Wednesday

AMB: (Vacant)
ECO/COM: Scott R. Loney
AGR: Theodore Horoschak (resident in Manama)

ROMANIA

Bucharest (E), Strada Tudor Arghezi 7-9, or AmConGen (Buch)
APO NY 09757
Tel 12-40-40   Telex 11416

AMB: David B. Funderburk
DCM: Samuel E. Fry
POL: Francis B. Corry
ECO: Alan Parker
COM: E. Scott Bozek
AGR: Larry Panasuk

RWANDA

Kigali (E), Blvd. de la Revolution, B.P. 28
Tel 5601

AMB: John Blane
DCM: Donald V. Hester
ECO/COM/CON: Janet R. Malkemes
AID: Eugene R. Chiavaroli

SAUDI ARABIA

Jidda (E), Palestine Rd., Ruwais, P. O. Box 149 or
APO NY 09697
Tel (02) 6670080
Telex 401459 AMEMB SJ
Com. Off.: Palestine Rd. (opp. Embassy);
Tel (02) 6670040
Workweek: Saturday-Wednesday (all posts)

AMB: Richard W. Murphy
DCM: Roscoe S. Suddarth
POL: David G. Newton
ECO: Roger B. Merrick (resident in Riyadh)
COM: Robert L. Beckman

Dhahran (CG), Between Aramco Hqrs and Dhahran Int'l Airport
P.O. Box 81, Dhahran Airport, or APO NY 09616
Tel (03) 8913200
Telex 601925 AMCON SJ

CG: John J. Eddy
ECO: Frank R. Adams
COM: Alfred Anderson

Riyadh (LO), Sulaimaniah District P.O. Box 9041
APO NY 09038
Tel (01) 464-0012
Telex 201363 USRIAD SJ
USIS: P.O. Box 865

PO: Roger B. Merrick
COM: Thomas W. Adams
ECO: William C. Ramsey

SENEGAL

Dakar (E), B.P. 49, Avenue Jean XXIII
Tel 21-42-96   Telex 517 AMEMB SG

AMB: Charles W. Bray III
DCM: Edmund T. DeJarnette
POL: David M. Winn
ECO/COM: William H. Memier
AGR: James M. Benson (resident in Abidjan)
AID: David Shear

SEYCHELLES

Victoria (E), Box 148
APO NY 09030
Tel 23921/2

AMB: David J. Fischer

SIERRA LEONE

Freetown (E), Corner Walpole and Siaka Stevens St.
Tel 26481   Telex 3210

AMB: Arthur W. Lewis
CON/ECO/COM: William A. Muller

AGR: Walter A. Stern (resident in Abidjan)
AID: Alex Dickie, Jr.

SINGAPORE

Singapore (E), 30 Hill St.; Singapore 0617
FPO San Fran 96699
Tel 338-0251
US Agricultural Trade Office: Liat Tow-
ers Bldg., 15th Fl., Orchard Rd., Sin-
gapore 0923
Tel 7371233
Telex RS25706 TRIWHT

AMB: Harry E. Thayer
DCM: Morton S. Smith
ECO/POL: William E. Spruce
COM: Geoffrey H. Walser

SOMALIA

Mogadishu (E), Corso Primo Luglio
Tel 28011
Workweek: Sunday–Thursday

AMB: Robert B. Oakley
DCM: Joseph D. McLaughlin
POL: Leonard Scensny
ECO/COM: Paul B. Daley
AID: Louis A. Cohen

SOUTH AFRICA

Pretoria (E), Thibault House, 225 Pretorius
St.
Tel 28-4266   Telex 3-751

AMB: Herman W. Nickel
DCM: Walter E. Stadtler
POL: Timothy M. Carney
ECO: Roderick M. Wright
AGR: Guy L. Haviland

Cape Town (CG), Broadway Industries
Center, Heerengracht, Foreshore
Tel 214-280/7

CG: Richard C. Scissors
POL/ECO: Leonard J. Lange
ECO/COM: Mark S. Massey

Durban (CG), Durban Bay House, 29th Fl.,
333 Smith St., Durban 4001
Tel 324-737

CG: Harold W. Geisel
CON: Curtis M. Stewart

Johannesburg (CG), 11th Fl., Kine Center,
Commissioner and Kruis sts., P.O. Box
2155
Tel (011) 21-1684/7   Telex 8-9236

CG: George Trail II
POL/ECO: Elizabeth P. Sprio
ECO: Robert S. Deutsch
COM: (Vacancy)

SPAIN

Madrid (E), Serrano 75
APO NY 09285
Tel 276-3400/3600   Telex 27763

AMB: Thomas O. Enders
DCM: Robert E. Barbour
POL: Robert E. Service
ECO: J. Brayton Redecker
COM: John D. Perkins
POL/MIL: John H. King
CON: Blaine C. Tueller
AGR: Fred W. Traeger

Barcelona (CG), Via Layetana 33:
Box 5, APO NY 09285
Tel 319-9550   Telex 52672

CG: Albert N. Williams
COM: Kevin C. Brennan

Seville (CG), Paseo de las Delicias No. 7
APO NY 09282
Tel 23-1885   Telex 27780

CG: John E. Clark

Bilbao (C), Avenida del Ejercito, 11-3d Fl.,
Deusto-Bilbao 12
APO NY 09285
Tel 435-8308/9   Telex 32589

PO: Eileen M. Heaphy

SRI LANKA

Colombo (E), 44 Galle Rd., Colombo 3,
P.O. Box 106

Tel 21271, 21532
Telex 0803-21305 AMEMB CE
AMB: John H. Reed
DCM: Herbert G. Hagerty
POL: Walter H. Manger
ECO/COM: Dorothy J. Black
AGR: W. Garth Thorburn
(resident in New Delhi)
AID: Sarah J. Littlefield

SUDAN

Khartoum (E), Sharia Ali Abdul Latif:
P.O. Box 699, APO NY 09668
Tel 74700   Telex 22619 AMEM SD
AMB: Hume A. Horan
DCM: John S. Davison
POL: Alan L. Keiswetter
ECO: Stanley T. Myles
AID: Arthur Mudge

SURINAME

Paramaribo (E), Dr. Sophie Redmondstraat
129, P.O. Box 1821
Tel 76459, 76507
USIS: Dr. Sophie Redmondstraat 129
Tel 75051
AMB: Robert W. Duemling
DCM: T. Patrick Killough
POL: Gardel Fuertado
ECO: Bruce L. Pearson
CON/COM: Patrick Syring
AGR: Henry C. Bryan (resident in Caracas)

SWAZILAND

Mbabane (E), Central Bank Bldg., P.O.
Box 199, Warner Street
Tel 22281/2/3/4/5
AMB: Robert H. Phinny
DCM: Charles E. Lahiguera
AGR: Guy L. Haviland (resident in Pretoria)
AID: Robert G. Huesmann

SWEDEN

Stockholm (E), Strandvagen 101
Tel (08) 63.05.20
Telex 12060 AMEMB S

AMB: Franklin S. Forsberg
DCM: Sherrod McCall
POL: Jenonne R. Walker
ECO: Anne Pinkney
COM: William J. Lynch
AGR: William P. Huth

SWITZERLAND

Bern (E), Jubilaeumstrasse 93, 3005 Bern
Tel (031) 437011   Telex 32128
AMB: John D. Lodge
DCM: James W. Shinn
POL: Frank Tumminia
ECO: Richard A. Dugstad
COM: James N. May
AGR: Mattie R. Sharpless

Zurich (CG), Zollikerstrasse 141, 8008 Zurich
Tel (01) 552566   Telex 0045-53893
CG: Alfred P. Brainard

SYRIA

Damascus (E), Abu Rumaneh, Al Mansur
St. No. 2; P.O. Box 29
Tel 333052, 332557, 330416, 332814,
332315   Telex 411919 USDAMA SY
AMB: Robert P. Paganelli
DCM: William A. Rugh
POL: April C. Glaspie
ECO/COM: Bruce D. Strathearn
AGR: Clyde E. Gumbmann
AID: Thomas A. Pearson

TANZANIA

Dar es Salaam (E), 36 Laibon Rd. (off Bagamoyo Rd.); P.O. Box 9123
Tel 68894, 67983, 67979, 68033, 67992
Telex 41250 AMEMB DAR
AMB: David C. Miller, Jr.
DCM: Lewis R. McFarlane
POL: Robert A. Proctor
ECO/COM: Ronald L. Kates
AGR: Harold L. Norton (resident in Nairobi)
AID: Arthur Handley

THAILAND

Bangkok (E), 95 Wireless Rd.
APO San Fran 96346
Tel 252-5040/5171
Com. Off.: "R" Fl., Shell Bldg., 140 Wireless Rd.
Tel 251-9260/2
AMB: John G. Dean
DCM: J. Stapleton Roy
POL: Phillip Mayhew
ECO: Paul K. Stahnke
COM: Brooks Ryno
AGR: Robert C. Tetro
AID: Robert Halligan

Chiang Mai (C), Vidhayanond Rd.
Box C, APO San Fran 96346
Tel 234566/7

PO: Harlan Y. Lee

Songkhla (C), 9 Sadao Rd.
Box S, APO San Fran 96346
Tel 311-589

PO: G. Nicholas Manger III

Udorn (C), 35/6 Supakitjanya Rd.
Box UD, APO San Fran 96346
Tel 221548

PO: John Muehlke

TOGO

Lome (E), Rue Pelletier Caventou & Rue
Vouban; B.P. 852
Tel 29-91
AMB: Howard K. Walker
DCM: William J. Hudson
POL: John D. Bennett
ECO/COM: Scott D. Bellard
AID: Myron Golden

TRINIDAD AND TOBAGO

Port-of-Spain (E), 15 Queen's Park West,
P.O. Box 752
Tel 62-26371
Telex 22230 AMEB POS
AMB: Melvin H. Evans
DCM: A. Donald Bramante
POL/LAB: Lars H. Hydle
ECO/COM: Guido C. Fenzi
AGR: Harry C. Bryan (resident in Caracas)

TUNISIA

Tunis (E), 144 Ave. de la Liberte
Tel 282.566   Telex 13379 AMB TUN
AMB: Walter L. Cutler
DCM: G. Norman Anderson
POL: Lawrence E. Pope
ECO/COM: John A. Polansky, Jr.
AID: James R. Phippard

TURKEY

Ankara (E), 110 Ataturk Blvd.
APO NY 09254
Tel 26 54 70
Telex 43144 USIA TR

AMB: Robert Strausz-Hupe
DCM: Richard W. Boehm
POL: Jay P. Freres
ECO: Alfred J. White
COM: George Knowles
AGR: Alfred Persi (resident in Tel Aviv)

Istanbul (CG), 104-108 Mesrutlyet Caddesi, Tepebasl
APO NY 09380   Tel 436200/09
Telex 24306 USIC TR

CG: Daniel O. Newberry
POL: Roger L. Hart
ECO: Louis E. Kahn
COM: Glenn L. McCurdy, Jr.

Izmir (CG), 92 Ataturk Caddesi (3d Fl.)
APO NY 09224
Tel 149426, 131369

CG: Beauveau B. Nalle

Adana (C), Ataturk Caddesi
APO NY 09289
Tel 14702/3, 14818

PO: David C. Harr
POL/ECO: Glenn A. Knight

UGANDA

Kampala (E), British High Commission
Bldg., Obote Ave.; P.O. Box 7007
Tel 59791

AMB: Allen C. Davis
DCM: John E. Bennett
ECO/COM: Wilfred Charette
AID: Craig Buck

UNION OF SOVIET SOCIALIST REPUBLICS

Moscow (E), Ulitsa Chaykovskogo 19/21/23, or APO NY 09862
Tel (096) 252-24-51 thru 59
Telex 413160 USGSO SU

AMB: Arthur A. Hartman
DCM: Warren Zimmermann
POL: Curtis W. Kamman
ECO: Henry Clarke
COM: Robert Krause
AGR: Harlan J. Dirks

US Commercial Office (Moscow), Ulitsa Chaykovskogo 15
Tel 255-48-48, 255-46-60
Telex 412-205 USCO SU

Leningrad (CG) UL, Petra Lavrova St. 15
Box L, APO NY 09664
Tel (812) 274-8235
Telex 0522 SU CONSULATE

CG: William T. Shinn

UNITED ARAB EMIRATES

Abu Dhabi (E), Al-Sudan Street; P.O. Box 4009
Tel 336691
Com. Sec.: United Bank Building, Flat No 702 (Corner of Liwa Street and Corniche Road) Tel 345545 Telex 22229 AMEMBY
Workweek: Saturday-Wednesday

AMB: G. Quincy Lumsden, Jr.
DCM: David M. Ransom
POL: Andrea Farsakl
ECO: Bruce Carter
COM: Charles B. Kestenbaum

Dubai (BO), Dubai International Trade Center; P.O. Box 9343
Tel 471115
Telex 46031 BACCUS EM
Workweek: Saturday-Wednesday

COM: (Vacancy)
CONS: Bruce Nelson

UNITED KINGDOM

London, England (E), 24/31 Grosvenor Sq. W. 1A 1AE
Box 40, FPO NY 09510

Tel (01) 499-9000-1 Telex 266777
US Agricultural Trade Office: 101 Wigmore St.
Tel 4990024 Telex 296009 USAGOF

AMB: John J. Louis, Jr.
DCM: Edward J. Streator, Jr.
POL: Richard McCormack
ECO: Michael Calingaert
COM: Gerald M. Marks
AGR: Turner L. Oyloe

Belfast, Northern Ireland (CG), Queen's House, 14 Queen St., BT1 6EQ
Tel Belfast 228239 Telex 747512

CG: Michael Michaud
AGR: Turner L. Oyloe (resident in London)

Edinburgh, Scotland (CG), 3 Regent Ter. EH 7 5BW
Tel 031-556-8315 Telex 727303

CG: Norman A. Singer

UPPER VOLTA

Ouagadougou (E), B.P. 35
Tel 35442/4/6 Telex 5290 UV

AMB: Julius W. Walker, Jr.
DCM: Anthony S. Dalsimer
POL/ECO: Rodney Huff
AID: Emerson J. Melaven

URUGUAY

Montevideo (E), Calle Lauro Muller 1776
APO Miami 34035
Tel 40-90-51, 40-91-26

AMB: Thomas Aranda, Jr.
DCM: Richard H. Melton
POL: Jerome L. Hoganson
ECO: James H. Cheatham
LAB: Abelardo I. Perez
AGR: Lawrence Hall (resident in Buenos Aires)

VENEZUELA

Caracas (E), Avenida Francisco de Miranda and Avenida Principal de la Floresta
APO Miami 34037
Tel 284-7111/6111
Telex 25501 AMEMB VE
US Agricultural Trade Office: Tower C,

Centro Plaza, Los Palos Grandes, Caracas
Tel 2832599
Telex 29119 USATO VC

AMB: George W. Landau
DCM: Richard B. Moon
POL: Claus W. Ruser
ECO: Pierce K. Bullen
COM: David C. Lacey, Jr.
AGR: Harry C. Bryan

Maracaibo (C), Edificio Matema, 1 Piso, Avenida 15 Calle 78
APO Miami 34037
Tel (061) 522-2605/6
Telex 62213 USCON VE

PO: Arlen R. Wilson

YEMEN ARAB REPUBLIC

Sanaa (E), P.O. Box 1088
Tel 72790, 75826, 74407, 72506
Workweek: Saturday-Wednesday

AMB: David E. Zweifel
DCM: Allen L. Keiswetter
POL: Jack R. McCreary
ECO/COM: N. Nicholas Hendershot
AID: Charles F. Welden, Jr.

YUGOSLAVIA

Belgrade (E), Kneza Milosa 50
APO NY 09757
Tel 645655   Telex 11529

AMB: David Anderson
DCM: Harry J. Gilmore
POL: James L. Clunan
ECO: Russell O. Prickett
COM: Kurt F. Gross
AGR: Roger Lowen

Zagreb (CG), Brace Kavurica 2
Tel 444-800
Telex 21180 YU AMCON

CG: Don J. Donchi
POL/ECO/COM: Richard J. Redmond

ZAIRE

Kinshasa (E), 310 Avenue des Aviateurs
APO NY 09662
Tel 25881 thru 6

AMB: Peter D. Constable
DCM: Thomas E. McNamara
POL: Jennifer C. Ward
ECO: William J. Waller
AGR: Walter A. Stern (resident in Abidjan)
AID: Richard L. Podol

Lubumbashi (CG), 1029 Blvd. Kamanyola, B.P. 1196
APO NY 09662
Tel 2324/5

CG: Dennis A. Sandberg
ECO/COM: Christopher W. Murray

Bukavu (C), Mobutu Ave., B.P. 3037
APO NY 09662
Tel 2594

No permanent staff assigned. Consular services provided by visiting Embassy personnel on periodic basis.

ZAMBIA

Lusaka (E), P.O. Box 31617
Tel 214911   Telex AMEMB ZA 41970

AMB: Nicholas Platt
DCM: John A. Buche
POL: George S. Dragnich
ECO/COM: David E. Jensen
AGR: Harold L. Norton (resident in Nairobi)
AID: John A. Patterson

ZIMBABWE

Harare (E), 78 Enterprise Rd., Highlands, Salisbury
Tel 791586/7
Commercial Section: 5th Fl., Century House, 36 Baker Ave. West; P. O. Box 3180
Tel 705-835   Telex 4591 USFCS ZW

AMB: Robert V. Keeley
DCM: Edward G. Lanpher
POL: Phillip H. Ringdahl
ECO: Marc Wall
COM: Kurt F. Gross

AGR: Jack Williams (resident in Pretoria)
AID: Roy Stacy

TAIWAN

Unofficial commercial and other relations with the people of Taiwan are maintained through a private instrumentality, the American Institute in Taiwan, which has offices in Taipei and Kaohsiung. The addresses of these offices are:

American Institute in Taiwan (Taipei Office), 7/9 Lane 134, Hsin Yi Road, Section 3

Tel. 709-2000
Telex 23890 USTRADE
American Institute in Taiwan (Kaohsiung Office), 88 Wu Fu 3d Road
Tel 221-2928

The Taipei office of the institute operates a trade center located in the Taiwan Glass Bldg., 261 Nanking East Road, Section 3 (Tel 709-2051, Telex 23890).

For further information contact the Washington office of the American Institute in Taiwan, 1700 N. Moore St. (17th Fl.), Arlington, VA 22209.